TEACHER'S EDITION

ON THE

IOWA

TESTS OF
BASIC SKILLS®

LEVELS 6–7

ELEMENTARY · SECONDARY · ADULT · LIBRARY

A Harcourt Company

www.steck-vaughn.com

Acknowledgments

Executive Editor: Diane Sharpe
Project Editor: Janet Jerzycki
Editor: Amanda Johnson
Contributing Author: Jay Comras
Graphics Project Manager: Sheryl Bankford
Production: Go Media, Inc., Austin, Texas
Cover Design: D Childress/Alan Klemp
Illustrators: Sonya Cohen, Holly Cooper, Julie Gomoll, Adolph Gonzales, Gwendolyn Manney, Rachel Matthews

Test Best is a registered trademark of Steck-Vaughn Company.

Iowa Tests of Basic Skills® is a trademark of The Riverside Publishing Company. Such company has neither endorsed nor authorized this test-preparation book.

ISBN 0-8114-2867-2

9 10 11 12 13 14 - 2241 - 17 16 15 14 13

4500409369

Contents

About the Program

Test Best on the Iowa Tests of Basic Skills has been developed to refresh basic skills, familiarize students with test formats and directions, and teach test-taking strategies for the Iowa Tests of Basic Skills. *Test Best* provides teachers with materials to ensure that students take the test under optimal conditions—that test-wise students be able to concentrate on what they know without being overwhelmed by a testing situation with which they are unfamiliar.

Being well prepared for a test means knowing how to approach different types of questions and how to use time wisely. By using the *Test Best* books prior to the administration of the Iowa Tests of Basic Skills, students will learn such skills, as well as be able to control their anxiety about a test and to keep their concentration high throughout the testing period. Armed with the skills they have learned as they work through *Test Best on the Iowa Tests of Basic Skills*, students can truly perform well.

The Steck-Vaughn *Test Best* Series for Grades K–8

Test Best on the Iowa Tests of Basic Skills consists of nine student books. You will need to determine which book is best suited to the abilities and needs of your students. The series is organized as follows:

Book	Grade Level
Level 5	Kindergarten
Levels 6–7	Grade 1
Level 8	Grade 2
Level 9	Grade 3
Level 10	Grade 4
Level 11	Grade 5
Level 12	Grade 6
Level 13	Grade 7
Level 14	Grade 8

Objectives of the Series

To Increase Awareness of Test-Taking Strategies

Test-taking strategies should focus on three important test principles:
1. Time Use
   - Not spending too much time on any one question
   - Working rapidly but comfortably
2. Error Avoidance
   - Paying careful attention to directions
   - Determining clearly what is being asked
   - Marking answers in the appropriate place
   - Checking all answers
   - Being neat by avoiding making stray marks on the test
3. Reasoning
   - Reading the entire question or passage and all the choices before answering a question
   - Applying what has been learned

To Increase Awareness of Directions

It is important that students understand the directions for taking the tests. Therefore, one of the key objectives of the program is to familiarize students with directions. Doing so builds self-confidence and permits students to utilize their time more effectively.

To Increase Awareness of Content and Skills

Anxiety often results from a lack of information about the knowledge and skills the tests will cover. You and your students will find that increased awareness of content and skills are significant outcomes of the program.

To Increase Awareness of Format

By practicing the skills needed to meet your school's educational objectives, the students will gain invaluable experience with test formats. Such familiarity permits students to spend more time applying what they have learned.

To Understand How the Test Is Administered

Students are sometimes uncomfortable anticipating what will happen on the day of the tests. Becoming familiar with the procedures, directions, and the process of test taking helps reduce anxiety and uncertainty.

Format of the Books

Each of the nine student books is divided into units that correspond to those found in the Iowa Tests of Basic Skills. The units vary but can include Vocabulary, Word Analysis, Listening, Reading Comprehension, Spelling, Language Mechanics, Language Expression, Math Concepts and Estimation, Math Problems, Math Computation, Sources of Information, Reference Materials, and Maps and Diagrams. Within each of these units are the skills covered on the tests.

Each skill lesson generally includes

Directions—clear, concise, and similar to those found in the Iowa Tests of Basic Skills;

Try This—A skill strategy for students that enables them to approach each lesson exercise in a logical manner (This feature appears only in the Teacher's Edition of *Test Best on the Iowa Tests of Basic Skills, Levels 6–7*, since most of the material at this level is oral. Including Try This in the Teacher's Edition allows you to orally work through the Try This feature with students.);

A Sample—to familiarize students with test-taking items;

Think It Through—a specific explanation to students of the correct answer in the Sample item that tells why the correct answer is correct and why the incorrect answers are wrong (This feature, like Try This, appears only in the Teacher's Edition of *Test Best on the Iowa Tests of Basic Skills, Levels 6–7*.);

A Practice Section—a set of exercises based on the lesson and modeled on the kinds of test items found in the Iowa Tests of Basic Skills.

Each unit is followed by a Unit Test that covers all the skills in the unit lessons and affords students the opportunity to experience a situation close to the testing situation. Each book concludes with a series of Comprehensive Tests—one for each unit in the book. The *Test Best* Comprehensive Tests give students an opportunity to take a test under conditions that parallel those they will face when taking the Iowa Tests of Basic Skills.

The Teacher's Edition

The Teacher's Edition of *Test Best on the Iowa Tests of Basic Skills* contains a Scope and Sequence and reduced student pages complete with answers. The Teacher's Edition also provides a detailed plan of action and suggestions for teaching and administering each of the lessons and tests, including Sample items. Scripts are provided so that students become familiar with oral directions given on the tests themselves.

Also contained in the Teacher's Edition is an introductory lesson designed to acquaint students with the *Test Best on the Iowa Tests of Basic Skills* program. This lesson appears on pages 7 through 10 and should be used before beginning Lesson 1 with students.

Scope and Sequence

READING AND LISTENING SKILLS

Skill	Unit 1: Vocabulary	Lesson 1: Matching Word Meanings	Lesson 2: Choosing Correct Word Meanings	Unit 1 Test	Unit 2: Word Analysis	Lesson 3: Recognizing Letters	Lesson 4: Recognizing Beginning Sounds	Lesson 5: Matching Rhyming Words	Lesson 6: Making New Words	Lesson 7: Finding Missing Letters	Lesson 8: Matching Vowel Sounds	Unit 2 Test	Unit 3: Reading	Lesson 9: Recognizing Words	Lesson 10: Reading Pictures	Lesson 11: Matching Words and Pictures	Lesson 12: Understanding Pictures	Lesson 13: Reading Stories	Unit 3 Test	Unit 4: Listening	Lesson 14: Building Listening Skills	Unit 4 Test	COMPREHENSIVE TESTS 1, 2, 3, 4
Listening to words and choosing pictures to match		■		■																			■
Recognizing words that match pictures		■		■																			■
Using context to identify words that complete sentences			■	■																			■
Recognizing lowercase letters						■						■											■
Using pictures to recognize and match initial consonant sounds							■					■											■
Using words to recognize and match initial consonant and vowel sounds							■					■											■
Using pictures to recognize and match rhyming words								■				■											■
Recognizing and matching words that rhyme								■				■											■
Understanding how words change when letter substitutions are made									■			■											■
Identifying the letter or letters that are missing from words										■		■											■
Recognizing and matching vowel sounds											■	■											■
Recognizing words presented orally and in print														■				■					■
Recognizing words that correspond to pictures															■			■					■
Matching words and pictures used in context																■		■					■
Relating pictures to sentences																	■	■					■
Understanding stated detail																	■	■	■				■
Making inferences																	■	■	■				■
Determining the main idea																		■	■				■
Making generalizations																		■	■				■
Listening to and remembering details of material presented orally																					■	■	■
Drawing conclusions																					■	■	■
Understanding sequence																					■	■	■
Predicting outcomes																					■	■	■
Following directions																					■	■	■

LANGUAGE SKILLS

	Unit 5: Language	Lesson 15: Understanding Language	Lesson 16: Recognizing and Classifying Words	Lesson 17: Spelling	Lesson 18: Using Correct Capitalization	Lesson 19: Using Correct Punctuation	Lesson 20: Finding Mistakes in Language	Unit 5 Test	COMPREHENSIVE TEST 5
Listening to and remembering details of material presented orally		■						■	■
Understanding prepositions		■						■	■
Understanding singulars and plurals		■						■	■
Inferring characteristics shared by groups		■						■	■
Understanding comparatives and superlatives		■						■	■
Recognizing temporal and spatial relationships		■						■	■
Recognizing basic vocabulary			■					■	■
Understanding classification			■					■	■
Recognizing words spelled correctly				■				■	■
Identifying words spelled incorrectly				■				■	■
Identifying the need for capital letters in sentences					■			■	■
Identifying the need for punctuation marks in sentences						■		■	■
Identifying errors in the use of nouns, pronouns, verbs, adjectives, and adverbs							■	■	■
Recognizing errors in sentence structure							■	■	■

MATHEMATICS SKILLS

Mathematics Skills	Unit 6: Math Concepts	Lesson 21: Understanding Numeration	Lesson 22: Working with Numbers	Lesson 23: Working with Money	Lesson 24: Understanding Measurement	Lesson 25: Understanding Geometry	Unit 6 Test	Unit 7: Math Problems	Lesson 26: Solving Problems	Lesson 27: Using Number Sentences	Lesson 28: Working with Graphs and Tables	Unit 7 Test	Unit 8: Math Computation	Lesson 29: Adding	Lesson 30: Subtracting	Unit 8 Test	COMPREHENSIVE TESTS 6, 7, 8
Understanding patterns and sequences	■						■										■
Counting	■						■										■
Understanding one-to-one correspondence	■						■										■
Understanding properties of number systems	■						■										■
Recognizing different names for numbers	■						■										■
Understanding place value	■						■										■
Recognizing numbers		■					■										■
Understanding whole-number values		■					■										■
Identifying coins				■			■										■
Determining the value of groups of coins				■			■										■
Recognizing analog time					■		■										■
Measuring quantity, time, length, and weight					■		■										■
Understanding simple fractions					■		■										■
Recognizing and comparing basic shapes						■	■										■
Understanding geometric relationships						■	■										■
Solving one-step word problems									■			■					■
Solving multiple-step word problems									■			■					■
Distinguishing between necessary and extraneous data									■			■					■
Understanding symbols for operations and relationships										■		■					■
Recognizing and solving number sentences used to represent problems										■		■					■
Understanding number sentences used to represent number properties										■		■					■
Interpreting graphs and tables											■	■					■
Using data in graphic displays to solve problems											■	■					■
Adding two or more whole numbers presented orally														■		■	■
Adding two or more whole numbers written vertically or horizontally														■		■	■
Renaming														■	■	■	■
Subtracting two whole numbers presented orally															■	■	■
Subtracting two whole numbers written vertically or horizontally															■	■	■

STUDY SKILLS

	Unit 9: Sources of Information	Lesson 31: Alphabetizing	Lesson 32: Understanding Maps	Lesson 33: Using the Dictionary	Lesson 34: Using a Table of Contents	Unit 9 Test	COMPREHENSIVE TEST 9
Alphabetizing words by their first letter		■				■	■
Understanding sequence		■				■	■
Using maps to locate information			■			■	■
Determining direction and distance			■			■	■
Using a dictionary to determine word spellings and definitions				■		■	■
Using a table of contents to locate information					■	■	■

Introducing Students to *Test Best*

Use this orientation to familiarize students with the format of *Test Best on the Iowa Tests of Basic Skills, Levels 6–7,* and with steps for preparing for and taking the Iowa Tests of Basic Skills.

SAY: **At certain times during the school year, you may take one or more special tests. These tests show how well you are doing in certain subjects, compared with other students of your age group across the country.**

Point out to students that most people worry when they have to take a test. Explain that *Test Best* practice lessons and class discussions can help prepare them for the test, so there will be no reason to worry. Tell students that the tests will not affect school grades. The tests will tell students about themselves—about the skills they have learned and the skills they need to learn. Distribute the *Test Best* books to students. Tell students that *Test Best* will use the same kinds of questions that are on the special test, the Iowa Tests of Basic Skills. Using the *Test Best* books will be practice for taking the special test.

SAY: **Some test questions will be harder than others, and some may be new to you. But that's all right. You will be given enough time to work on each test.**

Allow students to skim through the books for a minute or two. Circulate around the room, making sure that all students are turned to the correct page as you examine the books.

SAY: **Now we will look at one of the lessons. Turn to Lesson 1 on page 1. You should be on the page with the scissors at the top. Across from the scissors the page has *Unit 1, Vocabulary*. That tells you the number and the name of the unit. This unit is about words. Just under the unit number and name it has *Lesson 1: Matching Word Meanings*. That tells you the number and the name of the lesson. This lesson is about word meanings. This is how a lesson page looks. What do you see just below the lesson number and name? (The letter *S* and the number *1*) This is <u>Sample 1</u>. A sample is a practice question. We will always work the samples together.**

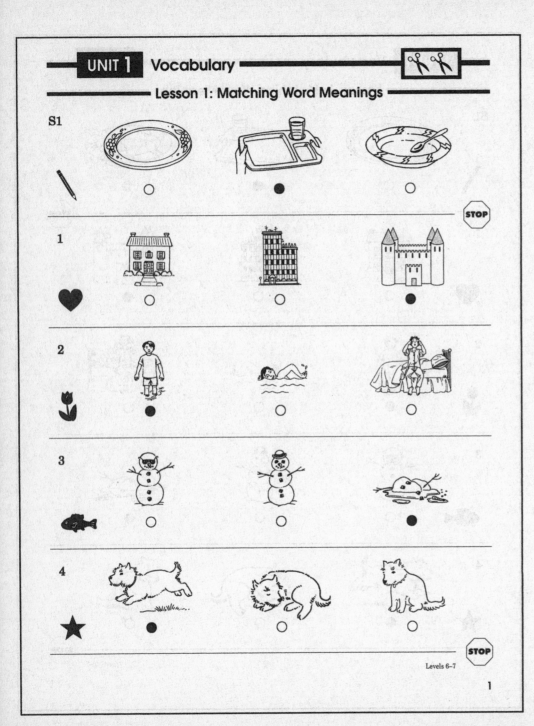

UNIT 1 Vocabulary

Lesson 1: Matching Word Meanings

S1

1

2

3

4

Levels 6–7

1

SAY: **What do you see in the row with <u>S1</u>? (Some pictures) The picture of the pencil at the beginning of the row is there to help you find your place on the page. What do you see just below each of the other pictures in the row? (A small circle) The pictures are the answer choices. When you decide on your answer, you will use your pencil to darken the circle, or answer space, for the answer choice. Let me show you how to darken the answer space.**

Draw a small circle on the chalkboard. Demonstrate the proper way to darken the answer space. Explain to students the importance of filling the answer space, pressing firmly with the pencil to make a dark mark, and erasing any stray marks that might be picked up as answers by the scoring machines.

Ask students if they have any questions.

SAY: **What do you see at the right, at the end of the row for <u>S1</u>? (A stop sign) What should you do when you see a stop sign? (Stop what you are doing.)**

Tell students that they will see stop signs throughout the lessons and on the Iowa Tests of Basic Skills. Explain that the stop sign is used to tell students to stop what they are doing, put their pencils down, and wait for further instructions from the teacher.

SAY: **Now look directly below the row for <u>S1</u>. What do you see? (The numbers *1, 2, 3, 4* and more pictures and answer circles) The numbers and pictures at the beginning of the rows stand for the lesson questions. The other pictures stand for the answer choices. I will ask you questions, and you will look at the answer choices. Then you will choose your answer.**

Now look at the bottom of the page. What do you see at the right, just below the last row of pictures? (A stop sign) What does the stop sign tell you to do? (Stop what you are doing, put your pencils down, and wait for further instructions from the teacher.)

Ask students if they have any questions about the lesson page.

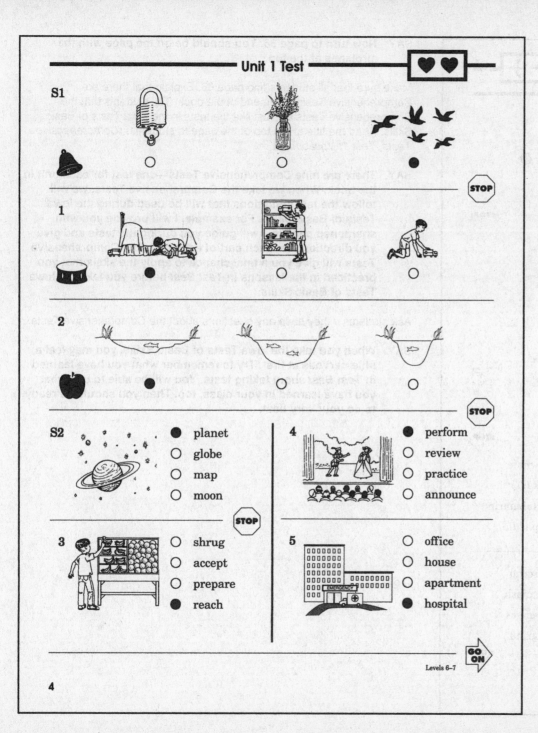

Unit 1 Test ♥♥

S1

○   ○   ●   **STOP**

1

○   ○   ○   **STOP**

2

○   ○   ○   **STOP**

S2
- ● planet
- ○ globe
- ○ map
- ○ moon

STOP

3
- ○ shrug
- ○ accept
- ○ prepare
- ● reach

4
- ● perform
- ○ review
- ○ practice
- ○ announce

5
- ○ office
- ○ house
- ○ apartment
- ● hospital

Levels 6–7

GO ON

4

SAY: **Now turn to page 4 in your books. You should be on the page with the hearts at the top.**

Make sure that all students find page 4. Explain that there is a unit test at the end of each unit that gives students an opportunity to practice taking a test.

Tell students to look at page 4. Have students locate <u>Sample 1</u> and <u>Sample 2</u> on the test. Tell students that you will always work the <u>Samples</u> together as a class. Explain that the unit test will include the skills you have practiced together in the unit lessons.

SAY: **Look at the bottom of page 4. What do you see at the bottom of the page? (An arrow with the words *GO ON*) This tells you to go to the next page.**

Ask students if they have any questions about the unit tests.

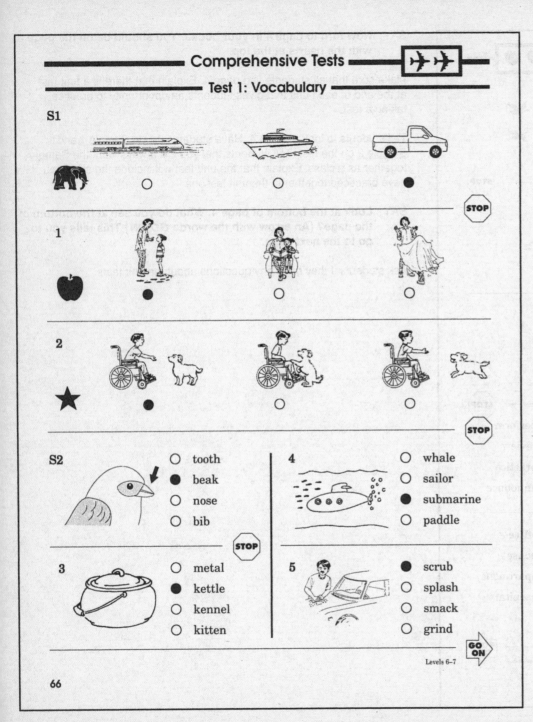

Comprehensive Tests

Test 1: Vocabulary

S1

1

2

S2
- ○ tooth
- ● beak
- ○ nose
- ○ bib

3
- ○ metal
- ● kettle
- ○ kennel
- ○ kitten

4
- ○ whale
- ○ sailor
- ● submarine
- ○ paddle

5
- ● scrub
- ○ splash
- ○ smack
- ○ grind

STOP

GO ON

Levels 6–7

SAY: Now turn to page 66. You should be on the page with the airplanes at the top.

Make sure that all students find page 66. Explain that there are Comprehensive Tests at the end of the book. Tell students that the Comprehensive Tests are just like the tests in the Iowa Tests of Basic Skills. Read the title at the top of the page to students. (*Comprehensive Tests, Test 1: Vocabulary*)

SAY: There are nine Comprehensive Tests—one test for each unit in the book. When we take the Comprehensive Tests, we will follow the test conditions that will be used during the Iowa Tests of Basic Skills. For example, I will provide you with sharpened pencils. I will guide you during the tests and give you directions for each part of each test. The Comprehensive Tests will give you a final chance to apply the skills that you practiced in the lessons in *Test Best* before you take the Iowa Tests of Basic Skills.

Ask students if they have any questions about the Comprehensive Tests.

SAY: When you take the Iowa Tests of Basic Skills, you may feel a little nervous at first. Try to remember what you have learned in *Test Best* about taking tests. You will be able to use what you have learned in your class, too. Then you should be ready to do your very best.

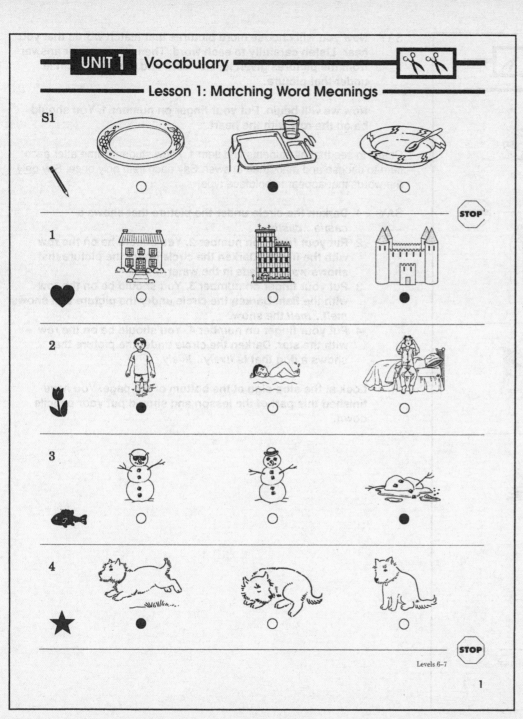

UNIT 1 Vocabulary

Lesson 1: Matching Word Meanings

Reading Skills: Listening to words and choosing pictures to match; recognizing words that match pictures

SAY: **Turn to Lesson 1, Matching Word Meanings, on page 1. You should be on the page with the scissors at the top.**

Check to see that all students find Lesson 1. Introduce the Try This feature.

SAY: **In the first part of Lesson 1, you will practice choosing pictures that match words that you hear.**

Listen carefully. When I say a word, you should <u>try this</u>: look carefully at each picture. Find the picture that matches the word that you hear. Then darken the circle under that picture. Put your finger on <u>S1</u>. You should be on the row with the pencil. This is <u>Sample 1</u>. We will work <u>Sample 1</u> together. Look at the three pictures in <u>Sample 1</u>. They are the answer choices. Listen carefully. Darken the circle under the picture that shows a *tray...tray.*

Do not identify the picture choices to the students. Allow students time to choose and mark their answer. Remind students to carefully fill in the answer circle and to completely erase any stray marks. Then introduce the Think It Through feature.

SAY: **Now we will <u>think it through</u>. We will check the answer. You should have darkened the circle under the second picture. It shows a flat surface with a raised edge that is used to carry things. A *tray* has a flat surface with a raised edge, and it is used to carry things. The first picture shows a *plate*. The last picture shows a *bowl*. The correct answer is the second picture. It shows a *tray*.**

Check to see that all students have filled in the correct answer space. If students have not filled in the correct answer space, caution them to completely erase their incorrect answer and to erase any stray marks before they darken the correct answer circle. Remind students that they were instructed to choose the picture that shows a *tray*. Ask students if they have any questions about <u>Sample 1</u> or about darkening the answer circle.

Lesson 1: Matching Word Meanings

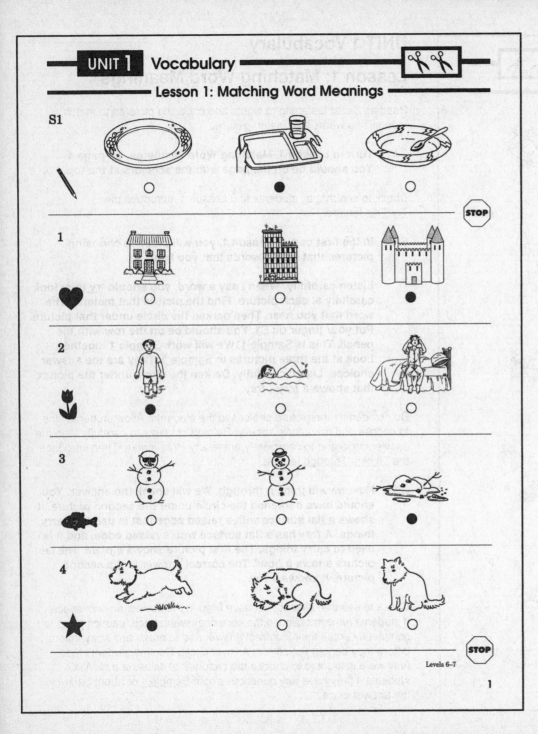

S1

1

2

3

4

Levels 6–7

SAY: **Now you will choose more pictures that match words that you hear. Listen carefully to each word. Then choose your answer from the pictures given for the word and darken the circle under that picture.**

Now we will begin. Put your finger on number 1. You should be on the row with the heart.

Check to see that all students find item 1. Allow students time after each item to choose and mark their answer. Say each item only once. Say only the words that appear in boldface type.

SAY: 1 **Darken the circle under the picture that shows a** *castle...castle.*

2 **Put your finger on number 2. You should be on the row with the flower. Darken the circle under the picture that shows** *wade...wade* **in the water.**

3 **Put your finger on number 3. You should be on the row with the fish. Darken the circle under the picture that shows** *melt...melt* **the snow.**

4 **Put your finger on number 4. You should be on the row with the star. Darken the circle under the picture that shows a dog that is** *lively...lively.*

Look at the stop sign at the bottom of the page. You have finished this part of the lesson and should put your pencils down.

1

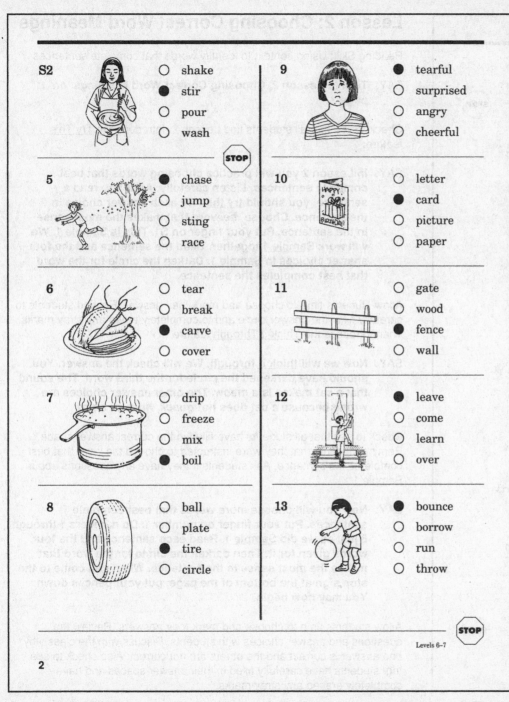

S2
- ○ shake
- ● stir
- ○ pour
- ○ wash

STOP

5
- ● chase
- ○ jump
- ○ sting
- ○ race

6
- ○ tear
- ○ break
- ● carve
- ○ cover

7
- ○ drip
- ○ freeze
- ○ mix
- ● boil

8
- ○ ball
- ○ plate
- ● tire
- ○ circle

9
- ● tearful
- ○ surprised
- ○ angry
- ○ cheerful

10
- ○ letter
- ● card
- ○ picture
- ○ paper

11
- ○ gate
- ○ wood
- ● fence
- ○ wall

12
- ● leave
- ○ come
- ○ learn
- ○ over

13
- ● bounce
- ○ borrow
- ○ run
- ○ throw

STOP

Levels 6–7

2

SAY: **Now turn to page 2.**

Check to see that all students find page 2.

SAY: **In the second part of Lesson 1, you will practice choosing words that match pictures.**

Listen carefully. When you look at a picture, you should try this: read each word beside it. Then decide which word matches the picture. Darken the circle for the word that matches what the picture shows.

Put your finger on S2. This is Sample 2. We will work Sample 2 together. Now look at the picture in Sample 2. There are four words beside the picture. Read the four words. Then darken the circle for the word that matches the picture.

Allow students time to choose and mark their answer. Remind students to carefully fill in the answer circle and to completely erase any stray marks.

SAY: **Now we will think it through. We will check the answer. You should have darkened the circle for the second word. The picture shows a woman stirring something in a bowl. Stir is the word that matches the picture.**

Check to see that all students have filled in the correct answer space. Remind students that they were instructed to choose the word that best matches the picture.

Ask students if they have any questions about Sample 2 or about darkening the answer circle.

SAY: **Now you will practice choosing more words that match pictures. Put your finger on number 5. Do numbers 5 through 13 just as we did Sample 2. Look at each picture and read the words beside it. Then darken the circle for the word that matches the picture. When you come to the stop sign at the bottom of the page, put your pencils down. You may now begin.**

Check to see that all students find item 5. Allow students time to choose and mark their answers.

Review the questions and answer choices with students. Discuss with the class why one answer is correct and the others are not correct. Also check to see that students have carefully filled in their answer spaces and have completely erased any stray marks.

Lesson 2: Choosing Correct Word Meanings

S1 A sound made by a cat is a . . .

○ quack   ○ hum   ● meow   ○ chirp

🛑 STOP

---

1 Something that unlocks a door is a . . .

● key   ○ knob   ○ hinge   ○ bell

2 To do something right away is to do it . . .

○ soon   ○ later   ○ never   ● now

3 To look in stores for things to buy is to . . .

○ hunt   ● shop   ○ find   ○ pay

4 Something that cannot be found is . . .

○ here   ○ broken   ● lost   ○ left

5 Something that has never been used is . . .

○ old   ○ clean   ○ different   ● new

6 To go fast is to . . .

○ rise   ○ repeat   ○ crawl   ● hurry

7 A room to cook food in is a . . .

○ stove   ○ bedroom   ● kitchen   ○ pan

8 To look at something very quickly is to . . .

● glance   ○ stare   ○ blink   ○ doze

🛑 STOP

Levels 6–7

3

Lesson 2: Choosing Correct Word Meanings

Reading Skill: Using context to identify words that complete sentences

SAY: **Turn to Lesson 2, Choosing Correct Word Meanings, on page 3.**

Check to see that all students find Lesson 2. Introduce the Try This feature.

SAY: **In Lesson 2 you will practice choosing words that best complete sentences. Listen carefully. After you read a sentence, you should try this: try each answer choice in the sentence. Choose the word that makes the most sense in the sentence. Put your finger on S1. This is Sample 1. We will work Sample 1 together. Read the sentence and the four answer choices in Sample 1. Darken the circle for the word that best completes the sentence.**

Allow students time to choose and mark their answer. Remind students to carefully fill in the answer circle and to completely erase any stray marks. Then introduce the Think It Through feature.

SAY: **Now we will think it through. We will check the answer. You should have darkened the circle for the third word. The sound that a cat makes is a _meow_. The other answer choices are wrong because a cat does not _quack_, _hum_, or _chirp_.**

Check to see that all students have filled in the correct answer space. Remind students that they were instructed to choose the word that best completes the sentence. Ask students if they have any questions about Sample 1 .

SAY: **Now you will choose more words that best complete sentences. Put your finger on number 1. Do numbers 1 through 8 just as we did Sample 1. Read each sentence and the four words given for it. Then darken the circle for the word that makes the most sense in the sentence. When you come to the stop sign at the bottom of the page, put your pencils down. You may now begin.**

Allow students time to choose and mark their answers. Review the questions and answer choices with students. Discuss with the class why one answer is correct and the others are not correct. Also check to see that students have carefully filled in their answer spaces and have completely erased any stray marks.

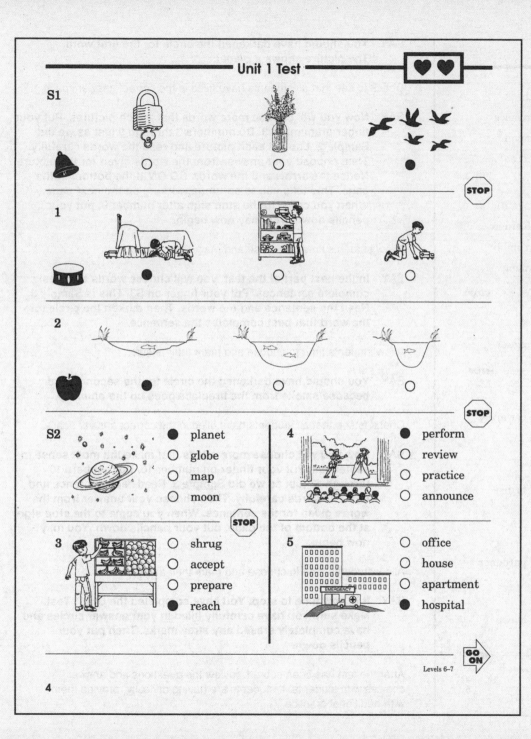

Unit 1 Test

SAY: **Turn to the Unit 1 Test on page 4. You should be on the page with the hearts at the top.**

Check to see that all students find the Unit 1 Test.

SAY: **In the first part of this test, you will choose pictures that match words that you hear. Put your finger on S1. You should be on the row with the bell. This is Sample 1. Look at the three pictures in Sample 1. Now listen carefully. Darken the circle under the picture that shows a *flock...flock*.**

Allow students time to choose and mark their answer. Remind students that they were instructed to choose the picture that shows a *flock*.

SAY: **You should have darkened the circle under the third picture because it shows a *flock* of birds.**

Check to see that all students have filled in the correct answer space. Ask students if they have any questions.

SAY: **Now you will choose more pictures that match words that you hear. Listen carefully to each word. Then choose your answer from the pictures given for the word. Put your finger on number 1. You should be on the row with the drum.**

Check to see that all students find item 1. Allow students time after each item to choose and mark their answer. Say each item only once. Say only the words that appear in boldface type.

SAY: 1 **Darken the circle under the picture that shows *search...search* for the toy.**
2 **Put your finger on number 2. You should be on the row with the apple. Darken the circle under the picture that shows the water that is *shallow...shallow*.**

Look at the stop sign at the end of the row. You have finished this part of the test and should put your pencils down.

In the next part of the test, you will choose words that match pictures. Put your finger on S2. This is Sample 2. Look at the picture. Then read the words beside it. Darken the circle for the word that matches the picture.

Allow students time to choose and mark their answer.

6		8	
	○ bridge		○ check
	○ train		○ menace
	● tunnel		● menu
	○ escape		○ note

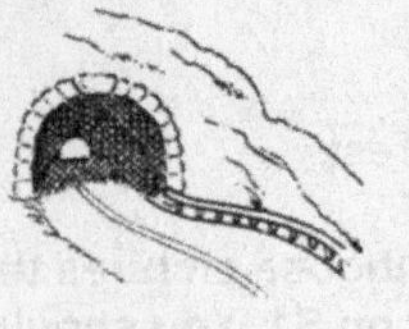

Hamburger $2
French Fries $1
Hot dog $1.50
Soda S $1.00
      L $1.50

7		9	
	○ mound		● gigantic
	○ gravel		○ average
	● garden		○ crumbly
	○ puddle		○ young

STOP

S3   Smoke from the
fireplace goes
up the . . .   ○ window ● chimney ○ stove   ○ closet

STOP

10   Someone who is
not frightened
easily is . . .   ● brave   ○ furious ○ smart   ○ cowardly

11   The part of your
body you think
with is your . . .   ○ scalp   ○ heart   ● brain   ○ bruise

12   Someone who helps
people who are
sick is a . . .   ○ teacher ○ farmer ● doctor   ○ gardener

13   Something that is
shiny is . . .   ○ simple ● bright ○ dull   ○ cheap

STOP

Levels 6-7

SAY: **You should have darkened the circle for the first word.
The picture shows a *planet*.**

Check to see that all students have filled in the correct answer space.

SAY: **Now you will choose more words that match pictures. Put your
finger on number 3. Do numbers 3 through 9 just as we did
Sample 2. Look at each picture and read the words carefully.
Then choose your answer from the words given for the picture.
Notice the arrow and the words *GO ON* at the bottom of the
page. This tells you to continue working on the next page.
When you come to the stop sign after number 9, put your
pencils down. You may now begin.**

Allow students time to choose and mark their answers.

SAY: **In the next part of the test, you will choose words that best
complete sentences. Put your finger on S3. This is Sample 3.
Read the sentence and the words. Then darken the circle for
the word that best completes the sentence.**

Allow students time to choose and mark their answer.

SAY: **You should have darkened the circle for the second word
because smoke from the fireplace goes up the *chimney*.**

Check to see that all students have filled in the correct answer space.

SAY: **Now you will choose more words that make the most sense in
sentences. Put your finger on number 10. Do numbers 10
through 13 just as we did Sample 3. Read each sentence and
the four words carefully. Then choose your answer from the
words given for the sentence. When you come to the stop sign
at the bottom of the page, put your pencils down. You may
now begin.**

Allow students time to choose and mark their answers.

SAY: **It is now time to stop. You have completed the Unit 1 Test.
Make sure you have carefully filled in your answer circles and
have completely erased any stray marks. Then put your
pencils down.**

After the test has been scored, review the questions and answer
choices with students. If students are having difficulty, provide them
with additional practice.

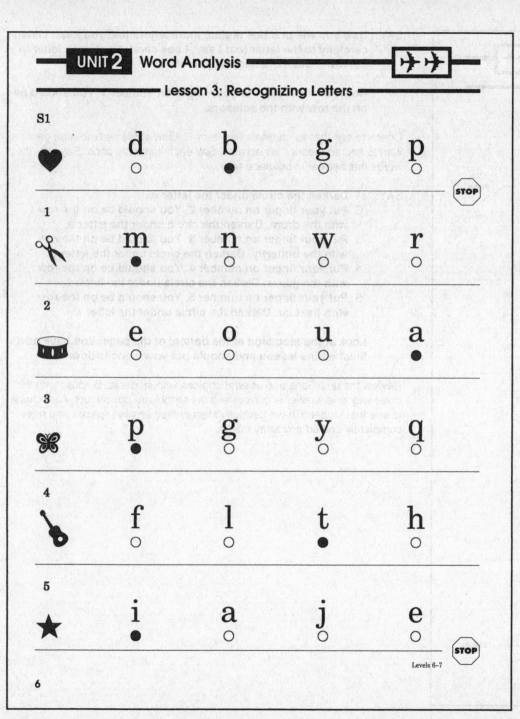

UNIT 2 Word Analysis

Lesson 3: Recognizing Letters

Reading Skill: Recognizing lowercase letters

SAY: **Turn to Lesson 3, Recognizing Letters, on page 6. You should be on the page with the airplanes at the top.**

Check to see that all students find Lesson 3. Introduce the Try This feature.

SAY: **In Lesson 3 you will practice finding letters that you hear.**

Listen carefully. When I say a letter, you should try this: look carefully at each letter in the row. Find the letter that you hear.

Put your finger on S1. You should be on the row with the heart. This is Sample 1. Now listen carefully. Look at the four letters in Sample 1. Darken the circle under the letter b.

Do not read the letter choices to the students. Allow students time to choose and mark their answer. Remind students to carefully fill in the answer circle and to completely erase any stray marks. Then introduce the Think It Through feature.

SAY: **Now we will think it through. We will check the answer. You should have darkened the circle under the second letter. The second letter is b. The first letter is d, the third letter is g, and the fourth letter is p.**

Check to see that all students have filled in the correct answer space. Remind students that they were instructed to find the letter b.

Ask students if they have any questions about Sample 1 or about darkening the answer circle.

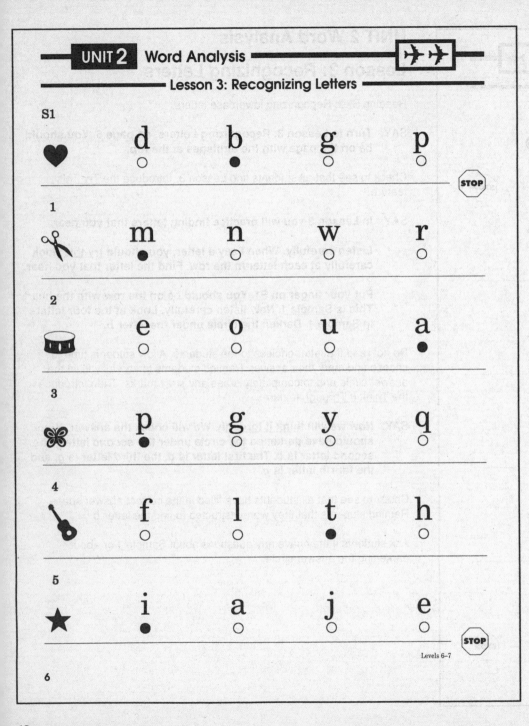

S1

♥   d ○   b ●   g ○   p ○   **STOP**

1

✂   m ●   n ○   w ○   r ○

2

🥁   e ○   o ○   u ○   a ●

3

🦋   p ●   g ○   y ○   q ○

4

🎸   f ○   l ○   t ●   h ○

5

★   i ●   a ○   j ○   e ○   **STOP**

Levels 6–7

6

SAY: **Now you will practice finding more letters that you hear. Listen carefully to the letter that I say. Look carefully at each letter in the row. Find the letter that you hear.**

Now we will begin. Put your finger on number 1. You should be on the row with the scissors.

Check to see that all students find item 1. Allow students time after each item to find and mark their answer. Say each item only once. Say <u>only</u> the words that appear in boldface type.

SAY: 1 **Darken the circle under the letter** *m*.
2 **Put your finger on number 2. You should be on the row with the drum. Darken the circle under the letter** *a*.
3 **Put your finger on number 3. You should be on the row with the butterfly. Darken the circle under the letter** *p*.
4 **Put your finger on number 4. You should be on the row with the guitar. Darken the circle under the letter** *t*.
5 **Put your finger on number 5. You should be on the row with the star. Darken the circle under the letter** *i*.

Look at the stop sign at the bottom of the page. You have now finished the lesson and should put your pencils down.

Review the questions and answer choices with students. Discuss with the class why one answer is correct and the others are not correct. Also check to see that students have carefully filled in their answer spaces and have completely erased any stray marks.

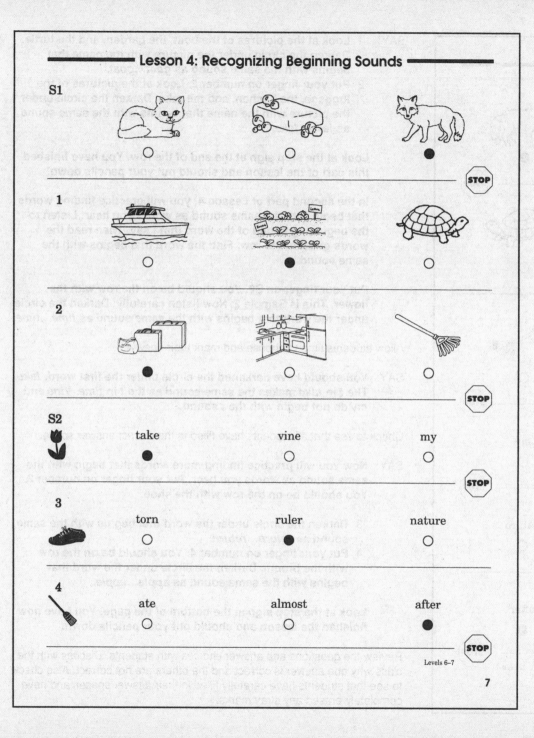

Lesson 4: Recognizing Beginning Sounds

Reading Skills: Using pictures to recognize and match initial consonant sounds; using words to recognize and match initial consonant and vowel sounds

SAY: **Turn to Lesson 4, Recognizing Beginning Sounds, on page 7.**

Check to see that all students find Lesson 4. Introduce the Try This feature.

SAY: **In the first part of Lesson 4, you will practice finding pictures with names that begin with the same sound as words you hear. Listen carefully. When I say a word, you should try this: listen to the beginning sound of the word. Remember that sound. Then find the picture with the name that begins with the same sound. Put your finger on S1. This is Sample 1. Look at the pictures of the kitten, the soap, and the fox. Now listen carefully. Darken the circle under the picture with the name that begins with the same sound as _fit...fit_.**

Allow students time to choose and mark their answer. Remind students to carefully fill in the answer circle and to completely erase any stray marks. Then introduce the Think It Through feature.

SAY: **Now we will think it through. We will check the answer. You should have darkened the circle under the third picture. _Fox_ is the correct answer. The _f_ in _fox_ makes the same sound as the _f_ in _fit_. _Kitten_ and _soap_ do not begin with the _f_ sound.**

Check to see that all students have filled in the correct answer space.

Ask students if they have any questions about Sample 1 or about darkening the answer circle.

SAY: **Now you will practice finding more pictures with names that begin with the same sound as words you hear. Listen carefully to the beginning sound of each word. Then look at the pictures given in the row. Find the picture that begins with the same sound as the word that you hear.**

Now we will begin. Put your finger on number 1.

Check to see that all students find item 1. Allow students time after each item to choose and mark their answer. Say each item only once. Say only the words that appear in boldface type.

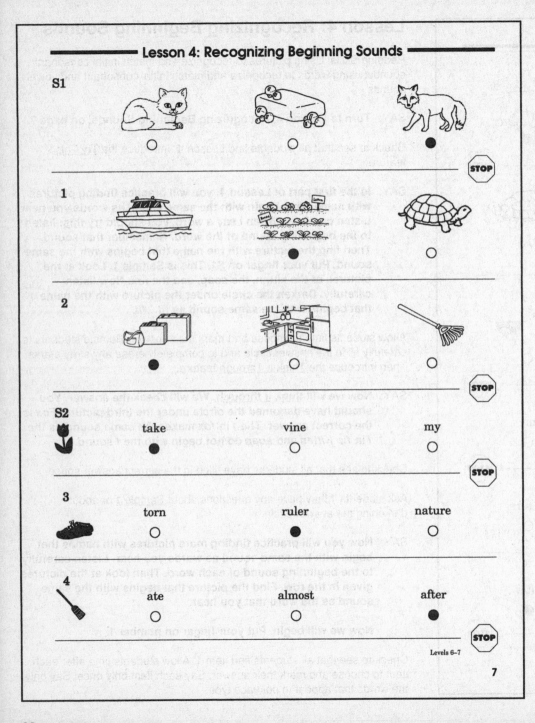

Lesson 4: Recognizing Beginning Sounds

S1

○   ○   ●

STOP

1

○   ●   ○

2

●   ○   ○

STOP

S2

take   vine   my
●   ○   ○

STOP

3

torn   ruler   nature
○   ●   ○

4

ate   almost   after
○   ○   ●

STOP

Levels 6–7

7

SAY: 1   **Look at the pictures of the boat, the garden, and the turtle. Darken the circle under the picture with the name that begins with the same sound as *goat...goat*.**

2   **Put your finger on number 2. Look at the pictures of the luggage, the kitchen, and the rake. Darken the circle under the picture with the name that begins with the same sound as *lake...lake*.**

Look at the stop sign at the end of the row. You have finished this part of the lesson and should put your pencils down.

In the second part of Lesson 4, you will practice finding words that begin with the same sound as words you hear. Listen to the beginning sound of the word that I say. Then read the words given in the row. Find the word that begins with the same sound.

Put your finger on S2. You should be on the row with the flower. This is Sample 2. Now listen carefully. Darken the circle under the word that begins with the same sound as *time...time*.

Allow students time to choose and mark their answer.

SAY: **You should have darkened the circle under the first word, *take*. The *t* in *take* makes the same sound as the *t* in *time*. *Vine* and *my* do not begin with the *t* sound.**

Check to see that all students have filled in the correct answer space.

SAY: **Now you will practice finding more words that begin with the same sound as words you hear. Put your finger on number 3. You should be on the row with the shoe.**

3   **Darken the circle under the word that begins with the same sound as *return...return*.**

4   **Put your finger on number 4. You should be on the row with the broom. Darken the circle under the word that begins with the same sound as *apple...apple*.**

Look at the stop sign at the bottom of the page. You have now finished the lesson and should put your pencils down.

Review the questions and answer choices with students. Discuss with the class why one answer is correct and the others are not correct. Also check to see that students have carefully filled in their answer spaces and have completely erased any stray marks.

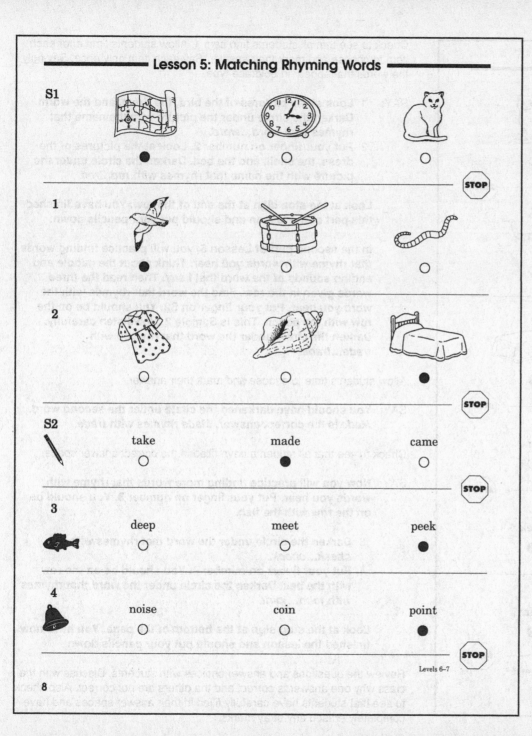

Lesson 5: Matching Rhyming Words

Reading Skills: Using pictures to recognize and match rhyming words; recognizing and matching words that rhyme

SAY: Turn to Lesson 5, Matching Rhyming Words, on page 8.

Check to see that all students find Lesson 5. Introduce the Try This feature.

SAY: In the first part of Lesson 5, you will practice finding pictures with names that rhyme with words you hear. When words rhyme, they have the same sounds in the middle and at the end. They begin with different sounds. *Hop* and *pop* rhyme. *Car* and *cape* do not rhyme.

Now listen carefully. When I say a word, you should try this: say the word to yourself. Think about the middle and ending sounds. Look at the three pictures given for the word. Then find the picture with the name that rhymes with the word you hear.

Put your finger on S1. This is Sample 1. There are pictures of a map, a clock, and a cat. Now listen carefully. Darken the circle under the picture with the name that rhymes with *clap...clap.*

Allow students time to choose and mark their answer. Remind students to carefully fill in the answer circle and to completely erase any stray marks. Then introduce the Think It Through feature.

SAY: Now we will think it through. We will check the answer. You should have darkened the circle under the first picture. *Map* is the correct answer. *Map* rhymes with *clap*.

Check to see that all students have filled in the correct answer space. Remind students that they were instructed to find the picture with the name that rhymes with *clap*.

Ask students if they have any questions about Sample 1 or about darkening the answer circle.

SAY: Now you will practice finding more pictures with names that rhyme with words you hear. Listen carefully to each word. Then find the picture with the name that rhymes with the word that you hear. Now we will begin. Put your finger on number 1.

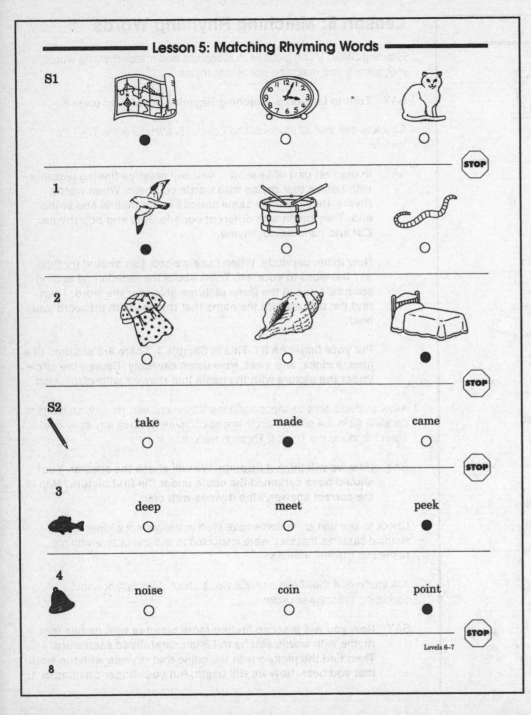

Lesson 5: Matching Rhyming Words

S1

STOP

1

STOP

2

STOP

S2

take   made   came

STOP

3

deep   meet   peek

4

noise   coin   point

STOP

Levels 6–7

8

Check to see that all students find item 1. Allow students time after each item to choose and mark their answer. Say each item only once. Say <u>only</u> the words that appear in boldface type.

SAY: 1 **Look at the pictures of the bird, the drum, and the worm. Darken the circle under the picture with the name that rhymes with *word...word*.**

2 **Put your finger on number 2. Look at the pictures of the dress, the shell, and the bed. Darken the circle under the picture with the name that rhymes with *red...red*.**

Look at the stop sign at the end of the row. You have finished this part of the lesson and should put your pencils down.

In the second part of Lesson 5, you will practice finding words that rhyme with words you hear. Think about the middle and ending sounds of the word that I say. Then read the three words given in the row. Find the word that rhymes with the word you hear. Put your finger on S2. You should be on the row with the pencil. This is Sample 2. Now listen carefully. Darken the circle under the word that rhymes with *trade...trade*.

Allow students time to choose and mark their answer.

SAY: **You should have darkened the circle under the second word. *Made* is the correct answer. *Made* rhymes with *trade*.**

Check to see that all students have filled in the correct answer space.

SAY: **Now you will practice finding more words that rhyme with words you hear. Put your finger on number 3. You should be on the row with the fish.**

3 **Darken the circle under the word that rhymes with *cheek...cheek*.**

4 **Put your finger on number 4. You should be on the row with the bell. Darken the circle under the word that rhymes with *joint...joint*.**

Look at the stop sign at the bottom of the page. You have now finished the lesson and should put your pencils down.

Review the questions and answer choices with students. Discuss with the class why one answer is correct and the others are not correct. Also check to see that students have carefully filled in their answer spaces and have completely erased any stray marks.

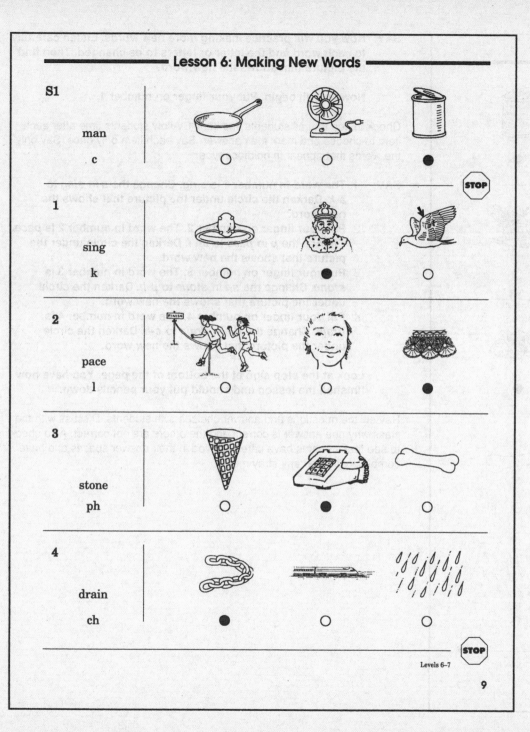

Lesson 6: Making New Words

Reading Skill: Understanding how words change when letter substitutions are made

SAY: **Turn to Lesson 6, Making New Words, on page 9.**

Check to see that all students find Lesson 6. Introduce the Try This feature.

SAY: **In Lesson 6 you will practice changing letters to make new words.**

Listen carefully. When I say a word, you should try this: say the word to yourself. Make a new word by changing the letter or letters I say. You can also read the word and the letter to be changed. Look at each picture in the row. Then find the picture that shows the new word.

Put your finger on S1. This is Sample 1. Now listen carefully. The word in Sample 1 is _man_. Change the _m_ in _man_ to a _c_. Darken the circle under the picture that shows the new word.

Allow students time to choose and mark their answer. Remind students to carefully fill in the answer circle and to completely erase any stray marks. Then introduce the Think It Through feature.

SAY: **Now we will think it through. We will check the answer. You should have darkened the circle under the picture of the _can_. When the _m_ in _man_ is changed to a _c_, the word becomes _can_.**

Check to see that all students have filled in the correct answer space. Remind students that they were instructed to find the picture that shows the new word that is made when the _m_ in _man_ is changed to a _c_.

Ask students if they have any questions about Sample 1 or about darkening the answer circle.

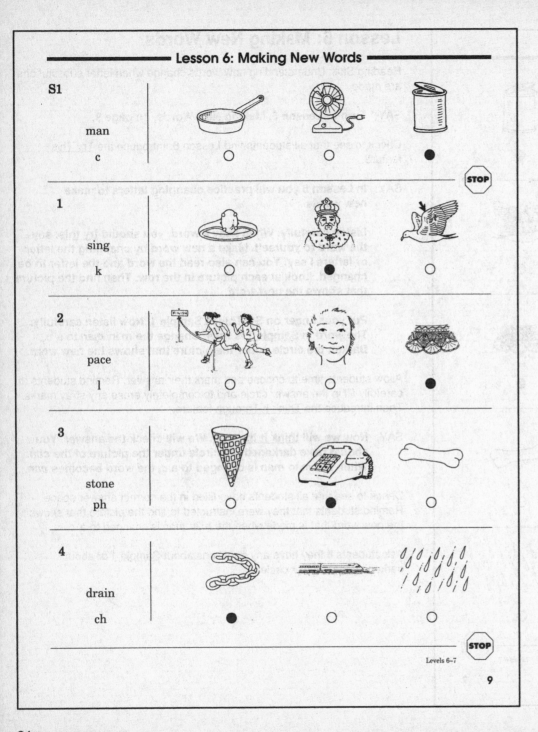

Lesson 6: Making New Words

S1

man

c

STOP

1

sing

k

2

pace

l

3

stone

ph

4

drain

ch

STOP

Levels 6–7

9

SAY: **Now you will practice making more new words. Listen carefully to each word and the letter or letters to be changed. Then find the picture that shows the new word.**

Now we will begin. Put your finger on number 1.

Check to see that all students find item 1. Allow students time after each item to choose and mark their answer. Say each item only once. Say <u>only</u> the words that appear in boldface type.

SAY: 1 **The word in number 1 is *sing*. Change the *s* in *sing* to a *k*. Darken the circle under the picture that shows the new word.**
  2 **Put your finger on number 2. The word in number 2 is *pace*. Change the *p* in *pace* to an *l*. Darken the circle under the picture that shows the new word.**
  3 **Put your finger on number 3. The word in number 3 is *stone*. Change the *s-t* in *stone* to *p-h*. Darken the circle under the picture that shows the new word.**
  4 **Put your finger on number 4. The word in number 4 is *drain*. Change the *d-r* in *drain* to *c-h*. Darken the circle under the picture that shows the new word.**

Look at the stop sign at the bottom of the page. You have now finished the lesson and should put your pencils down.

Review the questions and answer choices with students. Discuss with the class why one answer is correct and the others are not correct. Also check to see that students have carefully filled in their answer spaces and have completely erased any stray marks.

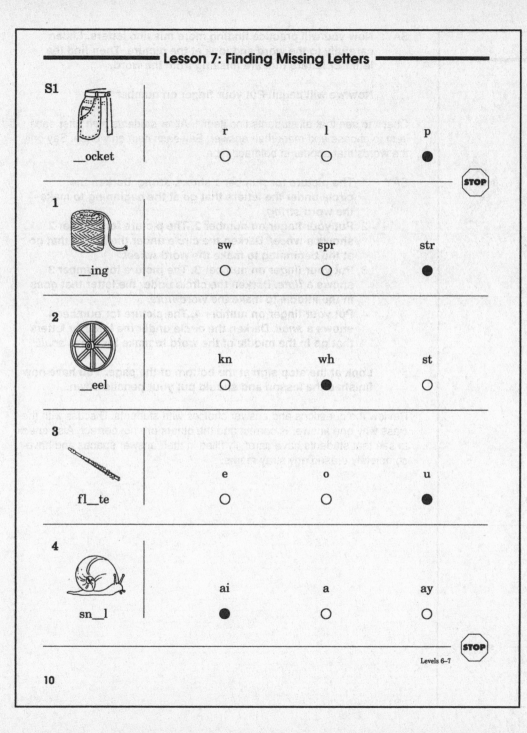

Lesson 7: Finding Missing Letters

Reading Skill: Identifying the letter or letters that are missing from words

SAY: **Turn to Lesson 7, Finding Missing Letters, on page 10.**

Check to see that all students find Lesson 7. Introduce the Try This feature.

SAY: **In Lesson 7 you will practice finding letters that are missing from words.**

Listen carefully. When I say a word, you should try this: say the word to yourself. Look at the picture and the part of the word that are shown at the beginning of the row. Then look at the letters that are given as answer choices. Find the letter or letters that are missing from the word.

Put your finger on S1. This is Sample 1. Now listen carefully. The picture for Sample 1 shows a *pocket*. Darken the circle under the letter that goes at the beginning to make the word *pocket*.

Allow students time to choose and mark their answer. Remind students to carefully fill in the answer circle and to completely erase any stray marks. Then introduce the Think It Through feature.

SAY: **Now we will think it through. We will check the answer. You should have darkened the circle under the *p*. The word *pocket* has a *p* at the beginning.**

Check to see that all students have filled in the correct answer space. Remind students that they were instructed to find the letter that goes at the beginning of the word to make *pocket*.

Ask students if they have any questions about Sample 1 or about darkening the answer circle.

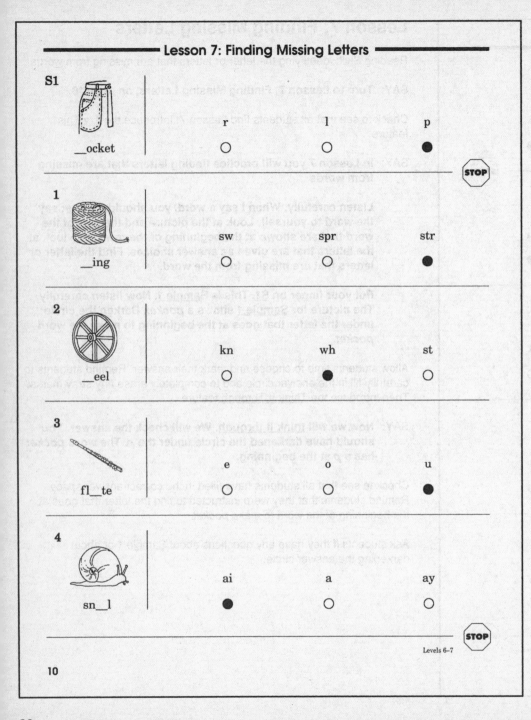

Lesson 7: Finding Missing Letters

S1

__ocket

r	l	p
○	○	●

STOP

1

__ing

sw	spr	str
○	○	●

2

__eel

kn	wh	st
○	●	○

3

fl__te

e	o	u
○	○	●

4

sn__l

ai	a	ay
●	○	○

STOP

10

SAY: **Now you will practice finding more missing letters. Listen carefully to the word and look at the picture. Then find the letter or letters that are missing from the word.**

Now we will begin. Put your finger on number 1.

Check to see that all students find item 1. Allow students time after each item to choose and mark their answer. Say each item only once. Say <u>only</u> the words that appear in boldface type.

SAY: 1 **The picture for number 1 shows *string*. Darken the circle under the letters that go at the beginning to make the word *string*.**

2 **Put your finger on number 2. The picture for number 2 shows a *wheel*. Darken the circle under the letters that go at the beginning to make the word *wheel*.**

3 **Put your finger on number 3. The picture for number 3 shows a *flute*. Darken the circle under the letter that goes in the middle to make the word *flute*.**

4 **Put your finger on number 4. The picture for number 4 shows a *snail*. Darken the circle under the letter or letters that go in the middle of the word to make the word *snail*.**

Look at the stop sign at the bottom of the page. You have now finished the lesson and should put your pencils down.

Review the questions and answer choices with students. Discuss with the class why one answer is correct and the others are not correct. Also check to see that students have carefully filled in their answer spaces and have completely erased any stray marks.

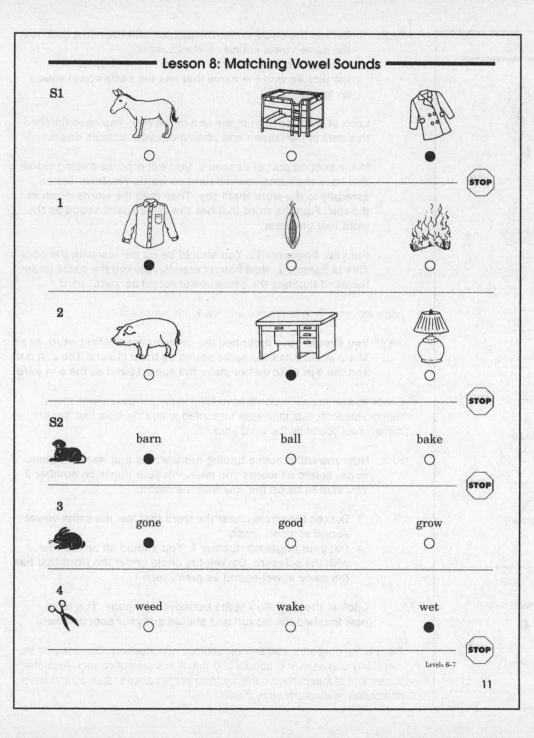

Lesson 8: Matching Vowel Sounds

Reading Skills: Recognizing and matching vowel sounds

SAY: **Turn to Lesson 8, Matching Vowel Sounds, on page 11.**

Check to see that all students find Lesson 8. Introduce the Try This feature.

SAY: **In the first part of Lesson 8, you will practice finding pictures with names that have the same vowel sound as words you hear. Listen carefully. When I say a word, you should try this: say the word to yourself. Think about the vowel sound in the word. Then look at the pictures given in the row. Find the picture with the name that has the same vowel sound as the word that you hear.**

Put your finger on S1. This is Sample 1. Now listen carefully. Darken the circle under the picture with the name that has the same vowel sound as hole...hole.

Allow students time to choose and mark their answer. Remind students to carefully fill in the answer circle and to completely erase any stray marks. Then introduce the Think It Through feature.

SAY: **Now we will think it through. We will check the answer. You should have darkened the circle under the picture of the coat. Coat has the same vowel sound as hole.**

Check to see that all students have filled in the correct answer space. Remind students that they were instructed to find the picture with the name that has the same vowel sound as hole.

Ask students if they have any questions about Sample 1 or about darkening the answer circle.

SAY: **Now you will practice finding more pictures with names that have the same vowel sound as words you hear. Listen carefully to the word that I say. Then find the picture with the name that has the same vowel sound as the word you hear.**

Now we will begin. Put your finger on number 1.

Check to see that all students find item 1. Allow students time after each item to choose and mark their answer. Say each item only once. Say only the words that appear in boldface type.

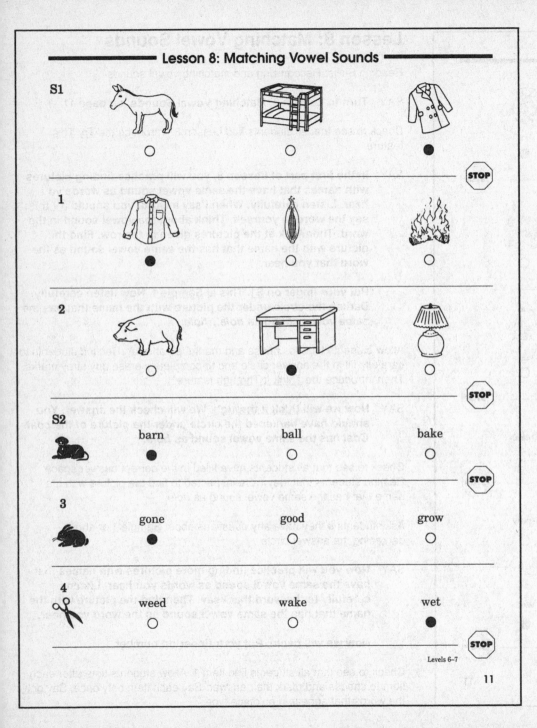

Lesson 8: Matching Vowel Sounds

S1

1

2

S2 barn ball bake

3 gone good grow

4 weed wake wet

Levels 6–7

11

SAY: 1 Darken the circle under the picture with the name that has the same vowel sound as *work...work*.

2 Put your finger on number 2. Darken the circle under the picture with the name that has the same vowel sound as *left...left*.

Look at the stop sign at the end of the row. You have finished this part of the lesson and should put your pencils down.

In the second part of Lesson 8, you will practice finding words that have the same vowel sound as words you hear. Listen carefully to the word that I say. Then read the words given in the row. Find the word that has the same vowel sound as the word that you hear.

Put your finger on S2. You should be on the row with the dog. This is Sample 2. Now listen carefully. Darken the circle under the word that has the same vowel sound as *yard...yard*.

Allow students time to choose and mark their answer.

SAY: **You should have darkened the circle under the first word, *barn*. The *a* in *barn* has the same sound as the *a* in *yard*. The *a* in *ball* and the *a* in *bake* do not make the same sound as the *a* in *yard*.**

Check to see that all students have filled in the correct answer space. Remind students that they were instructed to find the word that has the same vowel sound as the word *yard*.

SAY: **Now you will practice finding more words that have the same vowel sound as words you hear. Put your finger on number 3. You should be on the row with the rabbit.**

3 Darken the circle under the word that has the same vowel sound as *cost...cost*.

4 Put your finger on number 4. You should be on the row with the scissors. Darken the circle under the word that has the same vowel sound as *men...men*.

Look at the stop sign at the bottom of the page. You have now finished the lesson and should put your pencils down.

Review the questions and answer choices with students. Discuss with the class why one answer is correct and the others are not correct. Also check to see that students have carefully filled in their answer spaces and have completely erased any stray marks.

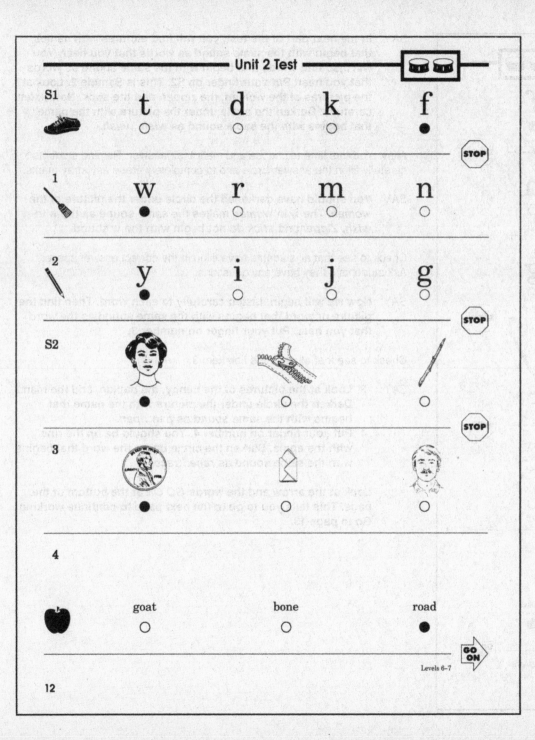

Unit 2 Test

SAY: **Turn to the Unit 2 Test on page 12. You should be on the page with the drums at the top.**

Check to see that all students find the Unit 2 Test.

SAY: **In the first part of this test, you will find letters that you hear. Put your finger on S1. You should be on the row with the shoe. This is Sample 1. Now listen carefully. Look at the four letters in Sample 1. Darken the circle under the letter f.**

Do not read the letter choices to the students. Allow students time to choose and mark their answer.

SAY: **You should have darkened the circle under the _fourth_ letter. The fourth letter is f. The first letter is t, the second letter is d, and the third letter is k.**

Check to see that all students have filled in the correct answer space. Ask students if they have any questions.

SAY: **Now you will find more letters that you hear. Listen carefully to the letter that I say. Then look at the letters listed in the row. Find the letter that you hear. Put your finger on number 1. You should be on the row with the broom.**

Check to see that all students find item 1. Allow students time after each item to choose and mark their answer. Say each item only once. Say only the words that appear in boldface type.

SAY: 1 **Darken the circle under the letter w.**
      2 **Put your finger on number 2. You should be on the row with the pencil. Darken the circle under the letter y.**

Look at the stop sign at the end of the row. You have finished this part of the test and should put your pencils down.

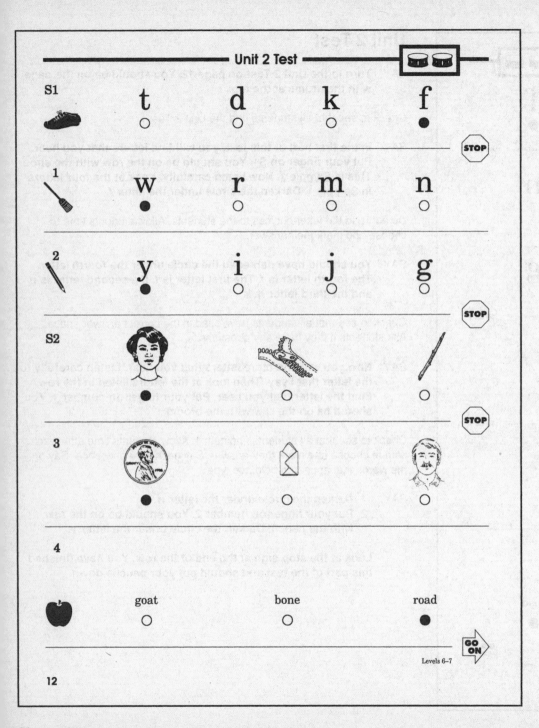

Unit 2 Test

S1
t   d   k   f
○   ○   ○   ●   **STOP**

1
w   r   m   n
●   ○   ○   ○

2
y   i   j   g
●   ○   ○   ○   **STOP**

S2
●   ○   ○   **STOP**

3
●   ○   ○

4
goat   bone   road
○   ○   ●

Levels 6–7

GO ON

12

Allow students time to choose and mark their answer. Remind students to carefully fill in the answer circle and to completely erase any stray marks.

SAY: **You should have darkened the circle under the picture of the *woman*. The *w* in *woman* makes the same sound as the *w* in *wish*. *Zipper* and *stick* do not begin with the *w* sound.**

Check to see that all students have filled in the correct answer space. Ask students if they have any questions.

SAY: **Now we will begin. Listen carefully to each word. Then find the picture or word that begins with the same sound as the word that you hear. Put your finger on number 3.**

Check to see that all students find item 3.

SAY: 3 **Look at the pictures of the penny, the napkin, and the man. Darken the circle under the picture with the name that begins with the same sound as *pan...pan.***
   4 **Put your finger on number 4. You should be on the row with the apple. Darken the circle under the word that begins with the same sound as *race...race.***

Look at the arrow and the words *GO ON* at the bottom of the page. This tells you to go to the next page to continue working. Go to page 13.

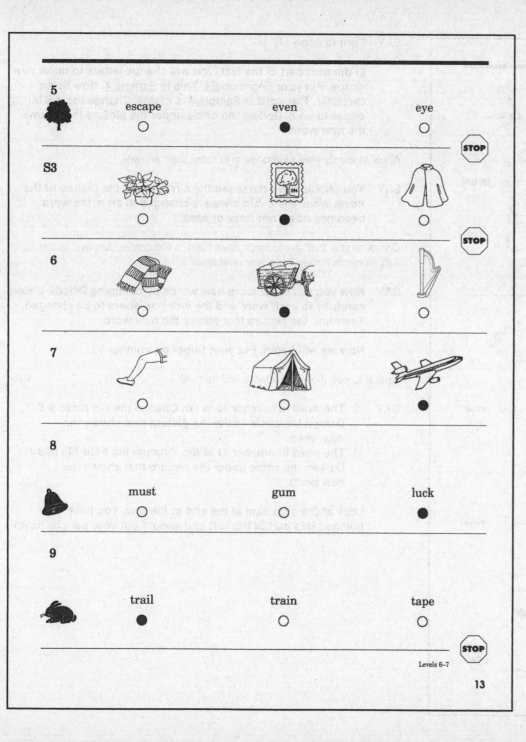

5

escape	even	eye
○	●	○

STOP

S3

○	●	○

STOP

6

○	○	○

7

○	○	●

8

must	gum	luck
○	○	●

9

trail	train	tape
●	○	○

STOP

Levels 6–7

13

Check to see that all students find page 13.

SAY: 5 **Put your finger on number 5. You should be on the row with the tree. Darken the circle under the word that begins with the same sound as** *easy...easy.*

Look at the stop sign at the end of the row. You have finished this part of the test and should put your pencils down.

In the next part of the test, you will find pictures with names that rhyme with words you hear. You will also find words that rhyme with words that you hear. *Hop* **and** *pop* **rhyme.** *Car* **and** *cape* **do not rhyme.**

Put your finger on S3. This is <u>Sample 3</u>. Look at the pictures of the plant, the stamp, and the cape. Now listen carefully. Darken the circle under the picture with the name that rhymes with *camp...camp.*

Allow students time to choose and mark their answer.

SAY: **You should have darkened the circle under the picture of the** *stamp. Stamp* **rhymes with** *camp.*

Check to see that all students have filled in the correct answer space. Ask students if they have any questions.

SAY: **Now we will begin. Listen carefully to each word. Then find the picture or word that rhymes with the word that you hear. Put your finger on number 6.**

Check to see that all students find item 6.

SAY: 6 **Look at the pictures of the scarf, the cart, and the harp. Darken the circle under the picture with the name that rhymes with** *dart...dart.*
7 **Put your finger on number 7. Look at the pictures of the leg, the tent, and the jet. Darken the circle under the picture with the name that rhymes with** *pet...pet.*
8 **Put your finger on number 8. You should be on the row with the bell. Darken the circle under the word that rhymes with** *duck...duck.*
9 **Put your finger on number 9. You should be on the row with the rabbit. Darken the circle under the word that rhymes with** *pail...pail.*

Look at the stop sign at the bottom of the page. You have now finished this part of the test and should put your pencils down.

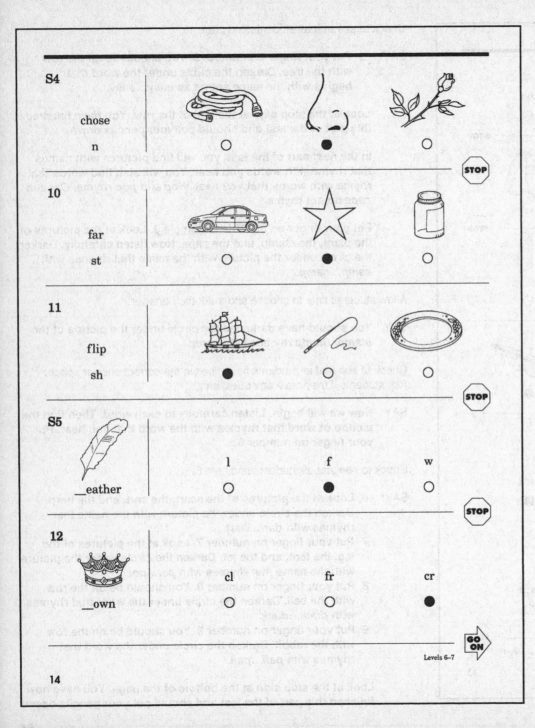

S4 chose
n

10 far
st

11 flip
sh

S5 ___eather
l   f   w

12 ___own
cl   fr   cr

Levels 6–7

14

SAY: **Turn to page 14.**

In the next part of the test, you will change letters to make new words. Put your finger on S4. This is Sample 4. Now listen carefully. The word in Sample 4 is *chose*. Change the *c-h* in *chose* to an *n*. Darken the circle under the picture that shows the new word.

Allow students time to choose and mark their answer.

SAY: **You should have darkened the circle under the picture of the *nose*. When the *c-h* in *chose* is changed to an *n*, the word becomes *nose*, not *hose* or *rose*.**

Check to see that all students have filled in the correct answer space. Ask students if they have any questions.

SAY: **Now you will make more new words by changing letters. Listen carefully to each word and the letter or letters to be changed. Then find the picture that shows the new word.**

Now we will begin. Put your finger on number 10.

Check to see that all students find item 10.

SAY: 10 **The word in number 10 is *far*. Change the *f* in *far* to *s-t*. Darken the circle under the picture that shows the new word.**
11 **The word in number 11 is *flip*. Change the *f-l* in *flip* to *s-h*. Darken the circle under the picture that shows the new word.**

Look at the stop sign at the end of the row. You have now finished this part of the test and should put your pencils down.

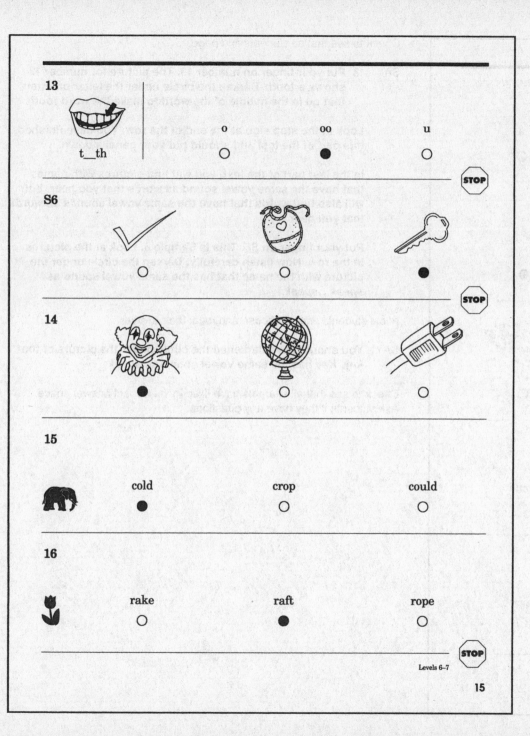

13

t__th

o	oo	u
○	●	○

STOP

S6

○   ○   ●

STOP

14

●   ○   ○

15

cold	crop	could
●	○	○

16

rake	raft	rope
○	●	○

STOP

Levels 6–7

15

SAY: **In the next part of the test, you will find letters that are missing from words. Put your finger on S5. This is Sample 5. Now listen carefully. The picture for Sample 5 shows a feather. Darken the circle under the letter that goes at the beginning to make the word *feather*.**

Allow students time to choose and mark their answer.

SAY: **You should have darkened the circle under the f. Feather has an f at the beginning.**

Check to see that all students have filled in the correct answer space. Ask students if they have any questions.

SAY: **Now you will find more missing letters. Listen carefully to the word and look at the picture. Then find the letter or letters that are missing from the word.**

Now we will begin. Put your finger on number 12.

Check to see that all students find item 12.

SAY: 12 **The picture for number 12 shows a *crown*. Darken the circle under the letters that go at the beginning to make the word *crown*.**

Look at the arrow and the words *GO ON* at the bottom of the page. This tells you to go to the next page and continue working on the test. Go to page 15.

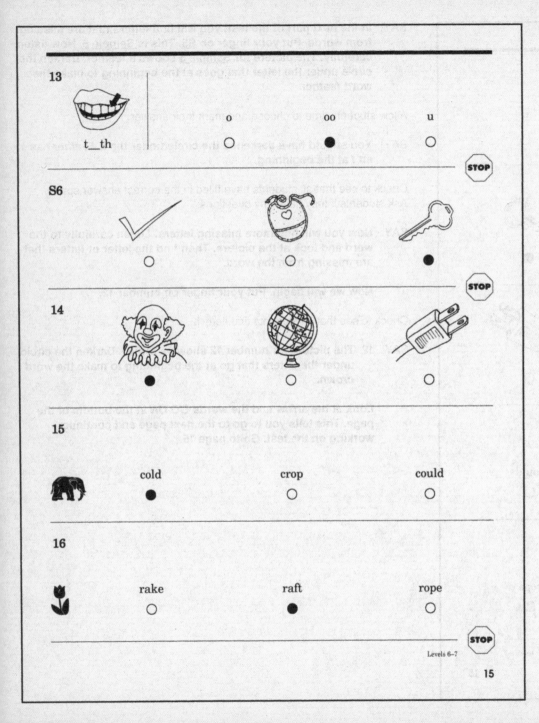

13

t__th

o   oo   u

○   ●   ○

STOP

S6

○   ●

STOP

14

●   ○   ○

15

cold   crop   could

●   ○   ○

16

rake   raft   rope

○   ●   ○

STOP

Levels 6–7

15

Check to see that all students find page 15.

SAY: 13 **Put your finger on number 13. The picture for number 13 shows a *tooth*. Darken the circle under the letter or letters that go in the middle of the word to make the word *tooth*.**

Look at the stop sign at the end of the row. You have finished this part of the test and should put your pencils down.

In the last part of the test, you will find pictures with names that have the same vowel sound as words that you hear. You will also find words that have the same vowel sounds as words that you hear.

Put your finger on S6. This is Sample 6. Look at the pictures in the row. Now listen carefully. Darken the circle under the picture with the name that has the same vowel sound as *speak...speak*.

Allow students time to choose and mark their answer.

SAY: **You should have darkened the circle under the picture of the *key*. *Key* has the same vowel sound as *speak*.**

Check to see that all students have filled in the correct answer space. Ask students if they have any questions.

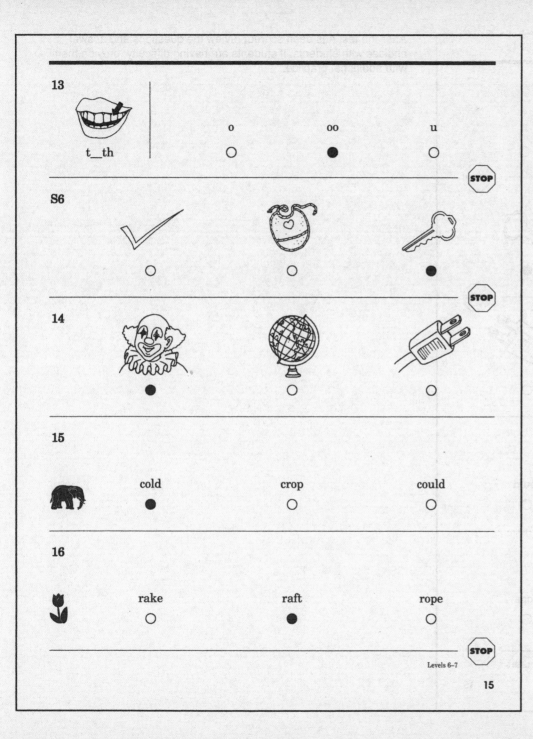

13

t__th

o	oo	u
○	●	○

STOP

S6

○	○	●

STOP

14

●	○	○

15

cold	crop	could
●	○	○

16

rake	raft	rope
○	●	○

STOP

Levels 6–7

15

SAY: **Now we will begin. Listen carefully to the word that I say. Then look at the pictures or words in the row. Find the picture or word that has the same vowel sound as the word that you hear. Put your finger on number 14.**

Check to see that all students find item 14.

SAY: 14 **Darken the circle under the picture with the name that has the same vowel sound as *proud...proud*.**

15 **Put your finger on number 15. You should be on the row with the elephant. Darken the circle under the word that has the same vowel sound as *croak...croak*.**

16 **Put your finger on number 16. You should be on the row with the flower. Darken the circle under the word that has the same vowel sound as *ran...ran*.**

Look at the stop sign at the bottom of the page. It is now time to stop. You have completed the Unit 2 Test. Make sure you have carefully filled in your answer circles and have completely erased any stray marks. Then put your pencils down.

After the test has been scored, review the questions and answer choices with students. If students are having difficulty, provide them with additional practice.

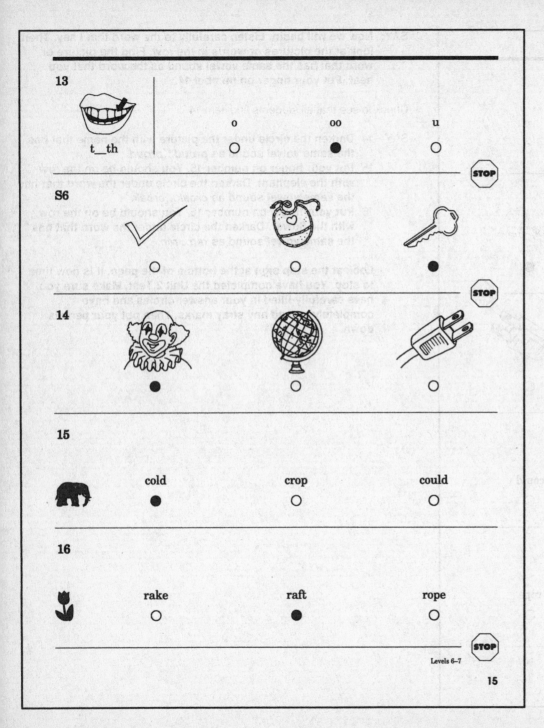

13

t__th

o	oo	u
○	●	○

STOP

S6

○	○	●

STOP

14

●	○	○

15

cold	crop	could
●	○	○

16

rake	raft	rope
○	●	○

STOP

Levels 6–7

15

UNIT 3 Reading

Lesson 9: Recognizing Words

S1

but	back	bat	boat
○	○	●	○

STOP

1

let	lid	lay	lip
○	●	○	○

2

pets	past	post	pots
○	○	○	●

3

horn	hear	hurt	hair
○	○	○	●

4

again	across	after	about
○	○	●	○

5

little	letter	ladder	lucky
○	○	●	○

6

green	grow	grass	groan
○	○	●	○

STOP

Levels 6–7

16

UNIT 3 Reading

Lesson 9: Recognizing Words

Reading Skill: Recognizing words presented orally and in print

SAY: **Turn to Lesson 9, Recognizing Words, on page 16. You should be on the page with the telephones at the top.**

Check to see that all students find Lesson 9. Introduce the <u>Try This</u> feature.

SAY: **In Lesson 9 you will practice finding words that you hear.**

Listen carefully. When I say a word and use it in a sentence, you should <u>try this</u>: look carefully at each word listed in the row. Then find the word that you hear.

Put your finger on <u>S1</u>. You should be on the row with the fish. This is <u>Sample 1</u>. Now listen carefully. The word for <u>Sample 1</u> is *bat*. John bought a new *bat*. Darken the circle under the word *bat*.

Allow students time to choose and mark their answer. Remind students to carefully fill in the answer circle and to completely erase any stray marks. Then introduce the <u>Think It Through</u> feature.

SAY: **Now we will <u>think it through</u>. We will check the answer. You should have darkened the circle under the *third* word. The third word is *bat*. The other words are *but*, *back*, and *boat*.**

Check to see that all students have filled in the correct answer space. Remind students that they were instructed to find the word *bat*.

Ask students if they have any questions about <u>Sample 1</u> or about darkening the answer circle.

Lesson 9: Recognizing Words

S1

but	back	bat	boat
○	○	●	○

STOP

1

let	lid	lay	lip
○	●	○	○

2

pets	past	post	pots
○	○	○	●

3

horn	hear	hurt	hair
○	○	○	●

4

again	across	after	about
○	○	●	○

5

little	letter	ladder	lucky
○	○	●	○

6

green	grow	grass	groan
○	○	●	○

STOP

Levels 6–7

16

SAY: Now you will practice finding more words that you hear. Listen carefully as I say each word and use it in a sentence. Then look carefully at each word listed in the row. Find the word that you hear.

Now we will begin. Put your finger on number 1. You should be on the row with the butterfly.

Check to see that all students find item 1. Allow students time after each item to choose and mark their answer. Say each item only once. Say <u>only</u> the words that appear in boldface type.

SAY: 1 The word for number 1 is *lid*. Open the *lid* of the box slowly. Darken the circle under the word *lid*.
2 Put your finger on number 2. You should be on the row with the drum. The word for number 2 is *pots*. Ana had to scrub all of the *pots*. Darken the circle under the word *pots*.
3 Put your finger on number 3. You should be on the row with the apple. The word for number 3 is *hair*. Please comb your *hair* before you leave. Darken the circle under the word *hair*.
4 Put your finger on number 4. You should be on the row with the elephant. The word for number 4 is *after*. We will leave *after* the movie. Darken the circle under the word *after*.
5 Put your finger on number 5. You should be on the row with the star. The word for number 5 is *ladder*. Marco needs a *ladder* to climb to the roof. Darken the circle under the word *ladder*.
6 Put your finger on number 6. You should be on the row with the flower. The word for number 6 is *grass*. Please do not walk on the *grass*. Darken the circle under the word *grass*.

Look at the stop sign at the bottom of the page. You have now finished the lesson and should put your pencils down.

Review the questions and answer choices with students. Discuss with the class why one answer is correct and the others are not correct. Also check to see that students have carefully filled in their answer spaces and have completely erased any stray marks.

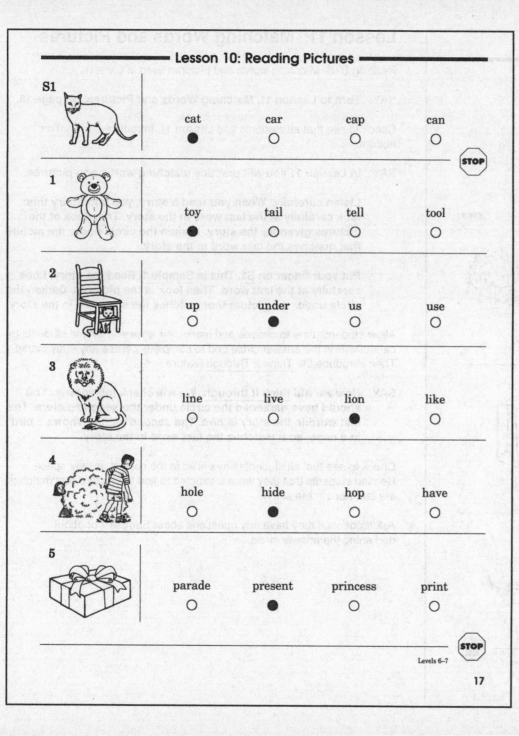

Lesson 10: Reading Pictures

Reading Skill: Recognizing words that correspond to pictures

SAY: **Turn to Lesson 10, Reading Pictures, on page 17.**

Check to see that all students find Lesson 10. Introduce the Try This feature.

SAY: **In Lesson 10 you will practice finding words that match pictures. Listen carefully. When you look at a picture, you should try this: read each word in the row carefully. Then find the word that matches the picture.**

Put your finger on S1. This is Sample 1. Look carefully at the picture. Then read the four words listed in the row. Darken the circle under the word that matches the picture.

Allow students time to choose and mark their answer. Remind students to carefully fill in the answer circle and to completely erase any stray marks. Then introduce the Think It Through feature.

SAY: **Now we will think it through. We will check the answer. You should have darkened the circle under the _first_ word. The picture shows a cat. The word _cat_ tells what the picture shows.**

Check to see that all students have filled in the correct answer space. Remind students that they were instructed to find the word that matches the picture.

Ask students if they have any questions about Sample 1 or about darkening the answer circle.

SAY: **Now you will practice finding more words that match pictures. Put your finger on number 1. Do numbers 1 through 5 just as we did Sample 1. Darken the circle under the word that matches the picture. When you come to the stop sign at the bottom of the page, put your pencils down. You may now begin.**

Check to see that all students find item 1. Allow students time to choose and mark their answers.

Review the questions and answer choices with students. Discuss with the class why one answer is correct and the others are not correct. Also check to see that students have carefully filled in their answer spaces and have completely erased any stray marks.

Lesson 11: Matching Words and Pictures

S1 Curtis fed his bird.

○ ● ○

STOP

1 Maria swims in a pool.

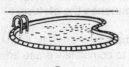  

● ○ ○

2 Jeff put the books in a box.

● ○ ○

3 Father heard a noise. It came from the chimney.

● ○ ○

Levels 6–7

GO ON

Lesson 11: Matching Words and Pictures

Reading Skill: Matching words and pictures used in context

SAY: **Turn to Lesson 11, Matching Words and Pictures, on page 18.**

Check to see that all students find Lesson 11. Introduce the Try This feature.

SAY: **In Lesson 11 you will practice matching words and pictures.**

Listen carefully. When you read a story, you should try this: look carefully at the last word in the story. Then look at the pictures given for the story. Darken the circle under the picture that matches the last word in the story.

Put your finger on S1. This is Sample 1. Read the story. Look carefully at the last word. Then look at the pictures. Darken the circle under the picture that matches the last word in the story.

Allow students time to choose and mark their answer. Remind students to carefully fill in the answer circle and to completely erase any stray marks. Then introduce the Think It Through feature.

SAY: **Now we will think it through. We will check the answer. You should have darkened the circle under the *second* picture. The last word in the story is *bird*. The second picture shows a bird in a cage, so it matches the last word in the story.**

Check to see that all students have filled in the correct answer space. Remind students that they were instructed to find the picture that matches the last word in the story.

Ask students if they have any questions about Sample 1 or about darkening the answer circle.

4 The children went to the zoo. They liked the seal.

     ○   ○   ●

---

5 When Mia went to the playground, she fell and hurt her arm.

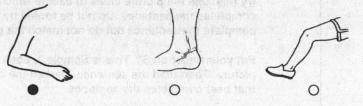

     ●   ○   ○

---

6 Before Beth left the house, she had to clean her bedroom.

     ●   ○   ○

---

7 Lee wants to travel in space. He is reading a book about rockets.

     ○   ●   ○

STOP

Levels 6–7

19

Now you will practice matching more words and pictures. Put your finger on number 1. Do numbers 1 through 7 just as we did Sample 1. Read each story carefully and look at the pictures. Darken the circle under the picture that matches the last word in the story. When you come to the arrow at the bottom of the page, continue working on the next page. When you come to the stop sign at the bottom of page 19, put your pencils down. You may now begin.

Allow students time to choose and mark their answers.

Review the questions and answer choices with students. Discuss with the class why one answer is correct and the others are not correct. Also check to see that students have carefully filled in their answer spaces and have completely erased any stray marks.

Lesson 12: Understanding Pictures

S1 The girl is sitting on a ___.

○ blanket   ○ stool   ● rock   ○ log

STOP

1 Dad and Angie are in the ___ store.

● shoe   ○ pet   ○ clothes   ○ music

2 Angie does not ___ the shoes.

○ clean   ● like   ○ lift   ○ wear

3 Dad has a shoe in ___ hand.

○ her   ○ my   ● his   ○ each

4 Ming hurt his ___.

○ arm   ● leg   ○ head   ○ lip

5 Ming hit a ___ when he was riding his bike.

○ road   ○ ride   ● rock   ○ hole

6 The ___ on Ming's bike is bent.

○ window   ● wheel   ○ wagon   ○ whistle

GO ON

Levels 6–7

Lesson 12: Understanding Pictures

Reading Skills: Relating pictures to sentences; understanding stated detail; making inferences

SAY: **Turn to Lesson 12, Understanding Pictures, on page 20.**

Check to see that all students find Lesson 12. Introduce the Try This feature.

SAY: **In Lesson 12 you will practice using picture clues to find words that best complete sentences.**

Listen carefully. When you read each sentence, you should try this: use the picture clues to decide which word best completes the sentence. Do not be fooled by words that complete the sentence but do not match the picture.

Put your finger on S1. This is Sample 1. Look carefully at the picture. Then read the sentence. Darken the circle for the word that best completes the sentence.

Allow students time to choose and mark their answer. Remind students to carefully fill in the answer circle and to completely erase any stray marks. Then introduce the Think It Through feature.

SAY: **Now we will think it through. We will check the answer. You should have darkened the circle for the word _rock_. The word _rock_ best completes the sentence and matches what is shown in the picture.**

Check to see that all students have filled in the correct answer space. Remind students that they were instructed to use picture clues to find the word that best completes the sentence.

Ask students if they have any questions about Sample 1 or about darkening the answer circle.

7 Eva is helping her ____.

● father   ○ mother   ○ sister   ○ aunt

8 She is helping to gather the ____.

○ chickens   ○ hay   ● eggs   ○ ducks

9 The hens lay the eggs in a ____ .

○ tree   ● nest   ○ pan   ○ shelf

10 If Eva drops an egg, it might ____.

○ keep   ● crack   ○ cook   ○ crawl

11 Two actors are on the ____.

● stage   ○ television   ○ chairs   ○ stairs

12 One of the actors is wearing a long ___.

○ dish   ● dress   ○ coat   ○ wig

13 The other people are ____ the play.

● watching   ○ singing   ○ writing   ○ reading

14 At the end of the play, the people will ____ their hands.

○ carry   ○ catch   ● clap   ○ call

STOP

Levels 6–7

SAY: **Now you will practice using picture clues to complete more sentences. Put your finger on number 1. Do numbers 1 through 14 just as we did <u>Sample 1</u>. Look carefully at the picture. Then read the sentence. Darken the circle for the word that best completes the sentence. When you come to the arrow at the bottom of the page, continue working on the next page. When you come to the stop sign at the bottom of page 21, put your pencils down. You may now begin.**

Allow students time to choose and mark their answers.

Review the questions and answer choices with students. Discuss with the class why one answer is correct and the others are not correct. Also check to see that students have carefully filled in their answer spaces and have completely erased any stray marks.

Lesson 13: Reading Stories

Lesson 13: Reading Stories

S1   It was late. Paul wanted to go home. His eyes kept closing. He was very sleepy.

Why did Paul want to go home?

○ He wanted to eat.

○ He wanted to see his dad.

● He wanted to go to bed.

 STOP

Yuko went to the circus. She saw many things. There were three dancing bears. One of them wore a skirt. She also saw an elephant walk on its back legs.

Yuko saw a tall clown in a little car. She laughed when the clown got stuck.

Yuko looked up to watch people walk on ropes. She sat very still. She was afraid they would fall.

Yuko wants to visit the circus again.

1   What is this story mainly about?

○ Clowns

● A trip to the circus

○ Elephants

2   How many legs did the elephant walk on?

○ One

● Two

○ Four

3   Why did Yuko laugh?

● She thought the clown was funny.

○ She thought the bears were funny.

○ She thought the people on ropes were funny.

4   Where did people walk on ropes?

○ On the ground

○ Over the water

● In the air

 GO ON

Levels 6–7

Lesson 13: Reading Stories

Reading Skills: Understanding stated detail; making inferences; determining the main idea; making generalizations

SAY: **Turn to Lesson 13, Reading Stories, on page 22.**

Check to see that all students find Lesson 13. Introduce the <u>Try This</u> feature.

SAY: **In Lesson 13 you will practice answering questions about stories that you read.**

Listen carefully. After you read a story, you should <u>try this</u>: carefully read the question and the answer choices. More than one answer choice may seem correct. Be sure to find the answer that goes best with the story.

Put your finger on <u>S1</u>. This is <u>Sample 1</u>. Read the story. Then read the question and the answer choices. Darken the circle for the correct answer.

Allow students time to choose and mark their answer. Remind students to carefully fill in the answer circle and to completely erase any stray marks. Then introduce the <u>Think It Through</u> feature.

SAY: **Now we will <u>think it through</u>. We will check the answer. You should have darkened the circle for the *third* answer choice. The last sentence in the story tells you that Paul was very sleepy. You can guess that the reason Paul wanted to go home was that *he wanted to go to bed*.**

Check to see that all students have filled in the correct answer space. Remind students that they were instructed to find the answer that best goes with the story.

Ask students if they have any questions about <u>Sample 1</u> or about darkening the answer circle.

The bell rang. Tim threw his books in his desk. He ran out of the room. He did not wait for his friends.

Tim wanted to get home quickly. That morning at breakfast, Tim's mother had told him there would be a surprise for him when he got home.

Tim raced in the front door. He stopped suddenly and shouted with joy, "Uncle Ed, I am so glad that you have come to visit!"

5 Why did the bell ring?

● School was over.

○ It was time to get up.

○ Someone was at the door.

6 Why did Tim run home?

○ He was scared.

○ He didn't want to miss the bus.

● He wanted to see his surprise.

7 How did Tim feel about his surprise?

○ He was scared.

● He was excited.

○ He was angry.

8 What was the surprise?

● A visit from Uncle Ed

○ A surprise birthday party

○ A new football

STOP

Levels 6–7

23

SAY: **Now you will practice answering questions about more stories that you read. Put your finger on number 1. Do numbers 1 through 8 just as you did <u>Sample 1</u>. Read the story. Then read the question and the answer choices. Darken the circle for the correct answer. When you come to the arrow at the bottom of the page, continue working on the next page. When you come to the stop sign at the bottom of page 23, put your pencils down. You may now begin.**

Allow students time to choose and mark their answers.

Review the questions and answer choices with students. Discuss with the class why one answer is correct and the others are not correct. Also check to see that students have carefully filled in their answer spaces and have completely erased any stray marks.

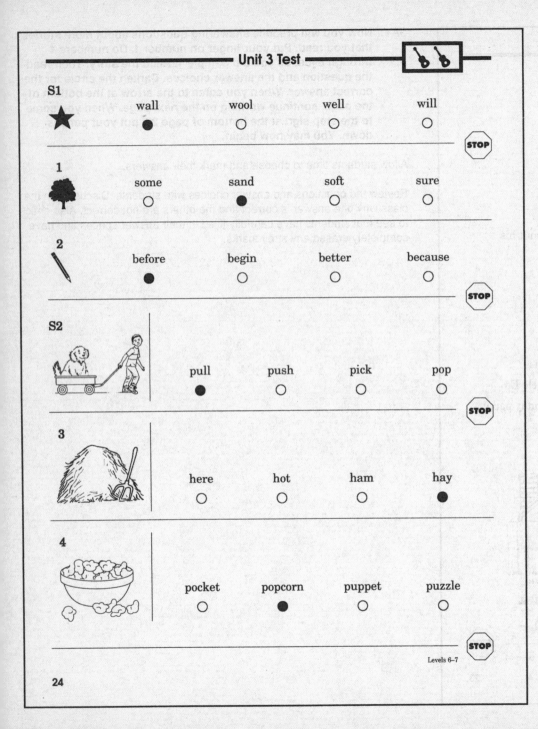

Unit 3 Test

SAY: **Turn to the Unit 3 Test on page 24. You should be on the page with the guitars at the top.**

Check to see that all students find the Unit 3 Test.

SAY: **In the first part of this test, you will find words that you hear. Put your finger on S1. You should be on the row with the star. This is Sample 1. Now listen carefully. The word for Sample 1 is** *wall.* **The baby colored on the** *wall.* **Darken the circle under the word** *wall.*

Allow students time to choose and mark their answer.

SAY: **You should have darkened the circle under the** *first* **word. The first word is** *wall.*

Check to see that all students have filled in the correct answer space. Ask students if they have any questions.

SAY: **Now you will find more words that you hear. Listen carefully as I say each word and use it in a sentence. Then look at each word listed in the row. Find the word that you hear.**

Now we will begin. Put your finger on number 1. You should be on the row with the tree.

Check to see that all students find item 1. Allow students time after each item to choose and mark their answer. Say each item only once. Say <u>only</u> the words that appear in boldface type.

SAY: 1 **The word for number 1 is** *sand.* **I have** *sand* **between my toes. Darken the circle under the word** *sand.*
2 **Put your finger on number 2. You should be on the row with the pencil. The word for number 2 is** *before.* **Sharpen your pencil** *before* **class begins. Darken the circle under the word** *before.*

Look at the stop sign at the end of the row. You have finished this part of the test and should put your pencils down.

Unit 3 Test

S1

wall   wool   well   will

●   ○   ○   ○

STOP

1

some   sand   soft   sure

○   ●   ○   ○

2

before   begin   better   because

●   ○   ○   ○

STOP

S2

pull   push   pick   pop

●   ○   ○   ○

STOP

3

here   hot   ham   hay

○   ○   ○   ●

4

pocket   popcorn   puppet   puzzle

○   ●   ○   ○

STOP

Levels 6–7

SAY: **In the next part of the test, you will find words that match pictures. Put your finger on S2. This is Sample 2. Read each word in the row. Then darken the circle under the word that matches the picture.**

Allow students time to choose and mark their answer. Remind students to carefully fill in the answer circle and to completely erase any stray marks.

SAY: **You should have darkened the circle under the *first* word. *Pull* is the correct answer because the boy in the picture is pulling a wagon.**

Check to see that all students have filled in the correct answer space. Ask students if they have any questions.

SAY: **Now you will find more words that match pictures. Put your finger on number 3. Do numbers 3 and 4 just as we did Sample 2. Look at each picture and read the words listed in the row. Darken the circle under the word that matches the picture. When you come to the stop sign at the bottom of the page, put your pencils down. You may now begin.**

Allow students time to choose and mark their answers.

S3   Mark went for a ride in a boat.

STOP

5   The rabbit hopped under the gate.

6   Jim is looking for his pen.

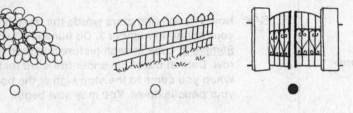

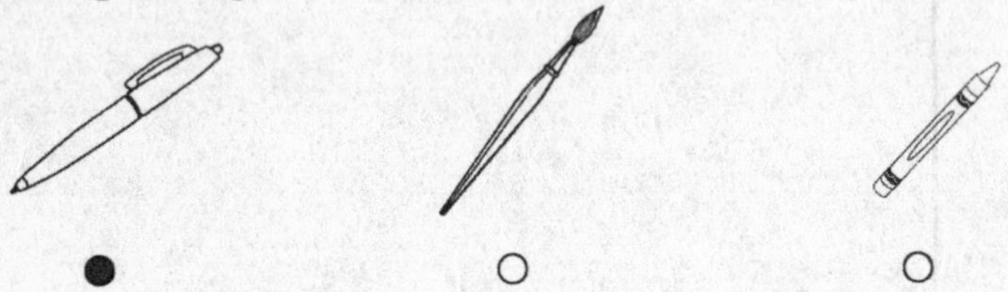

7   Dad said, "I can't see without my glasses."

STOP

Levels 6–7

25

SAY: **Now go to page 25.**

Check to see that all students find page 25.

SAY: **In the next part of the test, you will match pictures and words. Put your finger on S3. This is Sample 3. Read the story. Look carefully at the last word. Darken the circle under the picture that matches the last word in the story.**

Allow students time to choose and mark their answer.

SAY: **You should have darkened the circle under the second picture. The last word in the story is boat. The second picture shows a boat, so it matches the last word in the story.**

Check to see that all students have filled in the correct answer space. Ask students if they have any questions.

SAY: **Now you will match more pictures and words. Put your finger on number 5. Do numbers 5 through 7 just as we did Sample 3. Read each story carefully and look at the pictures. Darken the circle under the picture that matches the last word in the story. When you come to the stop sign at the bottom of the page, put your pencils down. You may now begin.**

Allow students time to choose and mark their answers.

S4 There are seven candles on the ____.

● cake   ○ cow   ○ cart   ○ cup

STOP

8 Al is ready to go to ____.

○ play   ○ eat   ● sleep   ○ school

9 Mother is reading Al a ____.

● story   ○ stamp   ○ stick   ○ show

10 Next Mother might ____ Al good night.

○ call   ○ come   ● kiss   ○ keep

11 There is a butterfly in the ____.

○ art   ● air   ○ ant   ○ age

12 Ling is holding a ____.

● net   ○ neck   ○ needle   ○ nail

13 Ling is ____ to reach the butterfly.

○ walking   ● jumping   ○ joking   ○ standing

14 She must move ____.

○ loudly   ○ happily   ○ slowly   ● quickly

STOP

Levels 6–7

SAY: **Now turn to page 26.**

Check to see that all students find page 26.

SAY: **In the next part of the test, you will use picture clues to find words that best complete sentences. Put your finger on S4. This is Sample 4. Now look carefully at the picture. Then read the sentence. Darken the circle for the word that best completes the sentence.**

Allow students time to choose and mark their answer. Remind students to carefully fill in the answer circle and to completely erase any stray marks.

SAY: **You should have darkened the circle for the word cake. The word cake best completes the sentence and matches what is shown in the picture.**

Check to see that all students have filled in the correct answer space. Ask students if they have any questions.

SAY: **Now you will use picture clues to complete more sentences. Put your finger on number 8. Do numbers 8 through 14 just as we did Sample 4. Look carefully at the picture. Then read the sentence. Darken the circle under the word that best completes the sentence. When you come to the stop sign at the bottom of the page, put your pencils down. You may now begin.**

Allow students time to choose and mark their answers.

S5   Terri and her dad made little holes in the ground. They put a seed in each hole. Then they covered the seeds. Terri poured water on the ground. She said, "Now we will have good things to eat."

What were Terri and her dad doing?

○ Eating seeds

○ Watering flowers

● Planting a garden

Mr. Han asked Ned to do some jobs. Ned liked to help Mr. Han. Mr. Han always gave him a dollar for each job.

Ned got out the hose, a bucket, and some soap. First, he washed the windows. Then he washed the doors and trunk. Finally, Ned washed the tires. He was very careful to get all the mud off.

When Ned was done, Mr. Han looked at the car. "You worked very hard. I will give you two dollars," said Mr. Han. "Tomorrow you will need a rake. I will pay you two more dollars if you do as well."

"Thank you, Mr. Han. I will be back tomorrow after breakfast," said Ned.

15 What did Ned wash?

○ A bike

● A car

○ A house

16 Why did Ned get two dollars?

● He did a good job.

○ He wanted to buy candy.

○ He did two jobs.

17 What will Ned do the next day?

○ Trim trees

○ Mow the grass

● Rake leaves

18 When will Ned come to Mr. Han's house?

● In the morning

○ In the afternoon

○ At night

Levels 6–7

27

SAY: **Now go to page 27.**

Check to see that all students find page 27.

SAY: **In the last part of the test, you will answer questions about stories that you read. Put your finger on S5. This is Sample 5. Now listen carefully. Read the story in Sample 5. Then read the question and the answer choices. Darken the circle for the correct answer.**

Allow students time to choose and mark their answer. Remind students to carefully fill in the answer circle and to completely erase any stray marks.

SAY: **You should have darkened the circle for the *third* answer choice. The story tells you that Terri and her dad put seeds in the ground and that they will have good things to eat. You can guess that Terri and her dad were *planting a garden*.**

Check to see that all students have filled in the correct answer space. Ask students if they have any questions.

SAY: **Now you will answer questions about another story. Put your finger on number 15. Do numbers 15 through 18 just as we did Sample 5. Read the story. Then read the question and the answer choices. Darken the circle for the correct answer. When you come to the stop sign at the bottom of the page, put your pencils down. You may now begin.**

Allow students time to choose and mark their answers.

SAY: **It is now time to stop. You have completed the Unit 3 Test. Make sure you have carefully filled in your answer circles and have completely erased any stray marks. Then put your pencils down.**

After the test has been scored, review the questions and answer choices with students. If students are having difficulty, provide them with additional practice.

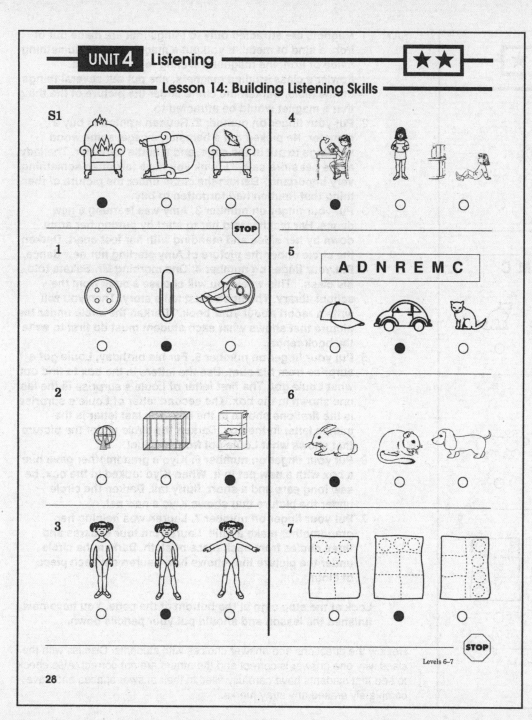

Lesson 14: Building Listening Skills

Listening Skills: Listening to and remembering details of material presented orally; drawing conclusions; understanding sequence; predicting outcomes; following directions

SAY: **Turn to Lesson 14, Building Listening Skills, on page 28. You should be on the page with the stars at the top.**

Check to see that all students find Lesson 14. Introduce the Try This feature.

SAY: **In Lesson 14 you will practice finding pictures that go with stories that you hear. When I read a story, you should try this: listen very carefully. Look at the pictures for the story. Then find the picture that goes with the story. Put your finger on S1. This is Sample 1. Listen carefully. Young children should not play with matches. Maria's little brother, Julio, struck a match. He dropped the burning match onto a chair. Darken the circle under the picture that shows what happened next.**

Do not identify the picture choices to the students. Allow students time to choose and mark their answer. Remind students to carefully fill in the answer circle and to completely erase any stray marks. Then introduce the Think It Through feature.

SAY: **Now we will think it through. We will check the answer. You should have darkened the circle under the *first* picture. It shows a chair that is on fire. You can guess that when Julio dropped the match on the chair, the chair began to burn.**

Check to see that all students have filled in the correct answer space. Ask students if they have any questions about Sample 1 or about darkening the answer circle.

SAY: **Now you will find more pictures that go with stories that you hear. Put your finger on number 1.**

Check to see that all students find item 1. Allow students time after each item to choose and mark their answer. Say each item only once. Say only the words that appear in boldface type.

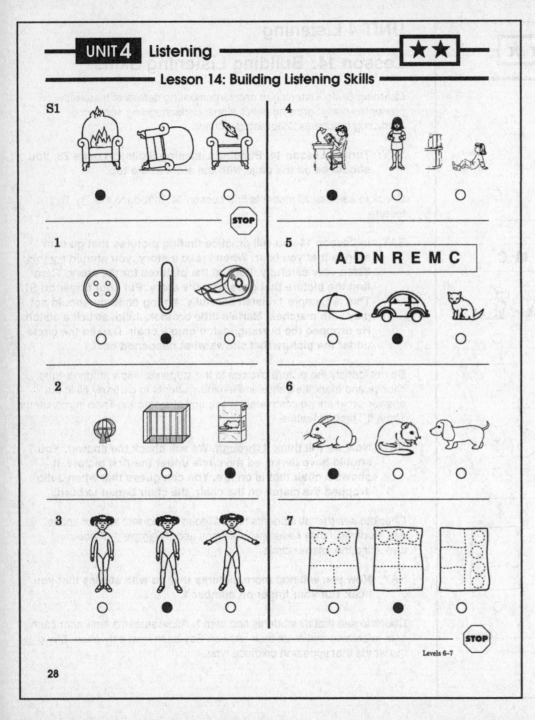

UNIT 4 Listening ★★

Lesson 14: Building Listening Skills

S1 (three chair pictures)

1 (button, paper clip, tape dispenser)

2 (hamster wheel, cage, box)

3 (three figures in poses)

4 (child at desk, child standing, child on floor)

5 A D N R E M C (cap, car, cat)

6 (rabbit, mouse, dog)

7 (cloth with squares and circles)

Levels 6–7

28

SAY:

1 **Magnets are attracted only to things that are made out of iron, a kind of metal. If you put a magnet next to something made of iron, the magnet will cling to it. When Mrs. Fowler's class studied magnets, she put out several things on the table. Darken the circle under the picture of the thing that a magnet would be attracted to.**

2 **Put your finger on number 2. Reuben wanted to buy a hamster. He picked out a hamster, a cage, some wood shavings to put in the cage, and a bottle for water. The lady at the pet store said, "I think you have forgotten something very important." Darken the circle under the picture of the thing that Reuben had forgotten to buy.**

3 **Put your finger on number 3. Amy was learning a new dance. Her teacher told her to start by putting her arms down by her sides and standing with her feet apart. Darken the circle under the picture of Amy starting her new dance.**

4 **Put your finger on number 4. One morning Mr. Sakata told his class, "This week you will choose a book from the school library. The book must tell a story. Then you will write a report about your book." Darken the circle under the picture that shows what each student must do first to write the book report.**

5 **Put your finger on number 5. For his birthday, Louie got a surprise from his aunt. Use the letters in the box to find out what Louie got. The first letter of Louie's surprise is the last one shown in the box. The second letter of Louie's surprise is the first one shown in the box. The last letter is the middle letter in the box. Darken the circle under the picture that shows what Louie got from his aunt.**

6 **Put your finger on number 6. Kiyo's grandmother gave him a box with a new pet in it. When Kiyo looked in the box, he saw long ears and a short, fluffy tail. Darken the circle under the picture that shows Kiyo's new pet.**

7 **Put your finger on number 7. Lauren was helping her grandmother make a quilt. Lauren cut four squares and three circles from each piece of cloth. Darken the circle under the picture that shows how Lauren cut each piece of cloth.**

Look at the stop sign at the bottom of the page. You have now finished the lesson and should put your pencils down.

Review the questions and answer choices with students. Discuss with the class why one answer is correct and the others are not correct. Also check to see that students have carefully filled in their answer spaces and have completely erased any stray marks.

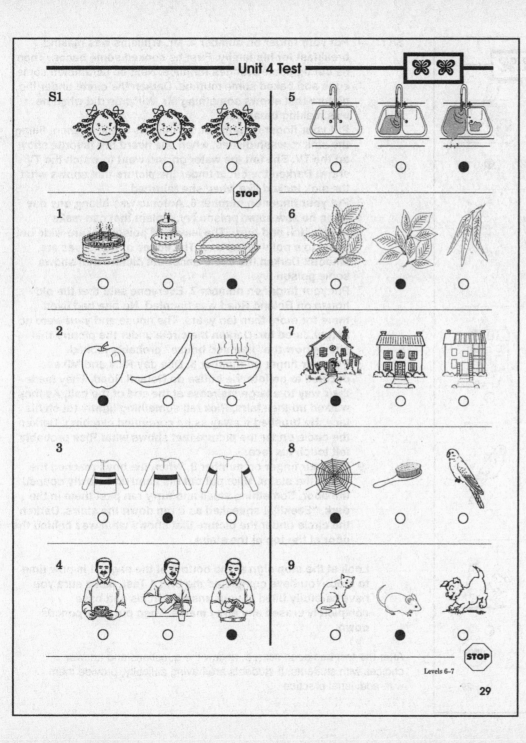

Unit 4 Test

SAY: **Turn to the Unit 4 Test on page 29. You should be on the page with the butterflies at the top.**

Check to see that all students find the Unit 4 Test.

SAY: **In this test you will find pictures that go with stories you hear. Put your finger on S1. This is Sample 1. Listen carefully. Mei drew a picture of herself. She drew a head with curly hair and two bows. Then she added eyes, a nose, and a big smile. Last she added freckles. Darken the circle under the picture that Mei drew of herself.**

Do not identify the picture choices to the students. Allow students time to choose and mark their answer.

SAY: **You should have darkened the circle under the _first_ picture. It shows a drawing of a Mei with curly hair, two bows, eyes, nose, a big smile, and freckles.**

Check to see that all students have filled in the correct answer space.

SAY: **Now you will find more pictures that go with stories you hear. Put your finger on number 1.**

Check to see that all students find item 1. Allow students time after each item to choose and mark their answer. Say each item only once. Say only the words that appear in boldface type.

SAY: 1 **Listen carefully. Mrs. Gonzales needed to buy a cake for her company's picnic. There were thirty people in the company. Darken the circle under the cake that Mrs. Gonzales probably bought.**

2 **Put your finger on number 2. B.J. had a loose tooth. He wiggled it but it would not come out. Finally his mother said, "B.J., I will give you something to eat that will help your tooth come out." Darken the circle under the picture that shows what B.J.'s mother probably gave him to eat.**

3 **Put your finger on number 3. Miguel needed a new shirt. His father took him to the store. The shirt with stripes around the sleeves was too big. The shirt with a stripe around the chest fit just right. The shirt with two stripes around the chest was too little. Darken the circle under the picture of the shirt that fit Miguel just right.**

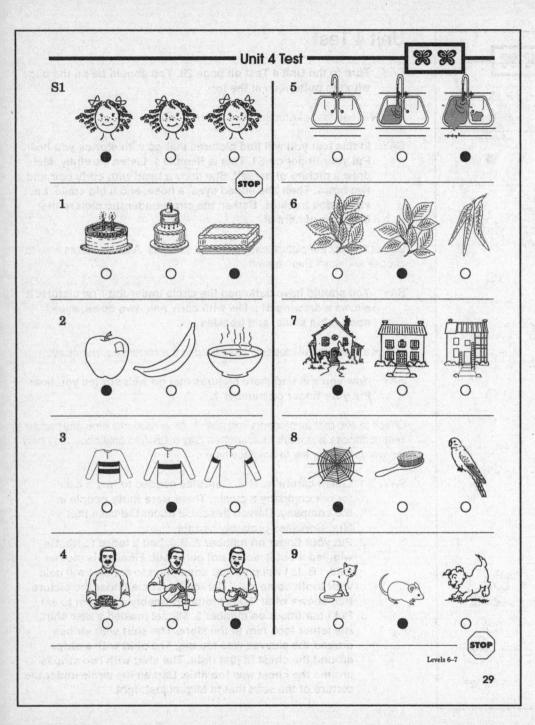

S1

5

1

6

2

7

3

8

4

9

Levels 6–7

29

SAY: 4 Put your finger on number 4. Mr. Williams was making breakfast for his family. First he cooked some bacon. Then he cut up some oranges for juice. Next he scrambled some eggs and baked some muffins. Darken the circle under the picture that shows something Mr. Williams did when he was making breakfast.

5 Put your finger on number 5. Tina was in the kitchen, filling the sink to wash dishes, when she heard her favorite show on the TV. She left the water on and went to watch the TV show. Darken the circle under the picture that shows what the sink looked like when she returned.

6 Put your finger on number 6. Antonio was hiking one day when he saw some poison ivy, a plant that can make people itch and burn. The leaves of poison ivy are wide but come to a point at the end. The edges of the leaves are smooth. Darken the circle under the picture that shows some poison ivy.

7 Put your finger on number 7. Everyone said that the old house on Roland Road was haunted. No one had lived there for more than ten years. The house and yard were no longer cared for. Darken the circle under the picture that shows how the "haunted house" probably looked.

8 Put your finger on number 8. One day Rick and Mike decided to go into the house on Roland Road. They made their way to a large staircase at the end of the hall. As they walked up the stairs, Rick felt something lightly touch his face. He brushed it away as he continued climbing. Darken the circle under the picture that shows what Rick probably felt touch his face.

9 Put your finger on number 9. When the boys reached the top of the stairs, Mike put out his hand and slowly opened the door. Something small and furry ran past them in the dark. "Eeek!" it squeaked as it ran down the stairs. Darken the circle under the picture that shows what was behind the door at the top of the stairs.

Look at the stop sign at the bottom of the page. It is now time to stop. You have completed the Unit 4 Test. Make sure you have carefully filled in your answer circles and have completely erased any stray marks. Then put your pencils down.

After the test has been scored, review the questions and answer choices with students. If students are having difficulty, provide them with additional practice.

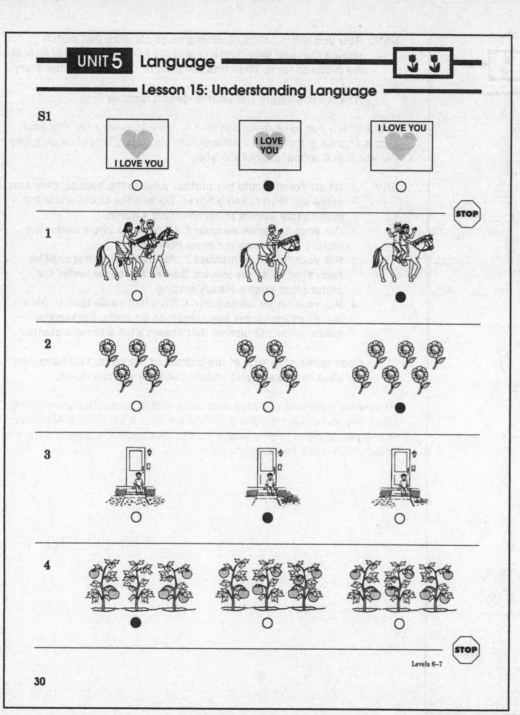

Lesson 15: Understanding Language

Language Skills: Listening to and remembering details of material presented orally; understanding prepositions; understanding singulars and plurals; inferring characteristics shared by groups; understanding comparatives and superlatives; recognizing temporal and spatial relationships

SAY: **Turn to Lesson 15, Understanding Language, on page 30. You should be on the page with the flowers at the top.**

Check to see that all students find Lesson 15. Introduce the Try This feature.

SAY: **In Lesson 15 you will practice choosing pictures that match stories that you hear.**

Listen carefully. When I tell a story, you should try this: think about what the story says. Then look carefully at each picture. Find the picture that matches the story.

Put your finger on S1. This is Sample 1. Now listen carefully. Eric drew a picture for his father. He drew a picture of a heart. He wrote *I love you* inside the heart. Darken the circle under the picture that Eric drew.

Do not identify the picture choices to the students. Allow students time to choose and mark their answer. Remind students to carefully fill in the answer circle and to completely erase any stray marks. Then introduce the Think It Through feature.

SAY: **Now we will think it through. We will check the answer. You should have darkened the circle under the *second* picture. It shows a heart with the words *I love you* written inside it.**

Check to see that all students have filled in the correct answer space. Remind students that they were instructed to choose the picture that shows what Eric drew.

Ask students if they have any questions about Sample 1 or about darkening the answer circle.

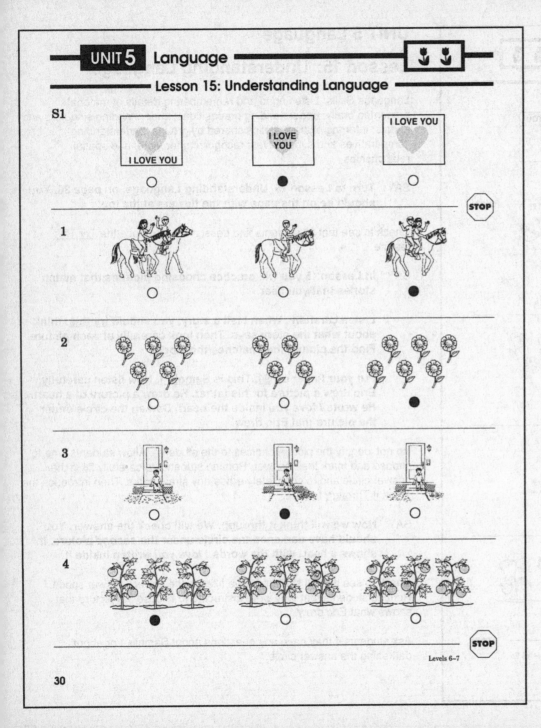

S1

1

2

3

4

Levels 6–7

SAY: **Now you will practice choosing more pictures that match stories that you hear. Listen carefully to each story and look at the pictures for it. Then find the picture that matches the story.**

Now we will begin. Put your finger on number 1.

Check to see that all students find item 1. Allow students time after each item to choose and mark their answer. Say each story only once. Say only the words that appear in boldface type.

SAY: 1 **When Yolanda and her mother went to the parade, they saw some children riding a horse. Darken the circle under the picture that shows children riding a horse.**
2 **Put your finger on number 2. Darken the circle under the picture that shows the most flowers.**
3 **Put your finger on number 3. Randy did not rest until he had raked all of the leaves. Darken the circle under the picture that shows Randy resting.**
4 **Put your finger on number 4. Kiyo had some tomato plants. Not all of the plants had tomatoes on them. Darken the circle under the picture that shows Kiyo's tomato plants.**

Look at the stop sign at the bottom of the page. You have now finished the lesson and should put your pencils down.

Review the questions and answer choices with students. Discuss with the class why one answer is correct and the others are not correct. Also check to see that students have carefully filled in their answer spaces and have completely erased any stray marks.

Lesson 16: Recognizing and Classifying Words

S1	○ nose	5	○ banana
	○ eye		○ peach
	● wagon		● tree
	○ mouth		○ orange

STOP

1	● dress	6	○ around
	○ white		○ on
	○ yellow		○ beside
	○ red		● bite

2	○ dog	7	○ big
	○ cat		● house
	○ bird		○ huge
	● story		○ large

3	○ May	8	○ milk
	● Saturday		○ water
	○ June		● meat
	○ April		○ juice

4	● bus	9	○ man
	○ one		● voice
	○ three		○ woman
	○ five		○ child

STOP

Levels 6–7

Lesson 16: Recognizing and Classifying Words

Language Skills: Recognizing basic vocabulary; understanding classification

SAY: **Turn to Lesson 16, Recognizing and Classifying Words, on page 31.**

Check to see that all students find Lesson 16. Introduce the Try This feature.

SAY: **In Lesson 16 you will practice choosing words that do not belong with other words.**

Listen carefully. While I say four words, you should try this: read each word silently. Find the word that does not belong with the other words.

Put your finger on S1. This is Sample 1. Now listen carefully. The words are *nose, eye, wagon,* and *mouth*. Darken the circle for the word that does not belong.

Allow students time to choose and mark their answer. Remind students to carefully fill in the answer circle and to completely erase any stray marks. Then introduce the Think It Through feature.

SAY: **Now we will think it through. We will check the answer. You should have darkened the circle for the third word. Nose, eye, and mouth are parts of the face. The word *wagon* does not belong because a wagon is not part of the face.**

Check to see that all students have filled in the correct answer space. Remind students that they were instructed to choose the word that does not belong with the others.

Ask students if they have any questions about Sample 1 or about darkening the answer circle.

Lesson 16: Recognizing and Classifying Words

S1 ○ nose ○ eye ● wagon ○ mouth	5 ○ banana ○ peach ● tree ○ orange
(STOP)	
1 ● dress ○ white ○ yellow ○ red	6 ○ around ○ on ○ beside ● bite
2 ○ dog ○ cat ○ bird ● story	7 ○ big ● house ○ huge ○ large
3 ○ May ● Saturday ○ June ○ April	8 ○ milk ○ water ● meat ○ juice
4 ● bus ○ one ○ three ○ five	9 ○ man ● voice ○ woman ○ child

(STOP)

Levels 6–7

31

SAY: Now you will practice choosing more words that do not belong with other words. Read each word silently as I say it aloud. Then find the word that does not belong.

Now we will begin. Put your finger on number 1.

Check to see that all students find item 1. Allow students time after each item to choose and mark their answer. Say each item only once. Say only the words that appear in boldface type.

SAY: 1 **The words for number 1 are *dress*, *white*, *yellow*, and *red*. Darken the circle for the word that does not belong.**
2 **Put your finger on number 2. The words for number 2 are *dog*, *cat*, *bird*, and *story*. Darken the circle for the word that does not belong.**
3 **Put your finger on number 3. The words for number 3 are *May*, *Saturday*, *June*, and *April*. Darken the circle for the word that does not belong.**
4 **Put your finger on number 4. The words for number 4 are *bus*, *one*, *three*, and *five*. Darken the circle for the word that does not belong.**
5 **Put your finger on number 5. The words for number 5 are *banana*, *peach*, *tree*, and *orange*. Darken the circle for the word that does not belong.**
6 **Put your finger on number 6. The words for number 6 are *around*, *on*, *beside*, and *bite*. Darken the circle for the word that does not belong.**
7 **Put your finger on number 7. The words for number 7 are *big*, *house*, *huge*, and *large*. Darken the circle for the word that does not belong.**
8 **Put your finger on number 8. The words for number 8 are *milk*, *water*, *meat*, and *juice*. Darken the circle for the word that does not belong.**
9 **Put your finger on number 9. The words for number 9 are *man*, *voice*, *woman*, and *child*. Darken the circle for the word that does not belong.**

Look at the stop sign at the bottom of the page. You have now finished the lesson and should put your pencils down.

Review the questions and answer choices with students. Discuss with the class why one answer is correct and the others are not correct. Also check to see that students have carefully filled in their answer spaces and have completely erased any stray marks.

Lesson 17: Spelling

S1	wint ●	along ○	ride ○

STOP

1	wind ○	blew ○	baloon ●

2	cros ●	street ○	now ○

3	piked ●	these ○	flowers ○

4	party ○	schol ●	today ○

5	walked ○	store ○	hirself ●

6	gren ●	frog ○	grass ○

7	you'll ○	late ○	hury ●

STOP

Levels 6–7

Lesson 17: Spelling

Language Skills: Recognizing words spelled correctly; identifying words spelled incorrectly

SAY: **Turn to Lesson 17, Spelling, on page 32.**

Check to see that all students find Lesson 17. Introduce the Try This feature.

SAY: **In Lesson 17 you will practice finding words that are not spelled correctly.**

Listen carefully. When I say three words and use them in a sentence, you should try this: read the words silently. Think about how the words should be spelled. Find the word that is not spelled correctly.

Put your finger on S1. This is Sample 1. Now listen carefully. The words are *went, along,* **and** *ride.* **I** *went along* **for the** *ride.* **Darken the circle under the word that is not spelled correctly.**

Allow students time to choose and mark their answer. Remind students to carefully fill in the answer circle and to completely erase any stray marks. Then introduce the Think It Through feature.

SAY: **Now we will think it through. We will check the answer. You should have darkened the circle under the first word.** *Went* **is the word that is not spelled correctly.** *Went* **should have an** *e* **where the** *i* **is.**

Check to see that all students have filled in the correct answer space. Remind students that they were instructed to find the word that is not spelled correctly.

Ask students if they have any questions about Sample 1 or about darkening the answer circle.

Lesson 17: Spelling

S1	wint ●	along ○	ride ○

STOP

1	wind ○	blew ○	baloon ●

2	cros ●	street ○	now ○

3	piked ●	these ○	flowers ○

4	party ○	schol ●	today ○

5	walked ○	store ○	hirself ●

6	gren ●	frog ○	grass ○

7	you'll ○	late ○	hury ●

Levels 6–7

STOP

32

SAY: **Now you will practice finding more words that are not spelled correctly. Read the words silently as I say them aloud and use them in a sentence. Think about how the words should be spelled. Darken the circle under the word that is not spelled correctly.**

Now we will begin. Put your finger on number 1.

Check to see that all students find item 1. As you read each item, make sure that you pronounce the three word choices clearly and that you stress the words as you read them in the sentence. Allow students time after each item to choose and mark their answer. Say each item only once. Say only the words that appear in boldface type.

SAY: 1 **The words for number 1 are** wind, blew, **and** balloon. **The** wind blew **the** balloon **away.**
2 **Put your finger on number 2. The words are** cross, street, **and** now. **I can** cross **the** street now.
3 **Put your finger on number 3. The words are** picked, these, **and** flowers. **Brian** picked these flowers.
4 **Put your finger on number 4. The words are** party, school, **and** today. **Roberto had a** party **at** school today.
5 **Put your finger on number 5. The words are** walked, store, **and** herself. **Elena** walked **to the** store **by** herself.
6 **Put your finger on number 6. The words are** green, frog, **and** grass. **The** green frog **sat on the** grass.
7 **Put your finger on number 7. The words are** you'll, late, **and** hurry. You'll **be** late **if you don't** hurry.

Look at the stop sign at the bottom of the page. You have now finished the lesson and should put your pencils down.

Review the questions and answer choices with students. Discuss with the class why one answer is correct and the others are not correct. Also check to see that students have carefully filled in their answer spaces and have completely erased any stray marks.

Lesson 18: Using Correct Capitalization

S1
- ○ Kevin was happy to
- ● know that mrs. Lam
- ○ found her two cats.

1
- ○ The Chang family will
- ● go to the beach. they
- ○ will stay for two weeks.

2
- ● please have your child
- ○ bring the money by
- ○ February 18.

3
- ○ On Monday mornings
- ● Diane and luke take
- ○ swimming classes.

4
- ○ Mia left her coat on the
- ○ playground last week.
- ● she cannot find it.

5
- ● My mother and i
- ○ painted my room blue.
- ○ It looks nice now.

6
- ● Jon and jeff went to the
- ○ fair. They went on many
- ○ rides and had fun.

7
- ○ Have you ever written a
- ● letter to Troy aikman
- ○ of the Dallas Cowboys?

8
- ○ My teacher asked us to
- ○ go to the library for her.
- ● we came back quickly.

9
- ● My brother tom does
- ○ not like my parrot Tiny
- ○ because Tiny is so loud.

10
- ○ I gave all my money to
- ● miss Mata. She did not
- ○ give me any change.

11
- ○ I am going to help my
- ● uncle shelby wash the
- ○ car on Sunday afternoon.

Levels 6–7

33

SAY: **Turn to Lesson 18, Using Correct Capitalization, on page 33.**

Check to see that all students find Lesson 18. Introduce the <u>Try This</u> feature.

SAY: **In Lesson 18 you will practice finding words that should begin with a capital letter.**

Listen carefully. I will read some sentences to you. While I read, you should <u>try this</u>: read along silently with me. Find the line that has a word that should begin with a capital letter. Remember to check all names of people and places. Check the first letter of each sentence. Check the days of the week and the months of the year. These words should all be capitalized.

Put your finger on <u>S1</u>. This is <u>Sample 1</u>. Now listen carefully. Kevin was happy to know that Mrs. Lam found her two cats. Darken the circle for the line that has a word that should begin with a capital letter.

Allow students time to choose and mark their answer. Remind students to carefully fill in the answer circle and to completely erase any stray marks. Then introduce the <u>Think It Through</u> feature.

SAY: **Now we will <u>think it through</u>. We will check the answer. You should have darkened the circle for the second line. <i>Mrs.</i> is part of Mrs. Lam's name. <i>Mrs.</i> should begin with a capital letter.**

Check to see that all students have filled in the correct answer space. Remind students that they were instructed to find the line that has a word that should begin with a capital letter.

Ask students if they have any questions about <u>Sample 1</u> or about darkening the answer circle.

Lesson 18: Using Correct Capitalization

S1
- ○ Kevin was happy to
- ● know that mrs. Lam
- ○ found her two cats.

(STOP)

1
- ○ The Chang family will
- ● go to the beach. they
- ○ will stay for two weeks.

2
- ● please have your child
- ○ bring the money by
- ○ February 18.

3
- ○ On Monday mornings
- ● Diane and luke take
- ○ swimming classes.

4
- ○ Mia left her coat on the
- ○ playground last week.
- ● she cannot find it.

5
- ● My mother and i
- ○ painted my room blue.
- ○ It looks nice now.

6
- ● Jon and jeff went to the
- ○ fair. They went on many
- ○ rides and had fun.

7
- ○ Have you ever written a
- ● letter to Troy aikman
- ○ of the Dallas Cowboys?

8
- ○ My teacher asked us to
- ○ go to the library for her.
- ● we came back quickly.

9
- ● My brother tom does
- ○ not like my parrot Tiny
- ○ because Tiny is so loud.

10
- ○ I gave all my money to
- ● miss Mata. She did not
- ○ give me any change.

11
- ○ I am going to help my
- ● uncle shelby wash the
- ○ car on Sunday afternoon.

(STOP)

Levels 6–7

33

Lesson 19: Using Correct Punctuation

S1 ○ The baby splashed cold
    ● water on his face He
    ○ clapped his hands.

STOP

1   ● D W was five last year.
    ○ He had a birthday
    ○ party at the park.

2   ○ My shadow dances on
    ● the wall as I walk It
    ○ moves as I move.

3   ● Hooray Today we are
    ○ going to the swimming
    ○ pool with our friends.

4   ○ Are you drawing a
    ○ picture of a brown
    ● dinosaur Bradley is.

5   ● Mrs Harper's class
    ○ will play a game with
    ○ Miss Burt's class.

6   ○ Can you tell me how to
    ● get to the office I need
    ○ to use the telephone.

7   ○ I have some wonderful
    ● news I'm going home
    ○ with my grandpa.

8   ○ Can you walk home
    ○ with me and spend the
    ● night Please say yes.

9   ○ Amy climbed over the
    ● fence She tore her shirt
    ○ and her shorts.

10 ● Wow That girl scored
    ○ all the points and
    ○ helped her school win.

11 ○ Last night I read a story
    ○ about wild things. Have
    ● you read that story

STOP

Levels 6–7

34

Lesson 19: Using Correct Punctuation

Language Skill: Identifying the need for punctuation marks in sentences

SAY: **Turn to Lesson 19, Using Correct Punctuation, on page 34.**

Check to see that all students find Lesson 19. Introduce the Try This feature.

SAY: **In Lesson 19 you will practice finding missing punctuation marks in sentences.**

Listen carefully. I will read some sentences to you. While I read, you should try this: read along silently with me. Find the line that is missing a punctuation mark.

Put your finger on S1. This is Sample 1. Now listen carefully. The baby splashed cold water on his face. He clapped his hands. Darken the circle for the line that is missing a punctuation mark.

Allow students time to choose and mark their answer. Remind students to carefully fill in the answer circle and to completely erase any stray marks. Then introduce the Think It Through feature.

SAY: **Now we will think it through. We will check the answer. You should have darkened the circle for the *second* line. *Face* is the last word in the first sentence. A period is needed at the end of the sentence.**

Check to see that all students have filled in the correct answer space. Remind students that they were instructed to find the line that is missing a punctuation mark.

Ask students if they have any questions about Sample 1 or about darkening the answer circle.

Lesson 19: Using Correct Punctuation

S1 ○ The baby splashed cold
   ● water on his face He
   ○ clapped his hands.

【STOP】

1 ● D W was five last year.
   ○ He had a birthday
   ○ party at the park.

2 ○ My shadow dances on
   ● the wall as I walk It
   ○ moves as I move.

3 ● Hooray Today we are
   ○ going to the swimming
   ○ pool with our friends.

4 ○ Are you drawing a
   ○ picture of a brown
   ● dinosaur Bradley is.

5 ● Mrs Harper's class
   ○ will play a game with
   ○ Miss Burt's class.

6 ○ Can you tell me how to
   ● get to the office I need
   ○ to use the telephone.

7 ○ I have some wonderful
   ● news I'm going home
   ○ with my grandpa.

8 ○ Can you walk home
   ○ with me and spend the
   ● night Please say yes.

9 ○ Amy climbed over the
   ● fence She tore her shirt
   ○ and her shorts.

10 ● Wow That girl scored
   ○ all the points and
   ○ helped her school win.

11 ○ Last night I read a story
   ○ about wild things. Have
   ● you read that story

【STOP】

Levels 6–7

34

SAY: **Now you will practice finding more missing punctuation marks in sentences. Read the sentences silently as I say them aloud. Find the line that is missing a punctuation mark. Then darken the circle for that line.**

Now we will begin. Put your finger on number 1.

Check to see that all students find item 1. Allow students time after each item to choose and mark their answer. Reread an item only if you make a mistake when saying it aloud. Say only the words that appear in boldface type.

SAY: 1 **D.W. was five last year. He had a birthday party at the park.**
2 **Put your finger on number 2. My shadow dances on the wall as I walk. It moves as I move.**
3 **Put your finger on number 3. Hooray! Today we are going to the swimming pool with our friends.**
4 **Put your finger on number 4. Are you drawing a picture of a brown dinosaur? Bradley is.**
5 **Put your finger on number 5. Mrs. Harper's class will play a game with Miss Burt's class.**
6 **Put your finger on number 6. Can you tell me how to get to the office? I need to use the telephone.**
7 **Put your finger on number 7. I have some wonderful news. I'm going home with my grandpa.**
8 **Put your finger on number 8. Can you walk home with me and spend the night? Please say yes.**
9 **Put your finger on number 9. Amy climbed over the fence. She tore her shirt and her shorts.**
10 **Put your finger on number 10. Wow! That girl scored all the points and helped her school win.**
11 **Put your finger on number 11. Last night I read a story about wild things. Have you read that story?**

Look at the stop sign at the bottom of the page. You have now finished the lesson and should put your pencils down.

Review the questions and answer choices with students. Discuss with the class why one answer is correct and the others are not correct. Also check to see that students have carefully filled in their answer spaces and have completely erased any stray marks.

S1
- ○ Justin and Kelly are
- ● not here. Them are
- ○ going to be late.

STOP

1
- ● Nick are not ready for
- ○ school yet. He still has to
- ○ comb his hair.

2
- ○ This card does not
- ○ belong to me. It belongs
- ● to hers.

3
- ○ The yellow butterfly is
- ● on that there tree. You
- ○ should leave it alone.

4
- ● Ana eated all the fruit.
- ○ Now we do not have
- ○ anything for a snack.

5
- ○ Mr. Lopez arrived on
- ○ time. His daughter
- ● weren't going.

6
- ● I haven't never seen
- ○ real snow. It does not
- ○ snow where I live.

7
- ● The gooses were
- ○ crossing the road to get
- ○ to the pond.

8
- ○ The man began to play
- ● the organ. I and Carmen
- ○ sang the song.

9
- ● The monkeys is
- ○ jumping from tree to
- ○ tree. They are fast.

10
- ○ The radio was still on
- ○ this morning when I
- ● woke up. Too noisy.

11
- ○ Last week at the
- ● circus, I seen a kitten
- ○ in a dress.

STOP

Levels 6–7

35

Lesson 20: Finding Mistakes in Language

Language Skills: Identifying errors in the use of nouns, pronouns, verbs, adjectives, and adverbs; recognizing errors in sentence structure

SAY: **Turn to Lesson 20, Finding Mistakes in Language, on page 35.**

Check to see that all students find Lesson 20. Introduce the <u>Try This</u> feature.

SAY: **In Lesson 20 you will practice finding mistakes in the way words are used.**

Listen carefully. I will read some sentences to you. While I read, you should <u>try this</u>: read along silently with me. Find the line that has a mistake in the way words are used.

Put your finger on <u>S1</u>. This is <u>Sample 1</u>. Now listen carefully. Justin and Kelly are not here. Them are going to be late. Darken the circle for the line that has a mistake in the way the words are used.

Allow students time to choose and mark their answer. Remind students to carefully fill in the answer circle and to completely erase any stray marks. Then introduce the <u>Think It Through</u> feature.

SAY: **Now we will <u>think it through</u>. We will check the answer. You should have darkened the circle for the second line. *Them* should be *they*. *They* are going to be late.**

Check to see that all students have filled in the correct answer space. Remind students that they were instructed to find the line that has a mistake in the way the words are used.

Ask students if they have any questions about <u>Sample 1</u> or about darkening the answer circle.

Lesson 20: Finding Mistakes in Language

S1 ○ Justin and Kelly are
    ● not here. Them are
    ○ going to be late.

STOP

1 ● Nick are not ready for
   ○ school yet. He still has to
   ○ comb his hair.

2 ○ This card does not
   ○ belong to me. It belongs
   ● to hers.

3 ○ The yellow butterfly is
   ● on that there tree. You
   ○ should leave it alone.

4 ● Ana eated all the fruit.
   ○ Now we do not have
   ○ anything for a snack.

5 ○ Mr. Lopez arrived on
   ○ time. His daughter
   ● weren't going.

6 ● I haven't never seen
   ○ real snow. It does not
   ○ snow where I live.

7 ● The gooses were
   ○ crossing the road to get
   ○ to the pond.

8 ○ The man began to play
   ● the organ. I and Carmen
   ○ sang the song.

9 ● The monkeys is
   ○ jumping from tree to
   ○ tree. They are fast.

10 ○ The radio was still on
   ○ this morning when I
   ● woke up. Too noisy.

11 ○ Last week at the
   ● circus, I seen a kitten
   ○ in a dress.

STOP

Levels 6–7

35

SAY: **Now you will practice finding more mistakes in the way words are used. Read the sentences silently as I say them aloud. Darken the circle for the line that has a mistake in the way the words are used.**

Now we will begin. Put your finger on number 1.

Check to see that all students find item 1. Allow students time after each item to choose and mark their answer. Reread an item only if you make a mistake when saying it aloud. Be sure that you do not emphasize the words that are used incorrectly. Say only the words that appear in boldface type.

SAY: 1 **Nick are not ready for school yet. He still has to comb his hair.**
      2 **Put your finger on number 2. This card does not belong to me. It belongs to hers.**
      3 **Put your finger on number 3. The yellow butterfly is on that there tree. You should leave it alone.**
      4 **Put your finger on number 4. Ana eated all the fruit. Now we do not have anything for a snack.**
      5 **Put your finger on number 5. Mr. Lopez arrived on time. His daughter weren't going.**
      6 **Put your finger on number 6. I haven't never seen real snow. It does not snow where I live.**
      7 **Put your finger on number 7. The gooses were crossing the road to get to the pond.**
      8 **Put your finger on number 8. The man began to play the organ. I and Carmen sang the song.**
      9 **Put your finger on number 9. The monkeys is jumping from tree to tree. They are fast.**
     10 **Put your finger on number 10. The radio was still on this morning when I woke up. Too noisy.**
     11 **Put your finger on number 11. Last week at the circus, I seen a kitten in a dress.**

Look at the stop sign at the bottom of the page. You have now finished the lesson and should put your pencils down.

Review the questions and answer choices with students. Discuss with the class why one answer is correct and the others are not correct. Also check to see that students have carefully filled in their answer spaces and have completely erased any stray marks.

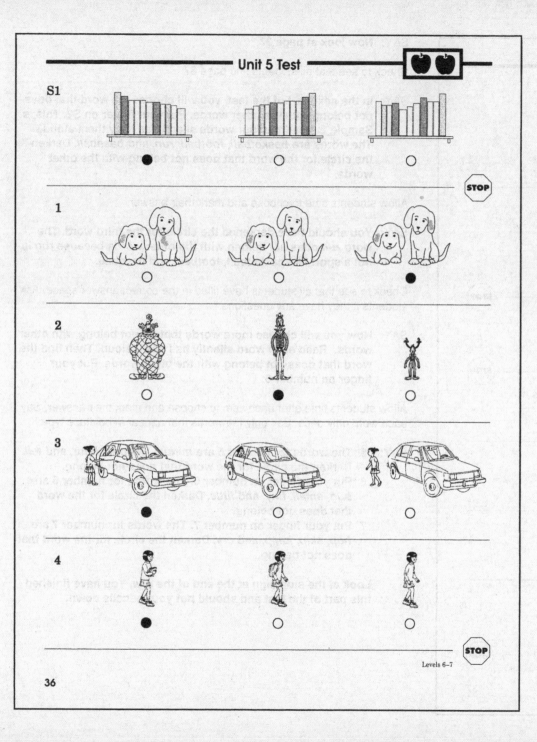

Unit 5 Test

SAY: **Turn to the Unit 5 Test on page 36. You should be on the page with the apples at the top.**

Check to see that all students find the Unit 5 Test.

SAY: **In the first part of this test, you will choose pictures that match stories that you hear. Put your finger on S1. This is Sample 1. Now listen carefully. Matthew was putting his books on a shelf in his room. He arranged them by their height, with the tallest books on the left. Darken the circle under the picture that shows Matthew's books.**

Do not identify the picture choices to the students. Allow students time to choose and mark their answer.

SAY: **You should have darkened the circle under the *first* picture. This picture shows the books arranged on the shelf by height, with the tallest books on the left.**

Check to see that all students have filled in the correct answer space. Ask students if they have any questions.

SAY: **Now you will choose more pictures that match stories that you hear. Listen carefully to each story and look at the pictures for it. Find the picture that matches the story. Put your finger on number 1.**

Check to see that all students find item 1. Allow students time after each item to choose and mark their answer. Say each story only once. Say only the words that appear in boldface type.

SAY: 1 **Each of Miko's puppies has a spot on its ear. Darken the circle under the picture that shows Miko's puppies.**
2 **Put your finger on number 2. When Alex went to the circus, he saw a clown that was tall and thin. Darken the circle under the picture of the clown that is tall and thin.**
3 **Put your finger on number 3. Shana will ride in the car. Darken the circle under the picture that shows that Shana will ride in the car.**
4 **Put your finger on number 4. Marisa could not find her backpack. She had to carry her books to school. Darken the circle under the picture that shows Marisa on her way to school.**

Look at the stop sign at the bottom of the page. You have finished this part of the test and should put your pencils down.

S2	○ basketball		6	● bug	
	○ football			○ small	
	● run			○ tiny	
	○ baseball			○ little	
		STOP			
5	○ minute		7	○ hop	
	○ second			○ skip	
	○ hour			○ jump	
	● tell			● cry	
		STOP			STOP

S3	thank ○	you ○	gifft ●
			STOP
8	she ○	chasd ●	woods ○
9	toold ●	everyone ○	fine ○
10	said ○	hous ●	fire ○
11	play ○	overe ●	four ○
			STOP

Levels 6–7

SAY: **Now look at page 37.**

Check to see that all students find page 37.

SAY: **In the next part of the test, you will choose the word that does not belong with the other words. Put your finger on S2. This is Sample 2. Read the four words silently as I say them aloud. The words are *basketball*, *football*, *run,* and *baseball.* Darken the circle for the word that does not belong with the other words.**

Allow students time to choose and mark their answer.

SAY: **You should have darkened the circle for the third word. The word *run* does not belong with the other words because run is not a sport like basketball, football, and baseball.**

Check to see that all students have filled in the correct answer space. Ask students if they have any questions.

SAY: **Now you will choose more words that do not belong with other words. Read each word silently as I say it aloud. Then find the word that does not belong with the other words. Put your finger on number 5.**

Allow students time after each item to choose and mark their answer. Say each word only once. Say only the words that appear in boldface type.

SAY: 5 **The words for number 5 are *minute, second, hour,* and *tell.* Darken the circle for the word that does not belong.**
6 **Put your finger on number 6. The words for number 6 are *bug, small, tiny,* and *little.* Darken the circle for the word that does not belong.**
7 **Put your finger on number 7. The words for number 7 are *hop, skip, jump,* and *cry.* Darken the circle for the word that does not belong.**

Look at the stop sign at the end of the row. You have finished this part of the test and should put your pencils down.

S2 ○ basketball
    ○ football
    ● run
    ○ baseball

6   ● bug
    ○ small
    ○ tiny
    ○ little

STOP

5   ○ minute
    ○ second
    ○ hour
    ● tell

7   ○ hop
    ○ skip
    ○ jump
    ● cry

STOP

S3   thank   you   gifft
          ○   ○   ●

STOP

8   she   chasd   woods
          ○   ○   ○

9   toold   everyone   fine
          ●   ○   ○

10   said   hous   fire
          ○   ●   ○

11   play   overe   four
          ○   ●   ○

STOP

Levels 6–7

37

SAY: **In the next part of the test, you will find words that are not spelled correctly. Put your finger on S3. This is <u>Sample 3</u>. Read the three words silently as I say them aloud and use them in a sentence. Darken the circle under the word that is not spelled correctly. The three words are *thank, you,* and *gift. Thank you* for the *gift.***

Allow students time to choose and mark their answer.

SAY: **You should have darkened the circle under the third word. *Gift* is the word that is not spelled correctly. *Gift* should have only one *f.***

Check to see that all students have filled in the correct answer space. Ask students if they have any questions.

SAY: **Now you will find more words that are not spelled correctly. Read the words silently as I say them and use them in a sentence. Then darken the circle under the word that is not spelled correctly. Put your finger on number 8.**

As you read each item, make sure that you pronounce the three word choices clearly and that you stress the words as you read them in the sentence. Allow students time after each item to choose and mark their answer. Say each item only once. Say <u>only</u> the words that appear in boldface type.

SAY: 8 **The words for number 8 are *she, chased,* and *woods. She chased* the rabbit through the *woods.***

9 **Put your finger on number 9. The words for number 9 are *told, everyone,* and *fine.* Noriku *told everyone* that she felt *fine.***

10 **Put your finger on number 10. The words for number 10 are *said, house,* and *fire.* They *said* the *house* was on *fire.***

11 **Put your finger on number 11. The words for number 11 are *play, over,* and *four.* The *play* was *over* at *four* o'clock.**

Look at the stop sign at the bottom of the page. You have finished this part of the test and should put your pencils down.

Check to see that all students find page 38.

SAY: **In the next part of the test, you will find words that should begin with a capital letter. Put your finger on S4. This is Sample 4. Read the sentences silently as I say them aloud. Then darken the circle for the line that has a word that should begin with a capital letter. Give this note to Lupe when you see her. It is very important.**

Allow students time to choose and mark their answer.

SAY: **You should have darkened the circle for the second line. The word** it **should begin with a capital letter because it is the first word in a sentence.**

Check to see that all students have filled in the correct answer space. Ask students if they have any questions.

SAY: **Now you will find other words that should begin with a capital letter. Read the sentences silently as I say them aloud. Then darken the circle for the line that has a word that should begin with a capital letter. Put your finger on number 12.**

Allow students time after each item to choose and mark their answer. Reread an item only if you make a mistake when saying it aloud. Say only the words that appear in boldface type.

SAY: 12 **My rabbit's name is Mopsy, and my pig's name is Charlotte.**
13 **Put your finger on number 13. Did you know that the Garcia family was moving to Texas?**
14 **Put your finger on number 14. I have never been able to set this clock. Koji and I asked Dad to do it.**
15 **Put your finger on number 15. Brian and Audry are playing with the girl who lives next door.**
16 **Put your finger on number 16. My soccer coach is Mrs. McBride. She knows all the rules.**

Look at the stop sign at the bottom of this column. You have finished this part of the test and should put your pencils down.

S4
○ Give this note to Lupe
● when you see her. it is
○ very important.

🛑 STOP

12
○ My rabbit's name is
○ Mopsy, and my pig's
● name is charlotte.

13
○ Did you know that the
● garcia family was
○ moving to Texas?

14
○ I have never been able
○ to set this clock. Koji
● and i asked Dad to do it.

15
● Brian and audry are
○ playing with the girl
○ who lives next door.

16
○ My soccer coach is
● mrs. McBride. She
○ knows all the rules.

🛑 STOP

S5
○ The elephant ate all
● the peanuts Then it
○ sprayed water on us.

🛑 STOP

17
○ Aunt Becky invited us
○ to spend the summer
● with her I hope we can.

18
○ Mora likes to eat red
● grapes, and A J likes to
○ eat pears.

19
○ Jason and I like to
● read poems We have
○ written some for Mom.

20
● Gosh This is the third
○ time this week I have
○ been late to school.

21
○ Leslie rented a movie
○ last night and watched
● it She took it back today.

🛑 STOP

Levels 6–7

S4
- ○ Give this note to Lupe
- ● when you see her. it is
- ○ very important.

(STOP)

12
- ○ My rabbit's name is
- ○ Mopsy, and my pig's
- ● name is charlotte.

13
- ○ Did you know that the
- ● garcia family was
- ○ moving to Texas?

14
- ○ I have never been able
- ○ to set this clock. Koji
- ● and i asked Dad to do it.

15
- ● Brian and audry are
- ○ playing with the girl
- ○ who lives next door.

16
- ○ My soccer coach is
- ● mrs. McBride. She
- ○ knows all the rules.

S5
- ○ The elephant ate all
- ● the peanuts Then it
- ○ sprayed water on us.

(STOP)

17
- ○ Aunt Becky invited us
- ○ to spend the summer
- ● with her I hope we can.

18
- ○ Mora likes to eat red
- ● grapes, and A J likes to
- ○ eat pears.

19
- ○ Jason and I like to
- ● read poems We have
- ○ written some for Mom.

20
- ● Gosh This is the third
- ○ time this week I have
- ○ been late to school.

21
- ○ Leslie rented a movie
- ○ last night and watched
- ● it She took it back today.

Levels 6–7

(STOP)   (STOP)

SAY: In the next part of the test, you will find missing punctuation marks in sentences. Put your finger on S5. This is Sample 5. Read the sentences silently as I say them aloud. Darken the circle for the line that is missing a punctuation mark. The elephant ate all the peanuts. Then it sprayed water on us.

Allow students time to choose and mark their answer.

SAY: **You should have darkened the circle for the *second* line. *Peanuts* is the last word in the first sentence. A period is needed at the end of the sentence.**

Check to see that all students have filled in the correct answer space. Ask students if they have any questions.

SAY: **Now you will find other missing punctuation marks in sentences. Read the sentences silently as I say them aloud. Darken the circle for the line that is missing a punctuation mark. Put your finger on number 17.**

Allow students time after each item to choose and mark their answer. Reread an item only if you make a mistake when saying it aloud. Say only the words that appear in boldface type.

SAY: 17 **Aunt Becky invited us to spend the summer with her. I hope we can.**
18 **Put your finger on number 18. Mora likes to eat red grapes, and A.J. likes to eat pears.**
19 **Put your finger on number 19. Jason and I like to read poems. We have written some for Mom.**
20 **Put your finger on number 20. Gosh! This is the third time this week I have been late to school.**
21 **Put your finger on number 21. Leslie rented a movie last night and watched it. She took it back today.**

Look at the stop sign at the bottom of this column. You have finished this part of the test and should put your pencils down.

S6
- The fox and the turtle
- ● is having a race. Who
- will win?

(STOP)

22
- ● I and Ming planted a
- little tree in our yard.
- We will take care of it.

23
- I was so excited about
- going to the store that I
- ● forgot mine money.

24
- Who will help me eat
- ● that there bread? I
- have jelly to put on it.

25
- ● Has you combed your
- hair? It doesn't look
- like you have.

26
- Mary Ellen went
- ● outside. She sawed
- snow on the ground.

27
- I bought a present for
- ● Ada. She won't never
- guess what it is.

28
- ● That song it is old. Can
- we look for a different
- one to sing?

29
- The dogs will not stop
- barking and growling.
- ● Running around.

30
- ● This is the bestest video
- game I have ever
- played. May I buy it?

31
- I will pass out the
- pencils and cards to
- ● the mans.

32
- ● The birds wasn't
- building their nests.
- They were laying eggs.

(STOP)

Levels 6–7

39

SAY: **Now look at page 39.**

Check to see that all students find page 39.

SAY: **In the last part of the test, you will find mistakes in the way words are used. Put your finger on S6. This is Sample 6. Read the sentences silently as I say them aloud. Darken the circle for the line that has a mistake in the way the words are used. The fox and the turtle is having a race. Who will win?**

Allow students time to choose and mark their answer.

SAY: **You should have darkened the circle for the *second* line. The sentence is about more than one animal. *Are* should be used when a sentence tells about more than one thing. The fox and the turtle *are* having a race.**

Check to see that all students have filled in the correct answer space. Ask students if they have any questions.

SAY: **Now you will find more mistakes in the way words are used. Read the sentences silently as I say them aloud. Then darken the circle for the line that has a mistake in the way the words are used. Put your finger on number 22.**

Allow students time after each item to choose and mark their answer. Reread an item only if you make a mistake when saying it aloud. Be sure you do not emphasize the words that are used incorrectly. Say only the words that appear in boldface type.

S6
- ○ The fox and the turtle
- ● is having a race. Who
- ○ will win?

STOP

22
- ● I and Ming planted a
- ○ little tree in our yard.
- ○ We will take care of it.

23
- ○ I was so excited about
- ○ going to the store that I
- ● forgot mine money.

24
- ○ Who will help me eat
- ● that there bread? I
- ○ have jelly to put on it.

25
- ● Has you combed your
- ○ hair? It doesn't look
- ○ like you have.

26
- ○ Mary Ellen went
- ● outside. She sawed
- ○ snow on the ground.

27
- ○ I bought a present for
- ● Ada. She won't never
- ○ guess what it is.

28
- ● That song it is old. Can
- ○ we look for a different
- ○ one to sing?

29
- ○ The dogs will not stop
- ○ barking and growling.
- ● Running around.

30
- ● This is the bestest video
- ○ game I have ever
- ○ played. May I buy it?

31
- ○ I will pass out the
- ○ pencils and cards to
- ● the mans.

32
- ● The birds wasn't
- ○ building their nests.
- ○ They were laying eggs.

STOP

Levels 6–7

39

SAY:
22 **I and Ming planted a little tree in our yard. We will take care of it.**
23 **Put your finger on number 23. I was so excited about going to the store that I forgot mine money.**
24 **Put your finger on number 24. Who will help me eat that there bread? I have jelly to put on it.**
25 **Put your finger on number 25. Has you combed your hair? It doesn't look like you have.**
26 **Put your finger on number 26. Mary Ellen went outside. She sawed snow on the ground.**
27 **Put your finger on number 27. I bought a present for Ada. She won't never guess what it is.**
28 **Put your finger on number 28. That song it is old. Can we look for a different one to sing?**
29 **Put your finger on number 29. The dogs will not stop barking and growling. Running around.**
30 **Put your finger on number 30. This is the bestest video game I have ever played. May I buy it?**
31 **Put your finger on number 31. I will pass out the pencils and cards to the mans.**
32 **Put your finger on number 32. The birds wasn't building their nests. They were laying eggs.**

Look at the stop sign at the bottom of the page. It is now time to stop. You have completed the Unit 5 Test. Make sure you have carefully filled in your answer circles and have completely erased any stray marks. Then put your pencils down.

After the test has been scored, review the questions and answer choices with students. If students are having difficulty, provide them with additional practice.

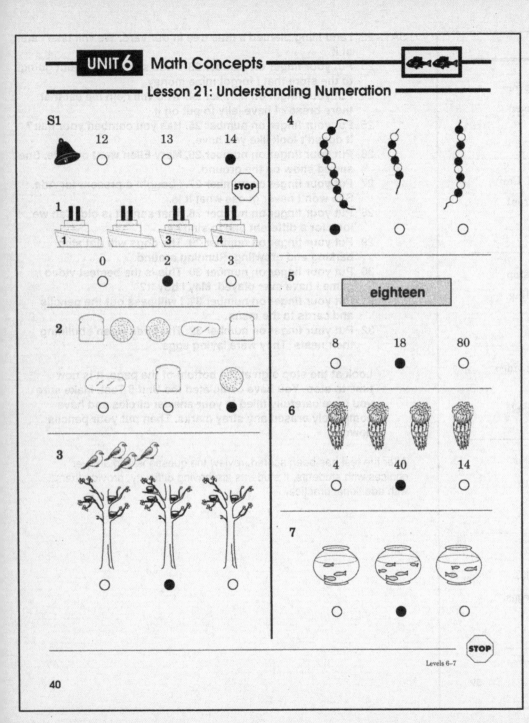

UNIT 6 Math Concepts

Lesson 21: Understanding Numeration

Mathematics Skills: Understanding patterns and sequences; counting; understanding one-to-one correspondence; understanding properties of number systems; recognizing different names for numbers; understanding place value

SAY: **Turn to Lesson 21, Understanding Numeration, on page 40. You should be on the page with the fish at the top.**

Check to see that all students find Lesson 21. Introduce the Try This feature.

SAY: **In Lesson 21 you will practice answering math questions about numbers, patterns, and objects.**

Listen carefully. When I read a question, you should try this: look at each picture or number for the question. Then find the picture or number that answers the question.

Put your finger on S1. You should be on the row with the bell. This is Sample 1. Now listen carefully. What number comes just before 15? Darken the circle under the number that comes just before 15.

Allow students time to choose and mark their answer. Remind students to carefully fill in the answer circle and to completely erase any stray marks. Then introduce the Think It Through feature.

SAY: **Now we will think it through. We will check the answer. You should have darkened the circle under the last number in the row. It is the number 14. If you count to 15, the number that comes just before 15 is 14.**

Check to see that all students have filled in the correct answer space. Remind students that they were instructed to find the number that comes just before 15.

Ask students if they have any questions about Sample 1 or about darkening the answer circle.

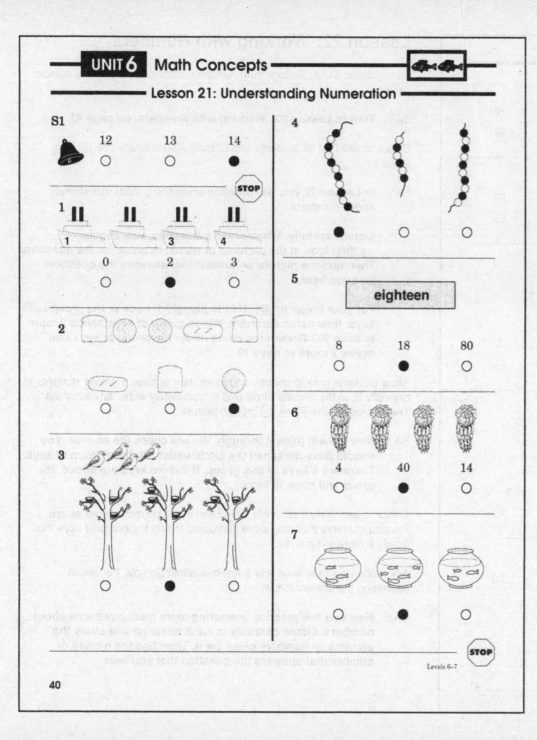

S1

| 12 | 13 | 14 |

1

| 1 | | 3 | 4 |

| 0 | 2 | 3 |

2

3

4

5

eighteen

| 8 | 18 | 80 |

6

| 4 | 40 | 14 |

7

Levels 6–7

40

SAY: Now you will practice answering more math questions about numbers, patterns, and objects. Listen carefully to each question and study each picture or number given for it. Then find the picture or number that answers the question that you hear.

Now we will begin. Put your finger on number 1.

Check to see that all students find item 1. Allow students time after each item to choose and mark their answer. Say each item only once. Say only the words that appear in boldface type.

SAY: 1 **Look at the boats in the row. One boat is missing its number. What number belongs on the boat? Darken the circle under the number that is missing.**

2 **Put your finger on number 2. Look at the pattern made by the sandwiches at the top. Which sandwich should come next in the pattern? Darken the circle under the sandwich that should come next in the pattern.**

3 **Put your finger on number 3. Look at the birds. Which tree will hold one bird in each nest, with no nests left over? Darken the circle under the tree that will hold one bird in each nest, with no nests left over.**

4 **Put your finger on number 4. Look at the strings of beads. Which string has 6 dark beads? Darken the circle under the string that has 6 dark beads.**

5 **Put your finger on number 5. Look at the word in the shaded box. Which number means the same as the word in the shaded box? Darken the circle under the number that means the same as the word in the shaded box.**

6 **Put your finger on number 6. Look at the bunches of carrots. Each bunch has 10 carrots. How many carrots are there altogether? Darken the circle under the number that tells how many carrots there are altogether.**

7 **Put your finger on number 7. Look at the bowls of fish. Which bowl has exactly 5 fish? Darken the circle under the bowl that has exactly 5 fish.**

Look at the stop sign at the bottom of the page. You have now finished the lesson and should put your pencils down.

Review the questions and answer choices with students. Discuss with the class why one answer is correct and the others are not correct. Also check to see that students have carefully filled in their answer spaces and have completely erased any stray marks.

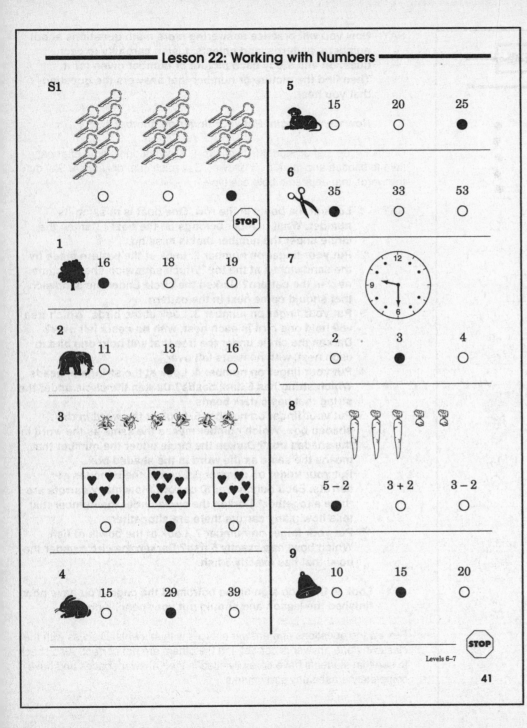

Lesson 22: Working with Numbers

Mathematics Skills: Recognizing numbers; understanding whole-number values

SAY: **Turn to Lesson 22, Working with Numbers, on page 41.**

Check to see that all students find Lesson 22. Introduce the Try This feature.

SAY: **In Lesson 22 you will practice answering math questions about numbers.**

Listen carefully. When I read a question, you should try this: look at the pictures or numbers given for the question. Then find the picture or number that answers the question that you hear.

Put your finger on S1. This is Sample 1. Look at the groups of keys. Now listen carefully. Which group of keys needs 2 more to have 10? Darken the circle under the group of keys that needs 2 more to have 10.

Allow students time to choose and mark their answer. Remind students to carefully fill in the answer circle and to completely erase any stray marks. Then introduce the Think It Through feature.

SAY: **Now we will think it through. We will check the answer. You should have darkened the circle under the *third* group of keys. There are 8 keys in this group. If 2 more keys are added, the group will have 10 keys.**

Check to see that all students have filled in the correct answer space. Remind students that they were instructed to find the group of keys that needs 2 more to have 10.

Ask students if they have any questions about Sample 1 or about darkening the answer circle.

SAY: **Now you will practice answering more math questions about numbers. Listen carefully to each question and study the pictures or numbers given for it. Then find the picture or number that answers the question that you hear.**

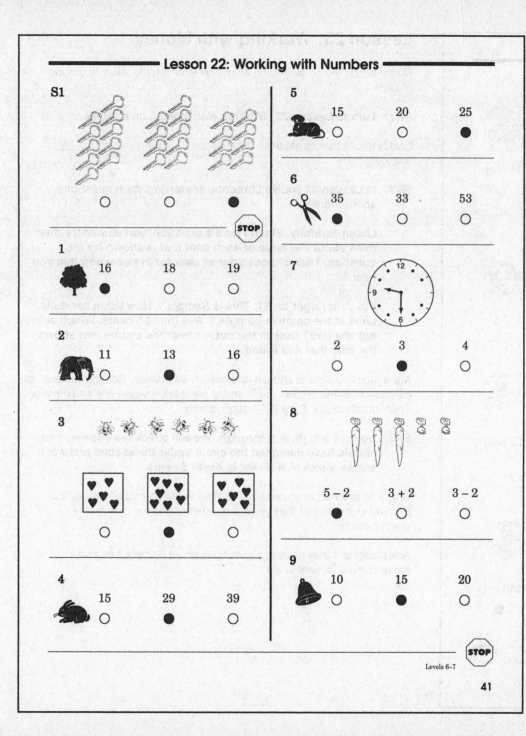

Lesson 22: Working with Numbers

S1

1
| 16 | 18 | 19 |

2
| 11 | 13 | 16 |

3

4
| 15 | 29 | 39 |

5
| 15 | 20 | 25 |

6
| 35 | 33 | 53 |

7
| 2 | 3 | 4 |

8
| 5 − 2 | 3 + 2 | 3 − 2 |

9
| 10 | 15 | 20 |

Levels 6–7

STOP

SAY: **Now we will begin. Put your finger on number 1. You should be on the row with the tree.**

Check to see that all students find item 1. Allow students time after each item to choose and mark their answer. Say each item only once. Say <u>only</u> the words that appear in boldface type.

SAY: 1 **Look at the numbers in the row. Which number is *16*? Darken the circle under the number *16*.**

2 **Put your finger on number 2. You should be on the row with the elephant. Which number is between 12 and 15? Darken the circle under the number that is between 12 and 15.**

3 **Put your finger on number 3. Look at the bees. Which box has one more heart than the number of bees? Darken the circle under the box that has one more heart than the number of bees.**

4 **Put your finger on number 4. You should be on the row with the rabbit. Which number is between 17 and 37? Darken the circle under the number that is between 17 and 37.**

5 **Put your finger on number 5. You should be on the row with the dog. Which number is closest in value to 23? Darken the circle under the number that is closest in value to 23.**

6 **Put your finger on number 6. You should be on the row with the scissors. Which number is *35*? Darken the circle under the number that is *35*.**

7 **Put your finger on number 7. Which number should be added to the clock? Darken the circle under the number that should be added to the clock.**

8 **Put your finger on number 8. Look at the picture of the carrots. What does the picture show? Darken the circle under the number expression that tells what the picture shows.**

9 **Put your finger on number 9. You should be on the row with the bell. Which number is closest in value to 13? Darken the circle under the number that is closest in value to 13.**

Look at the stop sign at the bottom of the page. You have now finished the lesson and should put your pencils down.

Review the questions and answer choices with students. Discuss with the class why one answer is correct and the others are not correct. Also check to see that students have carefully filled in their answer spaces and have completely erased any stray marks.

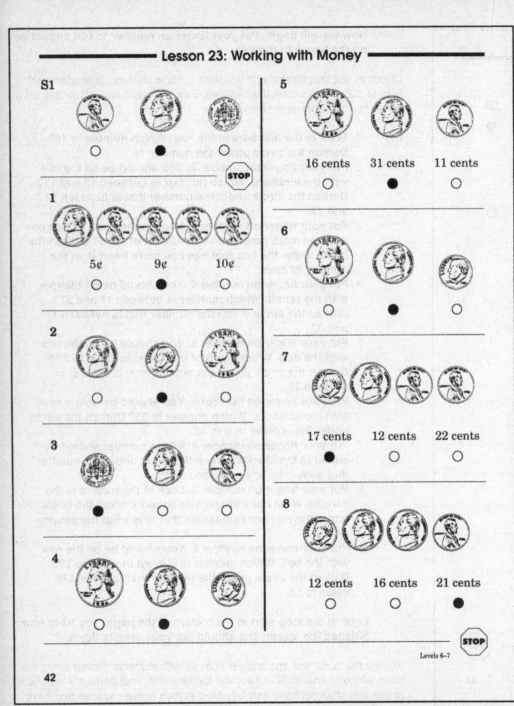

Lesson 23: Working with Money

Mathematics Skills: Identifying coins; determining the value of groups of coins

SAY: **Turn to Lesson 23, Working with Money, on page 42.**

Check to see that all students find Lesson 23. Introduce the <u>Try This</u> feature.

SAY: **In Lesson 23 you will practice answering math questions about money.**

Listen carefully. When I read a question, you should <u>try this</u>: think about the value of each coin that is shown for the question. Then choose your answer for the question that you hear.

Put your finger on <u>S1</u>. This is <u>Sample 1</u>. Now listen carefully. Look at the coins in <u>Sample 1</u>. Ava found 5 cents. Which coin did she find? Darken the circle under the picture that shows the coin that Ava found.

Allow students time to choose and mark their answer. Remind students to carefully fill in the answer circle and to completely erase any stray marks. Then introduce the <u>Think It Through</u> feature.

SAY: **Now we will <u>think it through</u>. We will check the answer. You should have darkened the circle under the second picture. It shows a _nickel_. A nickel is worth 5 cents.**

Check to see that all students have filled in the correct answer space. Remind students that they were instructed to find the coin that is worth 5 cents.

Ask students if they have any questions about <u>Sample 1</u> or about darkening the answer circle.

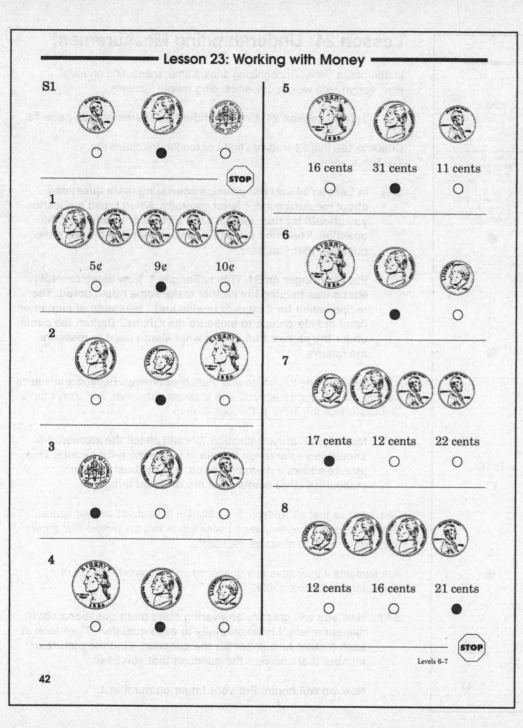

Lesson 23: Working with Money

S1

○ ● ○

STOP

1

5¢   9¢   10¢

○ ● ○

2

○ ● ○

3

● ○ ○

4

○ ● ○

5

16 cents 31 cents 11 cents

○ ● ○

6

○ ● ○

7

17 cents 12 cents 22 cents

● ○ ○

8

12 cents 16 cents 21 cents

○ ○ ●

STOP

Levels 6–7

42

SAY: Now you will practice answering more math questions about money. Listen carefully to each question. Think about the value of each coin that is shown for the question. Then choose your answer for the question that you hear.

Now we will begin. Put your finger on number 1.

Check to see that all students find item 1. Allow students time after each item to choose and mark their answer. Say each item only once. Say <u>only</u> the words that appear in boldface type.

SAY:
1. **Look at the coins in the row. How much are these coins worth altogether? Darken the circle under the amount that tells how much these coins are worth altogether.**
2. **Put your finger on number 2. Look at the coins. Which coin do you need 2 of to have 20 cents? Darken the circle under the picture of the coin that you need 2 of to have 20 cents.**
3. **Put your finger on number 3. Look at the coins. Alfredo found 10 cents. Darken the circle under the picture of the coin that Alfredo found.**
4. **Put your finger on number 4. Look at the coins in the row. Which coin do you need 2 of to have 10 cents? Darken the circle under the picture of the coin that you need 2 of to have 10 cents.**
5. **Put your finger on number 5. Look at the coins. How much are these coins worth altogether? Darken the circle under the amount that tells how much these coins are worth altogether.**
6. **Put your finger on number 6. Look at the coins. Which coin do you need 3 of to have 15 cents? Darken the circle under the coin that you need 3 of to have 15 cents.**
7. **Put your finger on number 7. Look at the coins in the row. How much are these coins worth altogether? Darken the circle under the amount that tells how much these coins are worth altogether.**
8. **Put your finger on number 8. Look at the coins in the row. How much are these coins worth altogether? Darken the circle under the amount that tells how much these coins are worth together.**

Look at the stop sign at the bottom of the page. You have now finished the lesson and should put your pencils down.

Review the questions and answer choices with students. Discuss with the class why one answer is correct and the others are not correct. Also check to see that students have carefully filled in their answer spaces and have completely erased any stray marks.

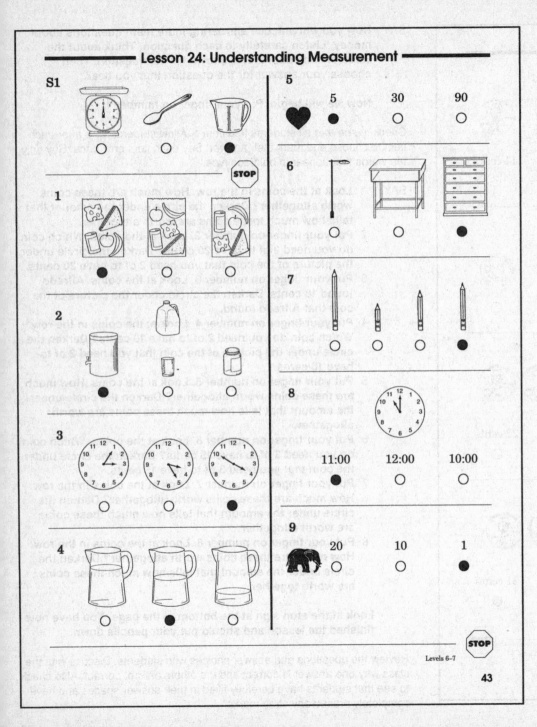

Lesson 24: Understanding Measurement

Mathematics Skills: Recognizing analog time; measuring quantity, time, length, and weight; understanding simple fractions

SAY: **Turn to Lesson 24, Understanding Measurement, on page 43.**

Check to see that all students find Lesson 24. Introduce the Try This feature.

SAY: **In Lesson 24 you will practice answering math questions about measurement. Listen carefully. When I read a question, you should try this: look at each picture or number for the question. Then find the picture or number that answers the question that you hear.**

Put your finger on S1. This is Sample 1. Now listen carefully. Marco was helping his mother make some raisin bread. The recipe called for 2 cups of raisins and 1 teaspoon of cinnamon. What did Marco use to measure the raisins? Darken the circle under the picture that shows what Marco used to measure the raisins.

Allow students time to choose and mark their answer. Remind students to carefully fill in the answer circle and to completely erase any stray marks. Then introduce the Think It Through feature.

SAY: **Now we will think it through. We will check the answer. You should have darkened the circle under the third picture. This picture shows a *measuring cup*. It is the best tool for measuring large amounts of dry or liquid things.**

Check to see that all students have filled in the correct answer space. Remind students that they were instructed to find the picture that shows what Marco used to measure the raisins.

Ask students if they have any questions about Sample 1 or about darkening the answer circle.

SAY: **Now you will practice answering more math questions about measurement. Listen carefully to each question. Then look at each picture or number for the question. Find the picture or number that answers the question that you hear.**

Now we will begin. Put your finger on number 1.

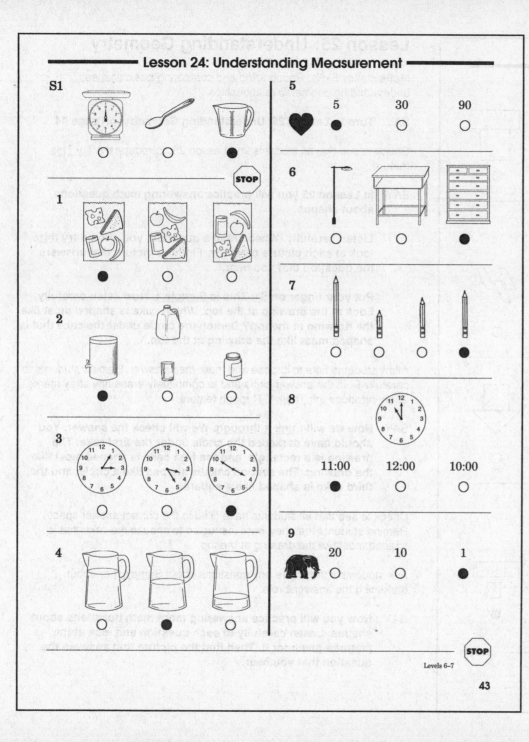

Lesson 24: Understanding Measurement

S1

1

2

3
11:00   12:00   10:00

4

5
5   30   90

6

7

8
11:00   12:00   10:00

9
20   10   1

STOP

Levels 6–7

43

Check to see that all students find item 1. Allow students time after each item to choose and mark their answer. Say each item only once. Say <u>only</u> the words that appear in boldface type.

SAY: 1 **Danielle packed her lunch for school. She put the items in a sack. She put all of the heavy items on the bottom and all of the light items on the top. Which picture shows Danielle's sack? Darken the circle under the picture that shows Danielle's sack.**

2 **Put your finger on number 2. Look at the container at the top. Which container holds more than the container at the top? Darken the circle under the container that holds more than the one at the top.**

3 **Put your finger on number 3. Look at the clocks. It was almost 4 o'clock by the time Blanca got home from school. Which clock shows almost 4 o'clock? Darken the circle under the picture of the clock that shows almost 4 o'clock.**

4 **Put your finger on number 4. Look at the pitchers in the row. Which pitcher is half full? Darken the circle under the pitcher that is half full.**

5 **Put your finger on number 5. You should be on the row with the heart. Which number tells about how many pounds a puppy weighs? Darken the circle under the number that tells about how many pounds a puppy weighs.**

6 **Put your finger on number 6. Look at the pictures of the street light, the desk, and the chest of drawers. Which one is about as tall as a boy? Darken the circle under the picture of the one that is about as tall as a boy.**

7 **Put your finger on number 7. Look at the pencils. Which pencil is the second tallest? Darken the circle under the pencil that is the second tallest.**

8 **Put your finger on number 8. Look at the clock. What time does the clock show? Darken the circle under the time that is shown on the clock.**

9 **Put your finger on number 9. You should be on the row with the elephant. Which number tells about how many pounds a loaf of bread weighs? Darken the circle under the number that tells about how many pounds a loaf of bread weighs.**

Look at the stop sign at the bottom of the page. You have now finished the lesson and should put your pencils down.

Review the questions and answer choices with students. Discuss with the class why one answer is correct and the others are not correct. Also check to see that students have carefully filled in their answer spaces and have completely erased any stray marks.

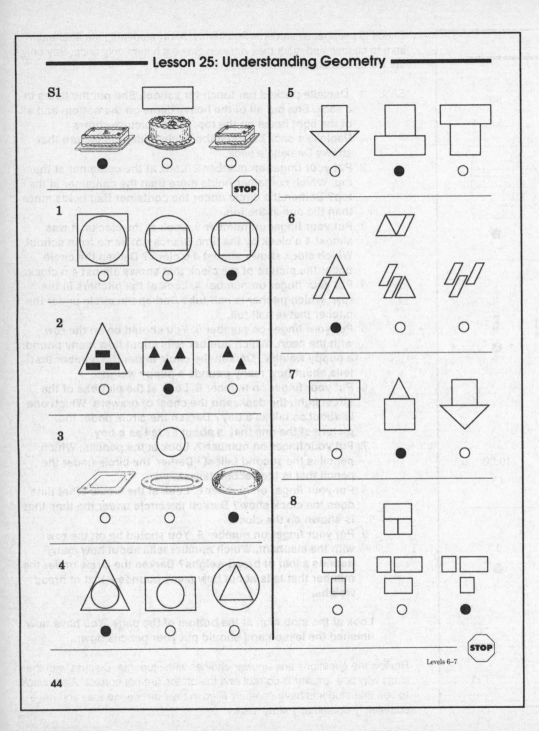

Lesson 25: Understanding Geometry

Mathematics Skills: Recognizing and comparing basic shapes; understanding geometric relationships

SAY: **Turn to Lesson 25, Understanding Geometry, on page 44.**

Check to see that all students find Lesson 25. Introduce the <u>Try This</u> feature.

SAY: **In Lesson 25 you will practice answering math questions about shapes.**

Listen carefully. When I read a question, you should <u>try this</u>: look at each picture carefully. Find the picture that answers the question that you hear.

Put your finger on <u>S1</u>. This is <u>Sample 1</u>. Now listen carefully. Look at the drawing at the top. Which cake is shaped most like the drawing at the top? Darken the circle under the cake that is shaped most like the drawing at the top.

Allow students time to choose and mark their answer. Remind students to carefully fill in the answer circle and to completely erase any stray marks. Then introduce the <u>Think It Through</u> feature.

SAY: **Now we will <u>think it through</u>. We will check the answer. You should have darkened the circle under the *first* cake. The drawing is a rectangle, and the first cake is shaped most like the drawing. The second cake is shaped like a circle, and the third cake is shaped like a square.**

Check to see that all students have filled in the correct answer space. Remind students that they were instructed to choose the cake that is shaped most like the drawing at the top.

Ask students if they have any questions about <u>Sample 1</u> or about darkening the answer circle.

SAY: **Now you will practice answering more math questions about shapes. Listen carefully to each question and look at the pictures given for it. Then find the picture that answers the question that you hear.**

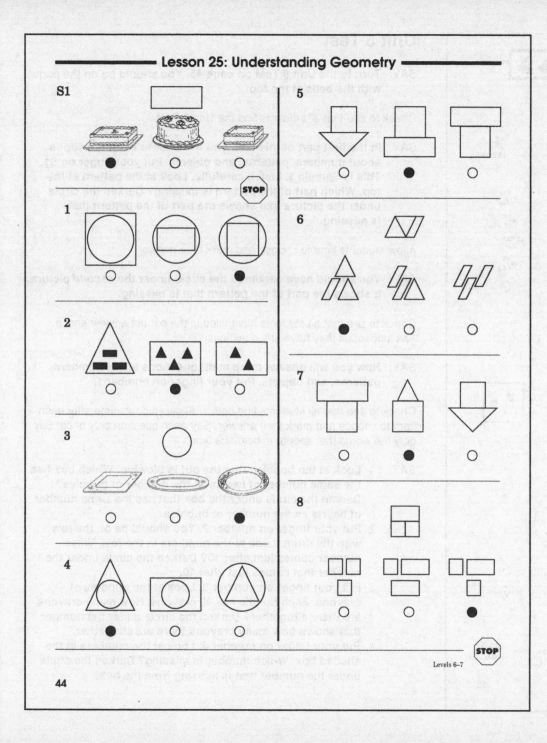

Lesson 25: Understanding Geometry

S1

1

2

3

4

5

6

7

8

Levels 6–7

44

SAY: **Now we will begin. Put your finger on number 1.**

Check to see that all students find item 1. Allow students time after each item to choose and mark their answer. Say each item only once. Say only the words that appear in boldface type.

SAY: 1 **Look at the pictures in the row. Which picture shows a square inside a circle? Darken the circle under the picture that shows a square inside a circle.**

2 **Put your finger on number 2. Look at the pictures in the row. Which picture shows 3 triangles inside a rectangle? Darken the circle under the picture that shows 3 triangles inside a rectangle.**

3 **Put your finger on number 3. Look at the drawing at the top. Which plate is shaped most like the drawing at the top? Darken the circle under the plate that is shaped most like the drawing at the top.**

4 **Put your finger on number 4. Look at the pictures. Which picture shows a circle inside a triangle? Darken the circle under the picture that shows a circle inside a triangle.**

5 **Put your finger on number 5. Look at the pictures. Which picture shows a square on top of a rectangle? Darken the circle under the picture that shows a square on top of a rectangle.**

6 **Put your finger on number 6. Look at the figure at the top. Which group of pieces could be put together to make the figure at the top? Darken the circle under the group of pieces that could be put together to make the figure at the top.**

7 **Put your finger on number 7. Look at the pictures in the row. Which picture shows a triangle on top of a square? Darken the circle under the picture that shows a triangle on top of a square.**

8 **Put your finger on number 8. Look at the figure at the top. Which group of pieces could be put together to make the figure at the top? Darken the circle under the group of pieces that could be put together to make the figure at the top.**

Look at the stop sign at the bottom of the page. You have now finished the lesson and should put your pencils down.

Review the questions and answer choices with students. Discuss with the class why one answer is correct and the others are not correct. Also check to see that students have carefully filled in their answer spaces and have completely erased any stray marks.

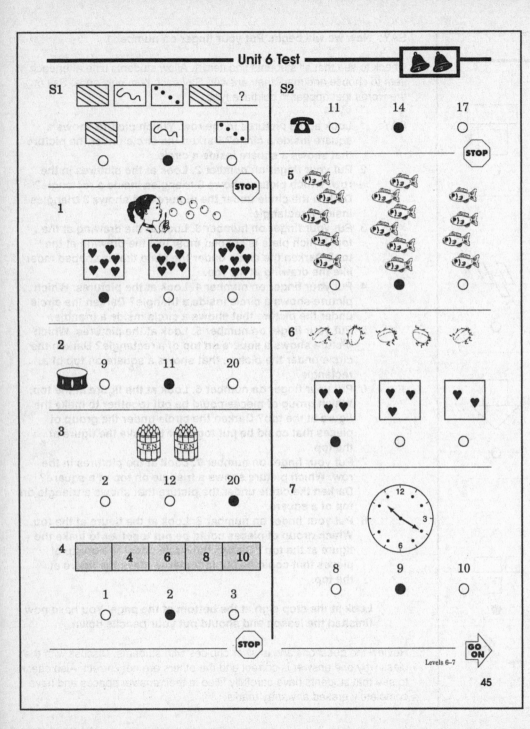

Unit 6 Test

SAY: **Turn to the Unit 6 Test on page 45. You should be on the page with the bells at the top.**

Check to see that all students find the Unit 6 Test.

SAY: **In the first part of this test, you will answer math questions about numbers, patterns, and objects. Put your finger on S1. This is Sample 1. Listen carefully. Look at the pattern at the top. Which part of the pattern is missing? Darken the circle under the picture that shows the part of the pattern that is missing.**

Allow students time to choose and mark their answer.

SAY: **You should have darkened the circle under the *second* picture. It shows the part of the pattern that is missing.**

Check to see that all students have filled in the correct answer space. Ask students if they have any questions.

SAY: **Now you will answer more math questions about numbers, patterns, and objects. Put your finger on number 1.**

Check to see that all students find item 1. Allow students time after each item to choose and mark their answer. Say each question only once. Say only the words that appear in boldface type.

SAY: 1 **Look at the bubbles that the girl is blowing. Which box has the same number of hearts as the number of bubbles? Darken the circle under the box that has the same number of hearts as the number of bubbles.**
2 **Put your finger on number 2. You should be on the row with the drum. Look at the numbers in the row. What number comes just after 10? Darken the circle under the number that comes just after 10.**
3 **Put your finger on number 3. Look at the bundles of crayons. Each bundle has 10 crayons. How many crayons are there altogether? Darken the circle under the number that shows how many crayons there are altogether.**
4 **Put your finger on number 4. Look at the numbers in the shaded box. Which number is missing? Darken the circle under the number that is missing from the box.**

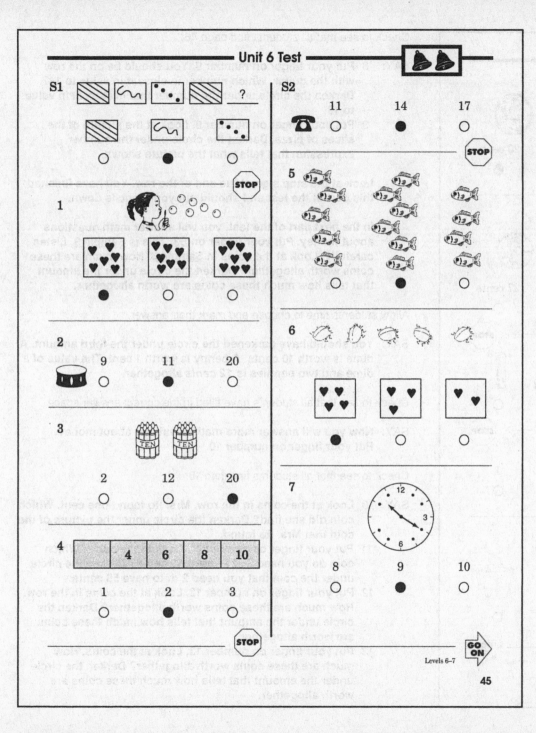

Unit 6 Test

S1

S2

Levels 6–7

Look at the stop sign at the bottom of this column. You have finished this part of the test and should put your pencils down.

In the next part of the test, you will answer math questions about numbers. Put your finger on <u>S2</u> at the top of the second column. You should be on the row with the telephone. This is <u>Sample 2</u>. Now listen carefully. Look at the numbers in the row. Which number is *14*? Darken the circle under the number *14*.

Allow students time to choose and mark their answer.

SAY: **You should have darkened the circle under the second number because it is *14*. The other numbers are *11* and *17*.**

Check to see that all students have filled in the correct answer space.

SAY: **Now you will answer more math questions about numbers. Listen carefully to each question and study each picture or number given for it. Then find the picture or number that answers the question that you hear.**

Now we will begin. Put your finger on number 5.

Check to see that all students find item 5.

SAY: 5 **Look at the groups of fish. Which group of fish needs 3 more to have 9? Darken the circle under the group of fish that needs 3 more to have 9.**
6 **Put your finger on number 6. Look at the bugs. Which box has one less heart than the number of bugs? Darken the circle under the box that has one less heart than the number of bugs.**
7 **Put your finger on number 7. What number should be added to the clock? Darken the circle under the number that should be added to the clock.**

Notice the arrow and with the words *GO ON* at the bottom of the page. This tells you to go to the next page to continue working. Turn to page 46.

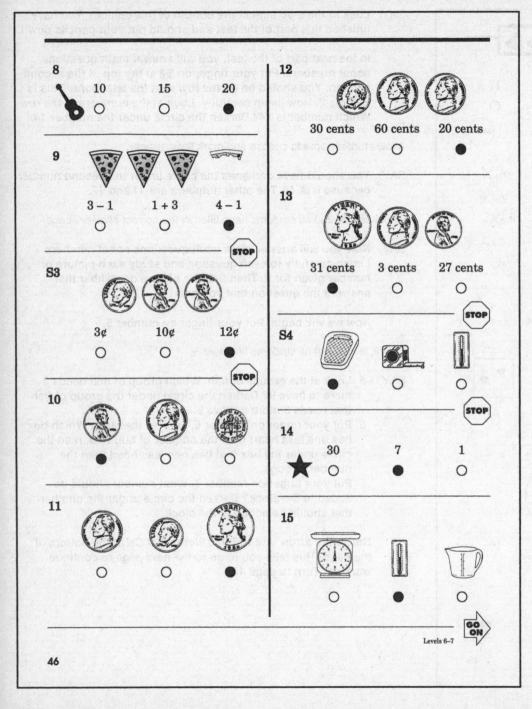

8

10 ○   15 ○   20 ●

9

3 − 1 ○   1 + 3 ○   4 − 1 ●   STOP

S3

3¢ ○   10¢ ○   12¢ ●   STOP

10

● ○ ○

11

○ ○ ●

12

30 cents ○   60 cents ○   20 cents ●

13

31 cents ●   3 cents ○   27 cents ○   STOP

S4

● ○ ○   STOP

14

30   7   1
★ ○   ●   ○

15

○   ●   ○

GO ON

Levels 6–7

46

SAY: 8 **Put your finger on number 8. You should be on the row with the guitar. Which number is closest in value to 18? Darken the circle under the number that is closest in value to 18.**

9 **Put your finger on number 9. Look at the picture of the slices of pizza. Darken the circle under the number expression that tells what the picture shows.**

Look at the stop sign at the end of the row. You have finished this part of the test and should put your pencils down.

In the next part of the test, you will answer math questions about money. Put your finger on S3. This is Sample 3. Listen carefully. Look at the coins in Sample 3. How much are these coins worth altogether? Darken the circle under the amount that tells how much these coins are worth altogether.

Allow students time to choose and mark their answer.

SAY: **You should have darkened the circle under the third amount. A dime is worth 10 cents. A penny is worth 1 cent. The value of a dime and two pennies is *12 cents* altogether.**

Check to see that all students have filled in the correct answer space.

SAY: **Now you will answer more math questions about money. Put your finger on number 10.**

Check to see that all students find item 10.

SAY: 10 **Look at the coins in the row. Mrs. Ito found one cent. Which coin did she find? Darken the circle under the picture of the coin that Mrs. Ito found.**

11 **Put your finger on number 11. Look at the coins. Which coin do you need 2 of to have 50 cents? Darken the circle under the coin that you need 2 of to have 50 cents.**

12 **Put your finger on number 12. Look at the coins in the row. How much are these coins worth altogether? Darken the circle under the amount that tells how much these coins are worth altogether.**

13 **Put your finger on number 13. Look at the coins. How much are these coins worth altogether? Darken the circle under the amount that tells how much these coins are worth altogether.**

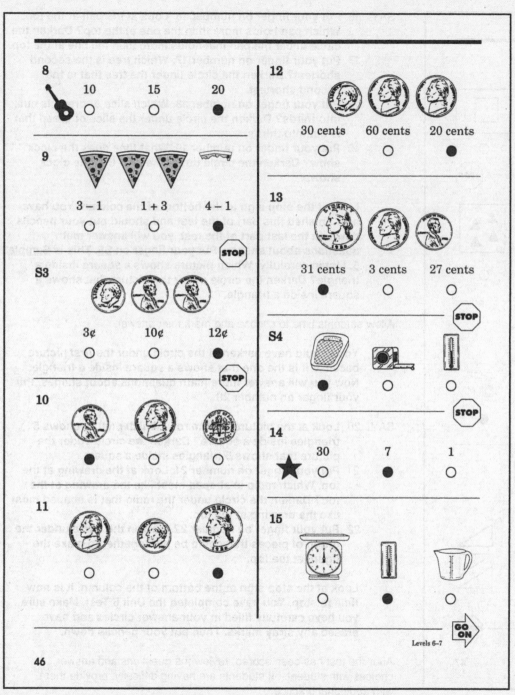

46

Levels 6-7

SAY: Look at the stop sign at the end of the row. You have now finished this part of the test and should put your pencils down.

In the next part of the test, you will answer math questions about measurement. Put your finger on <u>S4</u>. This is <u>Sample 4</u>. Listen carefully. The school nurse told Ping that she was 40 inches tall and weighed 39 pounds. What did the school nurse use to find out how much Ping weighed? Darken the circle under the picture that shows what the school nurse used to find out how much Ping weighed.

Allow students time to choose and mark their answer.

SAY: You should have darkened the circle under the first picture. It shows a *scale for weighing people*. The nurse probably used that scale to find out how much Ping weighed.

Check to see that all students have filled in the correct answer space.

SAY: Now you will answer more math questions about measurement. Listen carefully to each question. Then find the picture or number that answers the question that you hear. Now we will begin. Put your finger on number 14. You should be on the row with the star.

Check to see that all students find item 14.

SAY: 14 Roberto and his family were going on a camping trip. Roberto wanted to camp for a whole week. How many days will Roberto be gone on the camping trip if he stays a whole week? Darken the circle under the number that tells how many days Roberto will be gone on a camping trip if he stays a whole week.

15 Put your finger on number 15. What should you use to find out how hot it is outside? Darken the circle under the picture that shows what you should use to find out how hot it is outside.

Notice the arrow and the words *GO ON* at the bottom of the page. This tells you to go to the next page to continue working. Go to page 47.

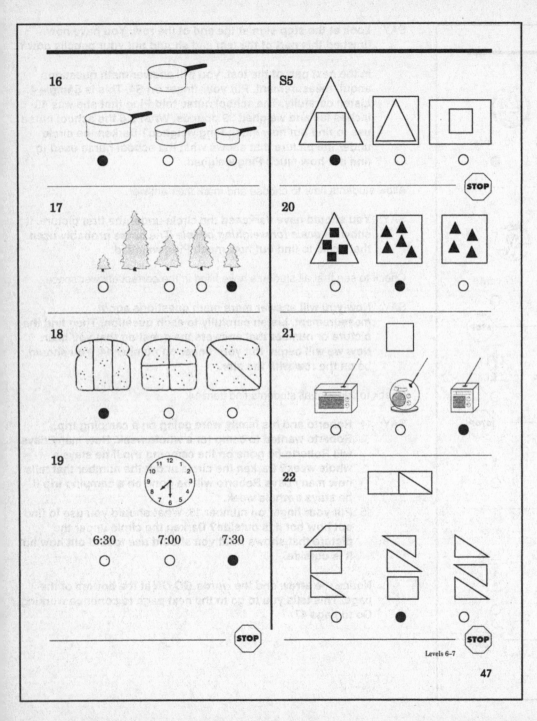

47

SAY: **16 Put your finger on number 16. Look at the pan at the top. Which pan holds more than the one at the top? Darken the circle under the pan that holds more than the one at the top.**

17 Put your finger on number 17. Which tree is the second shortest? Darken the circle under the tree that is the second shortest.

18 Put your finger on number 18. Which slice of bread is cut into thirds? Darken the circle under the slice of bread that is cut into thirds.

19 Put your finger on number 19. What time does the clock show? Darken the circle under the time that the clock shows.

Look at the stop sign at the bottom of the column. You have now finished this part of the test and should put your pencils down. In the last part of the test, you will answer math questions about shapes. Put your finger on S5. This is Sample 5. Listen carefully. Which picture shows a square inside a triangle? Darken the circle under the picture that shows a square inside a triangle.

Allow students time to choose and mark their answer.

SAY: **You should have darkened the circle under the *first* picture because it is the one that shows a square inside a triangle. Now you will answer more math questions about shapes. Put your finger on number 20.**

SAY: **20 Look at the pictures in the row. Which picture shows 5 triangles inside a square? Darken the circle under the picture that shows 5 triangles inside a square.**

21 Put your finger on number 21. Look at the drawing at the top. Which radio is shaped most like the drawing at the top? Darken the circle under the radio that is shaped most like the drawing at the top.

22 Put your finger on number 22. Darken the circle under the group of pieces that could be put together to make the figure at the top.

Look at the stop sign at the bottom of the column. It is now time to stop. You have completed the Unit 6 Test. Make sure you have carefully filled in your answer circles and have erased any stray marks. Then put your pencils down.

After the test has been scored, review the questions and answer choices with students. If students are having difficulty, provide them with additional practice.

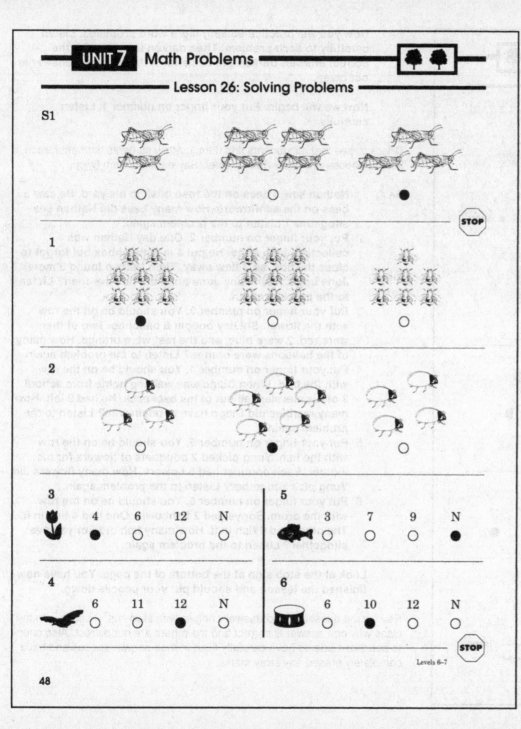

UNIT 7 Math Problems

Lesson 26: Solving Problems

Mathematics Skills: Solving one-step word problems; solving multiple-step word problems; distinguishing between necessary and extraneous data

Distribute scratch paper to students. Tell them that they may use the scratch paper to work the problems.

SAY: **Turn to Lesson 26, Solving Problems, on page 48. You should be on the page with the trees at the top.**

Check to see that all students find Lesson 26. Introduce the <u>Try This</u> feature.

SAY: **In Lesson 26 you will practice solving word problems. Listen carefully. When I say a problem, you should <u>try this</u>: use your scratch paper to work the problem. Then look at each picture or number for the problem. Darken the circle for the picture or number that answers the problem that you hear. Some problems have N as an answer choice. Darken the circle for the N if the correct answer is not given.**

Put your finger on <u>S1</u>. This is <u>Sample 1</u>. Now listen carefully to this problem. Nathan liked to collect insects. He had 5 grasshoppers in a jar. Then 2 grasshoppers jumped out. How many grasshoppers were left in the jar? Listen to the problem again. (Repeat the problem.) Darken the circle for the correct answer.

Allow students time to choose and mark their answer. Remind students to carefully fill in the answer circle and to completely erase any stray marks. Then introduce the <u>Think It Through</u> feature.

SAY: **Now we will <u>think it through</u>. We will check the answer. You should have darkened the circle for the *third* picture. It shows 3 grasshoppers. Five grasshoppers minus 2 grasshoppers equals 3 grasshoppers.**

Check to see that all students have filled in the correct answer space. Remind students that they were instructed to find the picture that shows how many grasshoppers were left in the jar. Ask students if they have any questions about <u>Sample 1</u> or about darkening the answer circle.

Lesson 26: Solving Problems

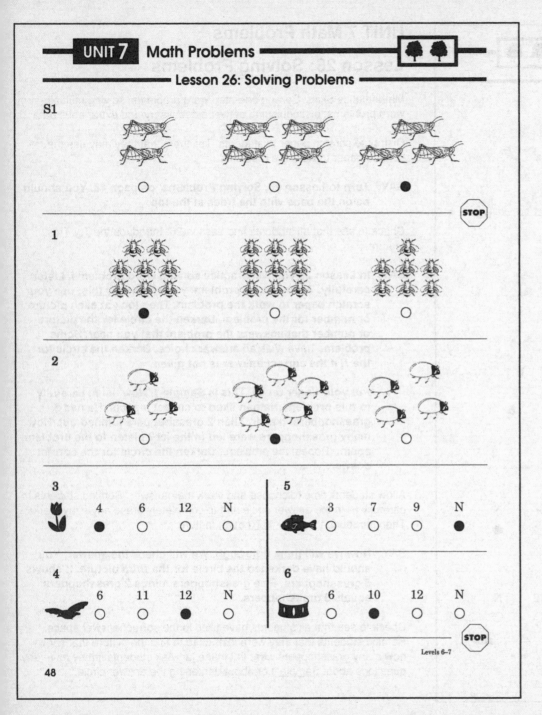

S1

1

2

🌷	4	6	12	N

3
🌷 4 ● 6 ○ 12 ○ N ○

5
🐟 3 ○ 7 ○ 9 ○ N ●

4
🦅 6 ○ 11 ○ 12 ● N ○

6
🥁 6 ○ 10 ● 12 ○ N ○

STOP

Levels 6–7

SAY: Now you will practice solving more word problems. Listen carefully to each problem. Then darken the circle for the correct answer. Darken the circle for *N* if the correct answer is not given.

Now we will begin. Put your finger on number 1. Listen carefully.

Check to see that all students find item 1. Allow students time after each item to choose and mark their answer. Say each problem <u>twice</u>.

SAY:
1 Nathan saw 3 bees on the rose bush in his yard. He saw 5 bees on the sunflowers. How many bees did Nathan see altogether? Listen to the problem again.
2 Put your finger on number 2. One day Nathan was collecting June bugs. He put 4 in a matchbox but forgot to close the box, so 2 flew away. Then Nathan found 3 more June bugs. How many June bugs did he have then? Listen to the problem again.
3 Put your finger on number 3. You should be on the row with the flower. Shelley bought 8 balloons. Two of them were red, 2 were blue, and the rest were orange. How many of the balloons were orange? Listen to the problem again.
4 Put your finger on number 4. You should be on the row with the bird. When Diego was walking home from school, 3 of his marbles fell out of his backpack. He had 9 left. How many marbles did Diego have to begin with? Listen to the problem again.
5 Put your finger on number 5. You should be on the row with the fish. Yung picked 2 bouquets of flowers for his mother. Each bouquet had 5 flowers. How many flowers did Yung pick altogether? Listen to the problem again.
6 Put your finger on number 6. You should be on the row with the drum. Sonya had 2 fishbowls. One had 4 fish in it. The other had 6 fish in it. How many fish did Sonya have altogether? Listen to the problem again.

Look at the stop sign at the bottom of the page. You have now finished the lesson and should put your pencils down.

Review the questions and answer choices with students. Discuss with the class why one answer is correct and the others are not correct. Also check to see that students have carefully filled in their answer spaces and have completely erased any stray marks.

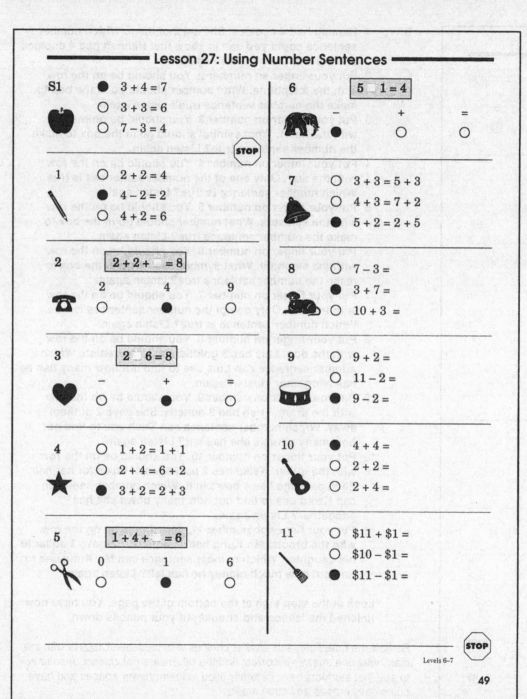

Lesson 27: Using Number Sentences

Mathematics Skills: Understanding symbols for operations and relationships; recognizing and solving number sentences used to represent problems; understanding number sentences used to represent number properties

Distribute scratch paper to students. Tell them that they may use the scratch paper to work the problems.

SAY: **Turn to Lesson 27, Using Number Sentences, on page 49.**

Check to see that all students find Lesson 27. Introduce the Try This feature.

SAY: **In Lesson 27 you will practice solving problems with number sentences. Listen carefully. When I say a problem, you should try this: use your scratch paper to work the problem. Then look at the answer choices carefully and darken the circle for the correct answer. Put your finger on S1. You should be on the row with the apple. This is Sample 1. Now listen to the problem. Three children went to the park and saw 4 of their friends. Which number sentence could you use to show that 3 children went to the park and saw 4 of their friends?** (Repeat the problem.) **Darken the circle for the correct answer.**

Allow students time to choose and mark their answer. Remind students to carefully fill in the answer circle and to completely erase any stray marks. Then introduce the Think It Through feature.

SAY: **Now we will think it through. We will check the answer. You should have darkened the circle for the first number sentence. Three children plus 4 children equals 7 children.**

Check to see that all students have filled in the correct answer space. Ask students if they have any questions about Sample 1 or about darkening the answer circle.

SAY: **Now you will practice solving more problems with number sentences. Listen carefully to each problem. Then darken the circle for the correct answer. Now we will begin. Put your finger on number 1. You should be on the row with the pencil.**

Check to see that all students find item 1. Allow students time after each item to choose and mark their answer. Say each problem twice.

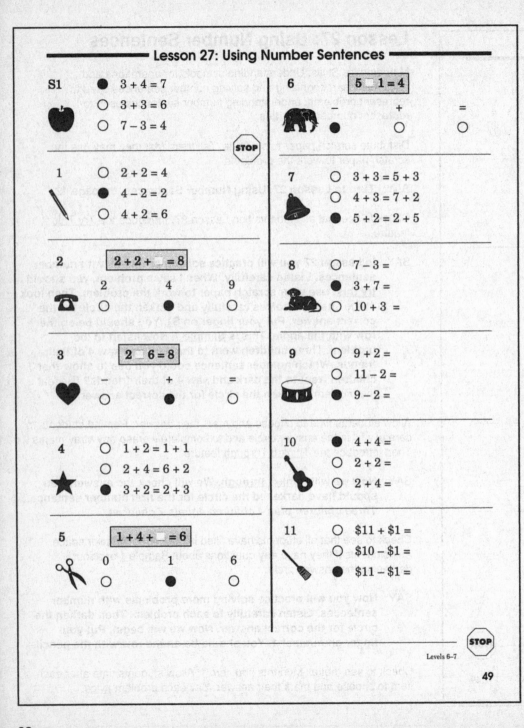

Lesson 27: Using Number Sentences

S1
- ● 3 + 4 = 7
- ○ 3 + 3 = 6
- ○ 7 − 3 = 4

(STOP)

1
- ○ 2 + 2 = 4
- ● 4 − 2 = 2
- ○ 4 + 2 = 6

2   2 + 2 + ☐ = 8

2	4	9
○	●	○

3   2 ☐ 6 = 8

−	+	=
○	●	○

4
- ○ 1 + 2 = 1 + 1
- ○ 2 + 4 = 6 + 2
- ● 3 + 2 = 2 + 3

5   1 + 4 + ☐ = 6

0	1	6
○	●	○

6   5 ☐ 1 = 4

−	+	=
●	○	○

7
- ○ 3 + 3 = 5 + 3
- ○ 4 + 3 = 7 + 2
- ● 5 + 2 = 2 + 5

8
- ○ 7 − 3 =
- ○ 3 + 7 =
- ○ 10 + 3 =

9
- ○ 9 + 2 =
- ○ 11 − 2 =
- ● 9 − 2 =

10
- ● 4 + 4 =
- ○ 2 + 2 =
- ○ 2 + 4 =

11
- ○ $11 + $1 =
- ○ $10 − $1 =
- ● $11 − $1 =

(STOP)

Levels 6–7

SAY:
1. **Hannah had 4 cookies. She ate 2 of them. Which number sentence could you use to show that Hannah had 4 cookies and ate 2 of them? Listen again.**
2. **Put your finger on number 2. You should be on the row with the telephone. What number should go in the box to make the number sentence true? Listen again.**
3. **Put your finger on number 3. You should be on the row with the heart. What symbol should go in the box to make the number sentence true? Listen again.**
4. **Put your finger on number 4. You should be on the row with the star. Only one of the number sentences is true. Which number sentence is true? Listen again.**
5. **Put your finger on number 5. You should be on the row with the scissors. What number should go in the box to make the number sentence true? Listen again.**
6. **Put your finger on number 6. You should be on the row with the elephant. What symbol should go in the box to make the number sentence true? Listen again.**
7. **Put your finger on number 7. You should be on the row with the bell. Only one of the number sentences is true. Which number sentence is true? Listen again.**
8. **Put your finger on number 8. You should be on the row with the dog. Luis has 3 goldfish and 7 angelfish. Which number sentence can Luis use to find out how many fish he has altogether? Listen again.**
9. **Put your finger on number 9. You should be on the row with the drum. Trish had 9 pencils. She gave 2 of them away. Which number sentence can Trish use to find out how many pencils she has left? Listen again.**
10. **Put your finger on number 10. You should be on the row with the guitar. Keiko has 2 packages of bows for her hair. Each package has 4 bows in it. Which number sentence can Keiko use to find out how many bows she has altogether? Listen again.**
11. **Put your finger on number 11. You should be on the row with the broom. Mr. Kung had 11 dollars. He gave 1 dollar to his daughter. Which number sentence can Mr. Kung use to find out how much money he has left? Listen again.**

Look at the stop sign at the bottom of the page. You have now finished the lesson and should put your pencils down.

Review the questions and answer choices with students. Discuss with the class why one answer is correct and the others are not correct. Also check to see that students have carefully filled in their answer spaces and have completely erased any stray marks.

Lesson 28: Working with Graphs and Tables

Cans of Food Collected for the City Food Drive

S1 How many cans will Lena collect if she collects one more can?

  3   5   6
  ○   ●   ○

STOP

1 Santos wants to collect as many cans as Taro. How many cans should Santos collect?

  3   4   5
  ●   ○   ○

2 How many more cans did Simon collect than Kevin?

  4   5   11
  ○   ●   ○

Favorite Vegetables of Grade 1 Children

Corn	
Potatoes	
Green Beans	
Carrots	

3 Which vegetable was chosen by four children?

  ○ Corn
  ○ Potatoes
  ● Green beans

4 Which vegetables were chosen by the same number of children?

  ○ Corn and carrots
  ○ Potatoes and green beans
  ● Potatoes and carrots

5 Which vegetable was chosen by twice as many children as those who chose corn?

  ○ Potatoes
  ● Green beans
  ○ Carrots

STOP

Levels 6–7

50

Lesson 28: Working with Graphs and Tables

Mathematics Skills: Interpreting graphs and tables; using data in graphic displays to solve problems

Distribute scratch paper to students. Tell them that they may use the scratch paper to work the problems.

SAY: **Turn to Lesson 28, Working with Graphs and Tables, on page 50.**

Check to see that all students find Lesson 28. Introduce the Try This feature.

SAY: **In Lesson 28 you will practice using graphs and tables to solve problems.**

Listen carefully. While I read a problem, you should try this: read the problem silently. Then look at the graph or table to find the information you need to solve the problem. Remember that you can use your scratch paper to work the problem. Darken the circle for the correct answer.

Put your finger on S1. This is Sample 1. Look at the graph at the top of the first column. It shows the number of cans of food that some children collected. Now listen carefully. How many cans will Lena collect if she collects one more can? Darken the circle for the correct answer.

Allow students time to choose and mark their answer. Remind students to carefully fill in the answer circle and to completely erase any stray marks. Then introduce the Think It Through feature.

SAY: **Now we will think it through. We will check the answer. You should have darkened the circle for the number 5. Lena has 4 cans. If she collects 1 more can, she will have 5 cans of food. Four cans plus 1 can equals 5 cans.**

Check to see that all students have filled in the correct answer space. Remind students that they were instructed to find the number of cans Lena will collect if she has 4 cans and collects 1 more.

Ask students if they have any questions about Sample 1 or about darkening the answer circle.

Lesson 28: Working with Graphs and Tables

Cans of Food Collected for the City Food Drive

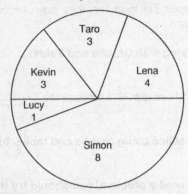

Taro 3
Kevin 3
Lena 4
Lucy 1
Simon 8

S1 How many cans will Lena collect if she collects one more can?

3 ○   5 ●   6 ○

STOP

1 Santos wants to collect as many cans as Taro. How many cans should Santos collect?

3 ●   4 ○   5 ○

2 How many more cans did Simon collect than Kevin?

4 ○   5 ●   11 ○

Favorite Vegetables of Grade 1 Children

Corn	
Potatoes	
Green Beans	
Carrots	

3 Which vegetable was chosen by four children?

○ Corn
○ Potatoes
● Green beans

4 Which vegetables were chosen by the same number of children?

○ Corn and carrots
○ Potatoes and green beans
● Potatoes and carrots

5 Which vegetable was chosen by twice as many children as those who chose corn?

○ Potatoes
● Green beans
○ Carrots

STOP

Levels 6–7

SAY: **Now you will practice using this graph to solve more problems. Read each problem silently as I say it aloud. Then look at the graph to find the information you need to solve the problem. Darken the circle for the correct answer.**

Now we will begin. Put your finger on number 1.

Check to see that all students find item 1. Allow students time after each item to choose and mark their answer. Say each problem only once. Say only the words that appear in boldface type.

SAY: 1 **Santos wants to collect as many cans as Taro. How many cans should Santos collect?**
   2 **Put your finger on number 2. How many more cans did Simon collect than Kevin?**

Now look at the graph at the top of the second column. One day some children in grade 1 made a graph that showed their favorite vegetables. One picture of a vegetable means that one child chose that vegetable as his or her favorite.

   3 **Put your finger on number 3. Which vegetable was chosen by four children?**
   4 **Put your finger on number 4. Which vegetables were chosen by the same number of children?**
   5 **Put your finger on number 5. Which vegetable was chosen by twice as many children as those who chose corn?**

Look at the stop sign at the bottom of the page. You have now finished the lesson and should put your pencils down.

Review the questions and answer choices with students. Discuss with the class why one answer is correct and the others are not correct. Also check to see that students have carefully filled in their answer spaces and have completely erased any stray marks.

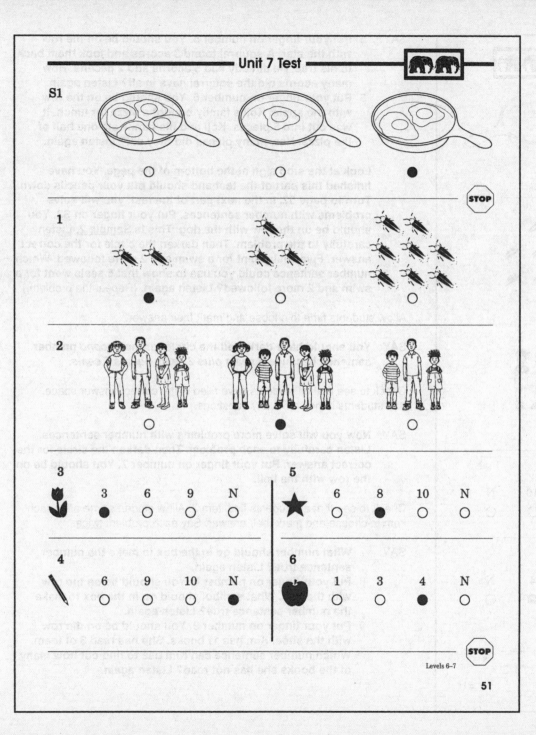

Unit 7 Test

Distribute scratch paper to students. Tell them that they may use the scratch paper to work the problems.

SAY: **Turn to the Unit 7 Test on page 51. You should be on the page with the elephants at the top.**

Check to see that all students find the Unit 7 Test.

SAY: **In the first part of this test, you will solve word problems. Put your finger on S1. This is Sample 1. Listen to the problem. Then darken the circle for the correct answer. Mr. Niwa cooked 3 eggs. He ate only 1. How many eggs were left? Listen to the problem again.** (Repeat the problem.)

Allow students time to choose and mark their answer.

SAY: **You should have darkened the circle for the *third* picture. It shows 2 eggs. Three eggs minus 1 egg equals 2 eggs.**

Check to see that all students have filled in the correct answer space. Ask students if they have any questions.

SAY: **Now you will solve more word problems. Darken the circle for each correct answer. Darken the circle for *N* if the correct answer is not given. Put your finger on number 1.**

Check to see that all students find item 1. Allow students time after each item to choose and mark their answer. Say each problem twice.

SAY: 1 **One night Maria saw 5 fireflies in her yard. One was in a tree, 2 were by the fence, and the rest were near her window. How many fireflies were near Maria's window? Listen again.**
2 **Put your finger on number 2. Mrs. Burns has 2 children. On weekdays she baby-sits her neighbor's 2 children. She also baby-sits her sister's child. How many children does Mrs. Burns care for, including her own children? Listen again.**
3 **Put your finger on number 3. You should be on the row with the flower. Sam has 6 teachers. Three of them are men. The rest are women. How many of Sam's teachers are women? Listen again.**
4 **Put your finger on number 4. You should be on the row with the pencil. Kristin has a necklace with 3 gold beads, 2 silver beads, and 3 black beads. How many beads does Kristin have on her necklace? Listen again.**

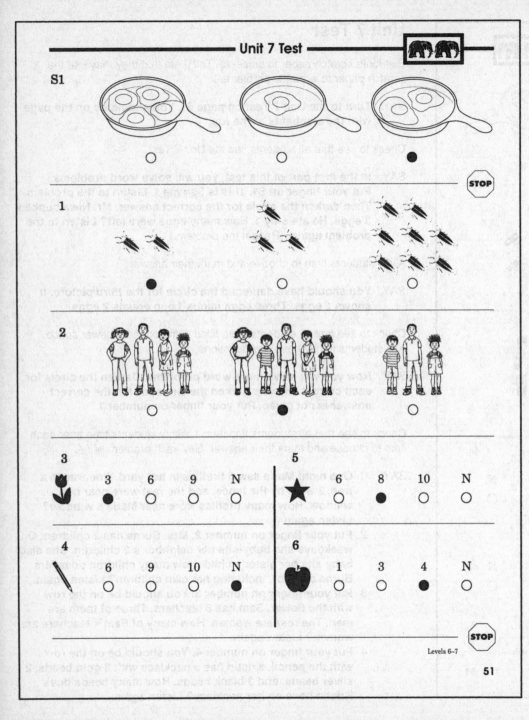

Unit 7 Test

S1

1

2

3

🌷 3 ● | 6 ○ | 9 ○ | N ○

4

✏ 6 ○ | 9 ○ | 10 ○ | N ●

5

★ 6 ○ | 8 ● | 10 ○ | N ○

6

🍎 1 ○ | 3 ○ | 4 ● | N ○

STOP

Levels 6–7

SAY:

5 Put your finger on number 5. You should be on the row with the star. A squirrel found 3 acorns and took them back to his tree. He already had 5 acorns and 2 pecans. How many acorns did the squirrel have in all? Listen again.

6 Put your finger on number 6. You should be on the row with the apple. Koji's family bought a pizza for lunch. It was cut into 8 pieces. Koji and his family ate one half of the pizza. How many pieces did they eat? Listen again.

Look at the stop sign at the bottom of the page. You have finished this part of the test and should put your pencils down. Turn to page 52. In the next part of the test, you will solve problems with number sentences. Put your finger on S2. You should be on the row with the dog. This is <u>Sample 2</u>. Listen carefully to the problem. Then darken the circle for the correct answer. Five seals went for a swim and 2 more followed. Which number sentence could you use to show that 5 seals went for a swim and 2 more followed? Listen again. (Repeat the problem.)

Allow students time to choose and mark their answer.

SAY: You should have darkened the circle for the *second* number sentence because *5 seals plus 2 seals equals 7 seals.*

Check to see that all students have filled in the correct answer space. Ask students if they have any questions.

SAY: Now you will solve more problems with number sentences. Listen carefully to each problem. Then darken the circle for the correct answer. Put your finger on number 7. You should be on the row with the bell.

Check to see that all students find item 7. Allow students time after each item to choose and mark their answer. Say each problem <u>twice</u>.

SAY:

7 What number should go in the box to make the number sentence true? Listen again.

8 Put your finger on number 8. You should be on the row with the fish. What symbol should go in the box to make the number sentence true? Listen again.

9 Put your finger on number 9. You should be on the row with the shoe. Kim has 11 books. She has read 3 of them. Which number sentence can Kim use to find out how many of the books she has not read? Listen again.

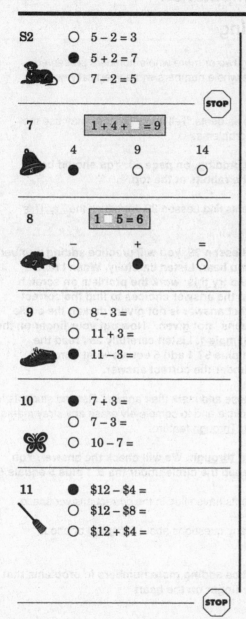

S2

- ○ $5 - 2 = 3$
- ● $5 + 2 = 7$
- ○ $7 - 2 = 5$

STOP

7 $1 + 4 + \boxed{} = 9$

    4   9   14
    ●   ○   ○

8 $1 \boxed{} 5 = 6$

    −   +   =
    ○   ●   ○

9
- ○ $8 - 3 =$
- ○ $11 + 3 =$
- ● $11 - 3 =$

10
- ● $7 + 3 =$
- ○ $7 - 3 =$
- ○ $10 - 7 =$

11
- ● $12 - 4 =$
- ○ $12 - 8 =$
- ○ $12 + 4 =$

STOP

		Stickers	Balloons
Jenny		14	2
Alex		9	5
Jeff		3	7
Anna		4	9

S3   Who has the most balloons?
- ○ Alex
- ○ Jeff
- ● Anna

STOP

12   How many stickers does Alex have?
- ○ 14
- ● 9
- ○ 5

13   How many more balloons than stickers does Anna have?
- ○ 13
- ● 5
- ○ 2

STOP   STOP

Levels 6–7

52

SAY: **10** Put your finger on number 10. You should be on the row with the butterfly. Lupe saw 7 spider monkeys and 3 squirrel monkeys at the zoo. Which number sentence can Lupe use to find out how many monkeys she saw at the zoo? Listen again.

11 Put your finger on number 11. You should be on the row with the broom. Lupe had 12 dollars to spend at the zoo. She came home with 4 dollars. Which number sentence can Lupe use to find out how much money she spent? Listen again.

Look at the stop sign at the bottom of the column. You have finished this part of the test and should put your pencils down. In the last part of the test, you will use a table to solve problems. Look at the table at the top of the second column. It shows how many balloons and stickers children in a class have received as rewards. Now put your finger on S3. This is Sample 3. Read the problem silently while I say it aloud. Then darken the circle for the correct answer. Who has the most balloons?

Allow students time to choose and mark their answer.

SAY: **You should have darkened the circle for *Anna*. Anna has 9 balloons, Alex has 5, and Jeff has 7. Nine is more than 5 or 7.**

Ask students if they have any questions.

SAY: **Now you will use this table to solve more problems. Read each problem silently as I say it aloud. Then darken the circle for the correct answer. Put your finger on number 12.**

Check to see that all students find item 12. Allow students time after each item to choose and mark their answer. Say each problem only once.

SAY: **12 How many stickers does Alex have?**
13 Put your finger on number 13. How many more balloons than stickers does Anna have?

It is now time to stop. You have completed the Unit 7 Test. Make sure you have carefully filled in your answer circles and have completely erased any stray marks. Then put your pencils down.

After the test has been scored, review the questions and answer choices with students. If students are having difficulty, provide them with additional practice.

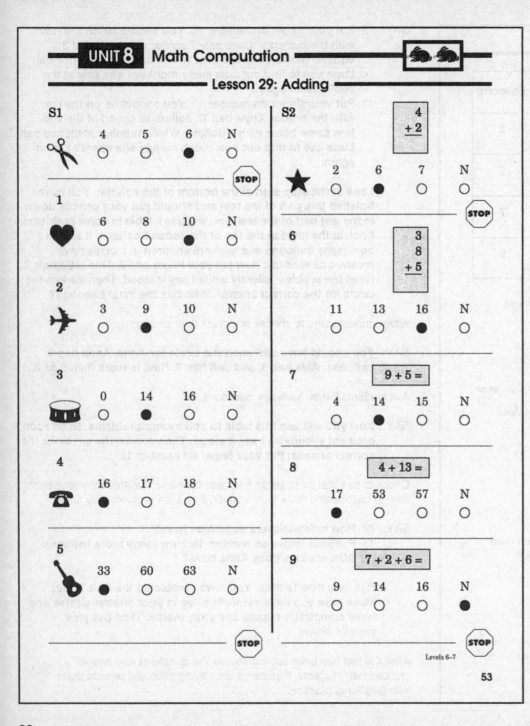

UNIT 8 Math Computation

Lesson 29: Adding

Mathematics Skills: Adding two or more whole numbers presented orally; adding two or more whole numbers written vertically or horizontally; renaming

Distribute scratch paper to students. Tell them that they may use the scratch paper to work the problems.

SAY: **Turn to Lesson 29, Adding, on page 53. You should be on the page with the rabbits at the top.**

Check to see that all students find Lesson 29. Introduce the Try This feature.

SAY: **In the first part of Lesson 29, you will practice adding numbers in problems that you hear. Listen carefully. When I read a problem, you should try this: work the problem on scratch paper. Then look at the answer choices to find the correct answer. If the correct answer is not given, darken the circle under N, which means "not given." Now put your finger on the scissors. This is Sample 1. Listen carefully as I read the problem. What is 1 plus 5? 1 add 5 equals what number? Darken the circle under the correct answer.**

Allow students time to choose and mark their answer. Remind students to carefully fill in the answer circle and to completely erase any stray marks. Then introduce the Think It Through feature.

SAY: **Now we will think it through. We will check the answer. You should have darkened the circle under the 6. 1 plus 5 equals 6.**

Check to see that all students have filled in the correct answer space.

Ask students if they have any questions about Sample 1 or about darkening the answer circle.

SAY: **Now you will practice adding more numbers in problems that you hear. Put your finger on the heart.**

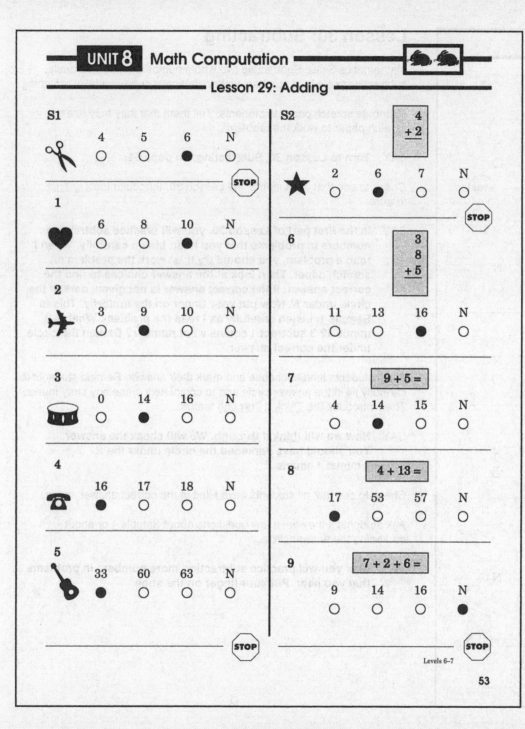

Check to see that all students find item 1. Allow students time after each item to choose and mark their answer. Say each problem only once. Say only the words that appear in boldface type.

SAY: 1 **What is 2 plus 8? 2 add 8 equals what number? Darken the circle under the correct answer.**
2 **Put your finger on the airplane. What is 6 plus 3? 6 add 3 equals what number? Darken the circle under the correct answer.**
3 **Put your finger on the drum. What is 7 plus 7? 7 add 7 equals what number? Darken the circle under the correct answer.**
4 **Put your finger on the telephone. What is 2 plus 14? 2 add 14 equals what number? Darken the circle under the correct answer.**
5 **Put your finger on the guitar. What is 3 plus 30? 3 add 30 equals what number? Darken the circle under the correct answer.**

Look at the stop sign at the bottom of this column. You have finished this part of the lesson and should put your pencils down. In the second part of this lesson, you will practice adding numbers in problems that you read. Put your finger on S2. You should be on the row with the star. This is Sample 2. The problem asks you to add 4 and 2. Work the problem. Then darken the circle under the correct answer. Darken the circle under N if the correct answer is not given.

Allow students time to choose and mark their answer.

SAY: **You should have darkened the circle under the 6. 4 plus 2 equals 6.**

Check to see that all students have filled in the correct answer space.

SAY: **Now you will practice adding more numbers in problems that you read. Put your finger on number 6. Do numbers 6 through 9 just as you did Sample 2. Read the problems carefully. When you come to the stop sign at the bottom of the column, put your pencils down. You may now begin.**

Allow students time to choose and mark their answers.

Review the questions and answer choices with students. Discuss with the class why one answer is correct and the others are not correct. Also check to see that students have carefully filled in their answer spaces and have completely erased any stray marks.

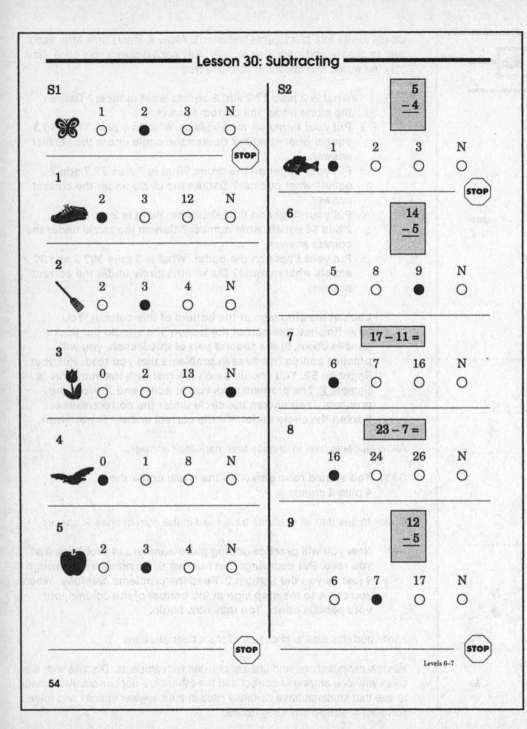

Lesson 30: Subtracting

Mathematics Skills: Subtracting two whole numbers presented orally; subtracting two whole numbers written vertically or horizontally; renaming

Distribute scratch paper to students. Tell them that they may use the scratch paper to work the problems.

SAY: **Turn to Lesson 30, Subtracting, on page 54.**

Check to see that all students find Lesson 30. Introduce the <u>Try This</u> feature.

SAY: **In the first part of Lesson 30, you will practice subtracting numbers in problems that you hear. Listen carefully. When I read a problem, you should <u>try this</u>: work the problem on scratch paper. Then look at the answer choices to find the correct answer. If the correct answer is not given, darken the circle under N. Now put your finger on the butterfly. This is <u>Sample 1</u>. Listen carefully as I read the problem. What is 3 minus 1? 3 subtract 1 equals what number? Darken the circle under the correct answer.**

Allow students time to choose and mark their answer. Remind students to carefully fill in the answer circle and to completely erase any stray marks. Then introduce the <u>Think It Through</u> feature.

SAY: **Now we will <u>think it through</u>. We will check the answer. You should have darkened the circle under the 2. 3 minus 1 equals 2.**

Check to see that all students have filled in the correct answer space.

Ask students if they have any questions about <u>Sample 1</u> or about darkening the answer circle.

SAY: **Now you will practice subtracting more numbers in problems that you hear. Put your finger on the shoe.**

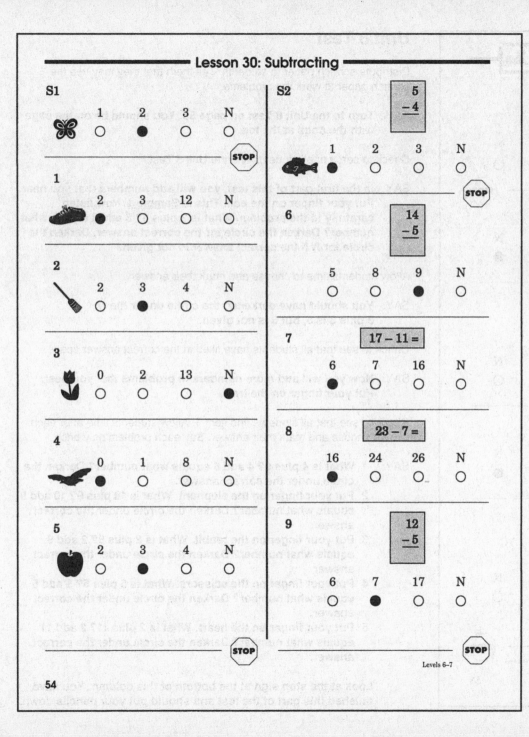

Lesson 30: Subtracting

Check to see that all students find item 1. Allow students time after each item to choose and mark their answer. Say each problem only once. Say only the words that appear in boldface type.

SAY: 1 **What is 7 minus 5? 7 subtract 5 equals what number? Darken the circle under the correct answer.**
2 **Put your finger on the broom. What is 6 minus 3? 6 subtract 3 equals what number? Darken the circle under the correct answer.**
3 **Put your finger on the flower. What is 7 minus 6? 7 subtract 6 equals what number? Darken the circle under the correct answer.**
4 **Put your finger on the bird. What is 8 minus 8? 8 subtract 8 equals what number? Darken the circle under the correct answer.**
5 **Put your finger on the apple. What is 10 minus 7? 10 subtract 7 equals what number? Darken the circle under the correct answer.**

Look at the stop sign at the bottom of this column. You have finished this part of the lesson and should put your pencils down. In the second part of this lesson, you will practice subtracting numbers in problems that you read. Put your finger on S2. You should be on the row with the fish. This is Sample 2. The problem asks you to subtract 4 from 5. Work the problem. Then darken the circle under the correct answer. Darken the circle under N if the correct answer is not given.

Allow students time to choose and mark their answer.

SAY: **You should have darkened the circle under the 1. 5 minus 4 equals 1.**

Check to see that all students have filled in the correct answer space.

SAY: **Now you will practice subtracting more numbers in problems that you read. Put your finger on number 6. Do numbers 6 through 9 just as you did Sample 2. Read the problems carefully. When you come to the stop sign at the bottom of the column, put your pencils down. You may now begin.**

Allow students time to choose and mark their answers.

Review the questions and answer choices with students. Discuss with the class why one answer is correct and the others are not correct. Also check to see that students have carefully filled in their answer spaces and have completely erased any stray marks.

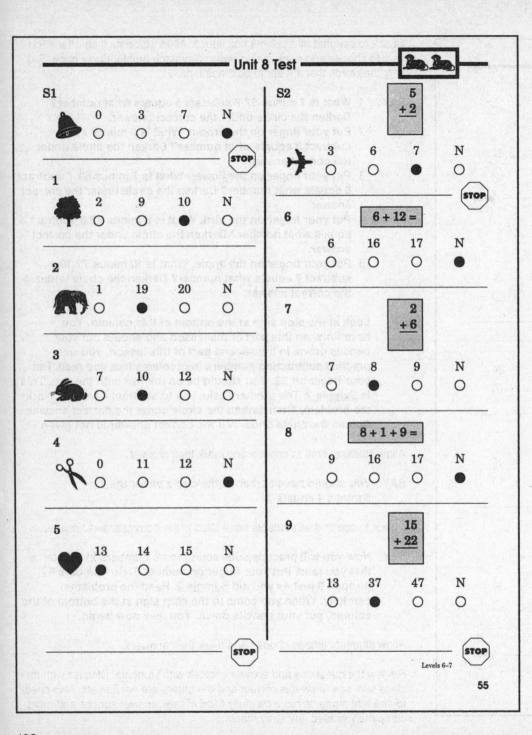

Unit 8 Test

Distribute scratch paper to students. Tell them that they may use the scratch paper to work the problems.

SAY: **Turn to the Unit 8 Test on page 55. You should be on the page with the dogs at the top.**

Check to see that all students find the Unit 8 Test.

SAY: **In the first part of this test, you will add numbers that you hear. Put your finger on the bell. This is <u>Sample 1</u>. Now listen carefully to the problem. What is 3 plus 3? 3 add 3 equals what number? Darken the circle for the correct answer. Darken the circle for _N_ if the correct answer is not given.**

Allow students time to choose and mark their answer.

SAY: **You should have darkened the circle under the _N_. 3 plus 3 is 6, but 6 is not given.**

Check to see that all students have filled in the correct answer space.

SAY: **Now you will add more numbers in problems that you hear. Put your finger on the tree.**

Check to see that all students find item 1. Allow students time after each item to choose and mark their answer. Say each problem only once.

SAY: 1 **What is 4 plus 6? 4 add 6 equals what number? Darken the circle under the correct answer.**
2 **Put your finger on the elephant. What is 10 plus 9? 10 add 9 equals what number? Darken the circle under the correct answer.**
3 **Put your finger on the rabbit. What is 2 plus 8? 2 add 8 equals what number? Darken the circle under the correct answer.**
4 **Put your finger on the scissors. What is 5 plus 5? 5 add 5 equals what number? Darken the circle under the correct answer.**
5 **Put your finger on the heart. What is 2 plus 11? 2 add 11 equals what number? Darken the circle under the correct answer.**

Look at the stop sign at the bottom of this column. You have finished this part of the test and should put your pencils down.

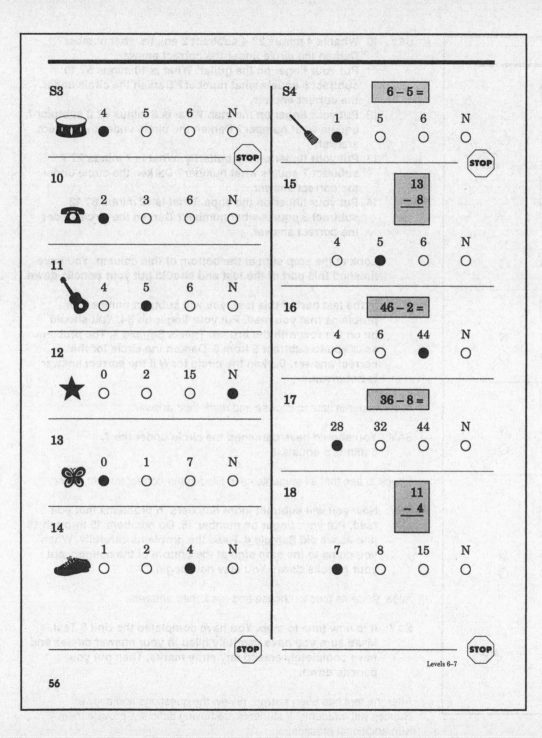

S3

4   5   6   N
●   ○   ○   ○

S4   **6 − 5 =**

1   5   6   N
●   ○   ○   ○

STOP   STOP

10

2   3   6   N
●   ○   ○   ○

15   **13 − 8**

4   5   6   N
○   ●   ○   ○

11

4   5   6   N
○   ●   ○   ○

16   **46 − 2 =**

4   6   44   N
○   ○   ●   ○

12

0   2   15   N
○   ○   ○   ●

17   **36 − 8 =**

28   32   44   N
●   ○   ○   ○

13

0   1   7   N
●   ○   ○   ○

18   **11 − 4**

7   8   15   N
●   ○   ○   ○

14

1   2   4   N
○   ○   ●   ○

STOP   STOP

Levels 6–7

56

SAY: **In the second part of this test, you will add numbers in problems that you read. Put your finger on S2. You should be on the row with the airplane. This is Sample 2. The problem asks you to add 5 and 2. Darken the circle for the correct answer. Darken the circle for *N* if the correct answer is not given.**

Allow students time to choose and mark their answer.

SAY: **You should have darkened the circle under the 7. 5 plus 2 equals 7.**

Check to see that all students have filled in the correct answer space.

SAY: **Now you will add more numbers in problems that you read. Put your finger on number 6. Do numbers 6 through 9 just as you did Sample 2. Read the problems carefully. When you come to the stop sign at the bottom of the column, put your pencils down. You may now begin.**

Allow students time to choose and mark their answers.

SAY: **You have finished this part of the test and should put your pencils down. Turn to page 56.**

In the next part of the test, you will subtract numbers in problems that you hear. Put your finger on the drum. This is Sample 3. Now listen carefully. What is 5 minus 1? 5 subtract 1 equals what number? Darken the circle for the correct answer. Darken the circle for *N* if the correct answer is not given.

Allow students time to choose and mark their answer.

SAY: **You should have darkened the circle under the 4. 5 minus 1 equals 4.**

Check to see that all students have filled in the correct answer space.

SAY: **Now you will subtract more numbers in problems that you hear. Listen carefully to each problem. Subtract the numbers. Then darken the circle under the correct answer. Put your finger on the telephone.**

Check to see that all students find item 10. Allow students time after each item to choose and mark their answer. Say each problem only once. Say only the words that appear in boldface type.

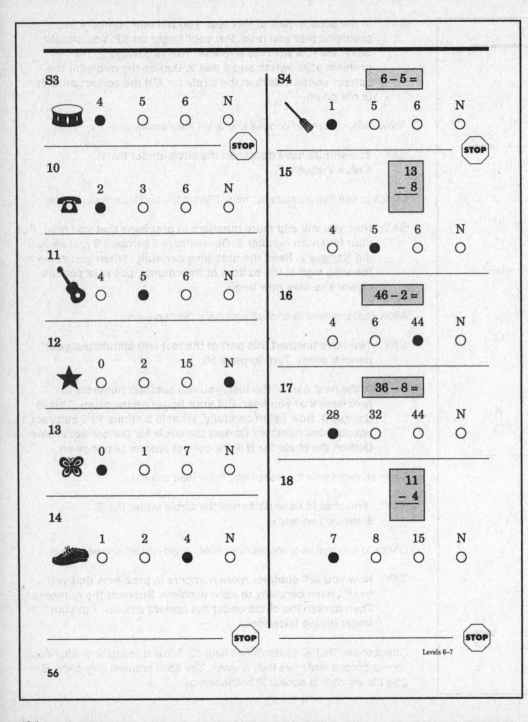

SAY: 10 **What is 4 minus 2? 4 subtract 2 equals what number? Darken the circle under the correct answer.**

11 **Put your finger on the guitar. What is 10 minus 5? 10 subtract 5 equals what number? Darken the circle under the correct answer.**

12 **Put your finger on the star. What is 8 minus 7? 8 subtract 7 equals what number? Darken the circle under the correct answer.**

13 **Put your finger on the butterfly. What is 7 minus 7? 7 subtract 7 equals what number? Darken the circle under the correct answer.**

14 **Put your finger on the shoe. What is 12 minus 8? 12 subtract 8 equals what number? Darken the circle under the correct answer.**

Look at the stop sign at the bottom of this column. You have finished this part of the test and should put your pencils down.

In the last part of this test, you will subtract numbers in problems that you read. Put your finger on S4. You should be on the row with the broom. This is Sample 4. The problem asks you to subtract 5 from 6. Darken the circle for the correct answer. Darken the circle for N if the correct answer is not given.

Allow students time to choose and mark their answer.

SAY: **You should have darkened the circle under the 1. 6 minus 5 equals 1.**

Check to see that all students have filled in the correct answer space.

SAY: **Now you will subtract more numbers in problems that you read. Put your finger on number 15. Do numbers 15 through 18 just as we did Sample 4. Read the problems carefully. When you come to the stop sign at the bottom of the column, put your pencils down. You may now begin.**

Allow students time to choose and mark their answers.

SAY: **It is now time to stop. You have completed the Unit 8 Test. Make sure you have carefully filled in your answer circles and have completely erased any stray marks. Then put your pencils down.**

After the test has been scored, review the questions and answer choices with students. If students are having difficulty, provide them with additional practice.

Lesson 31: Alphabetizing

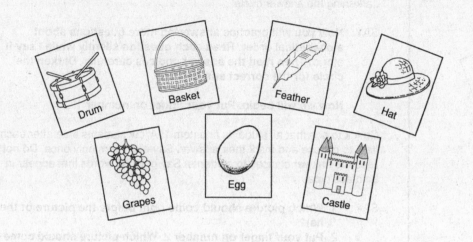

Drum

Basket

Feather

Hat

Grapes

Egg

Castle

S1 Which picture should be at the top of the page?

○ Hat

○ Feather

● Basket

STOP

1 Which picture should come right before the picture of the hat?

● Grapes

○ Castle

○ Egg

2 Which picture should come fourth on the page?

○ Feather

○ Grapes

● Egg

3 Which picture should come between the pictures of the feather and the hat?

○ Egg

● Grapes

○ Basket

STOP

Levels 6–7

57

UNIT 9 Sources of Information

Lesson 31: Alphabetizing

Study Skills: Alphabetizing words by their first letter; understanding sequence

SAY: **Turn to Lesson 31, Alphabetizing, on page 57. You should be on the page with the scissors at the top.**

Check to see that all students find Lesson 31. Introduce the <u>Try This</u> feature.

SAY: **In Lesson 31 you will practice answering questions about alphabetical order.**

Listen carefully. First I will tell you a story. Then I will read the questions that you see on the page. When I read a question, you should <u>try this</u>: read the question silently. Think about what the question asks. Then read the answer choices for the question. Look carefully at the first letter of each answer choice. Say the alphabet to yourself to find out where the first letter of each answer choice belongs in the alphabet. Find the answer choice that answers the question.

Put your finger on <u>S1</u>. This is <u>Sample 1</u>. Now listen carefully to the story. Mr. Rice told his class that they were going to make picture dictionaries. "First you should cut out some pictures from magazines," Mr. Rice said. "Then look at the pictures and think about the name of each one. Next, paste the pictures onto a sheet of paper. Be sure to paste them so that their names are in alphabetical order, starting at the top of the page." Jesse cut out the pictures that you see on this page. Which picture should be at the top of the page? Darken the circle for the correct answer.

Do not read the answer choices to the students. Allow students time to choose and mark their answer. Remind students to carefully fill in the answer circle and to completely erase any stray marks. Then introduce the <u>Think It Through</u> feature.

SAY: **Now we will <u>think it through</u>. We will check the answer. You should have darkened the circle for the third word. The picture of the *basket* should be at the top of the page because *b* comes before *f* and *h* in the alphabet.**

──────── Lesson 31: Alphabetizing ────────

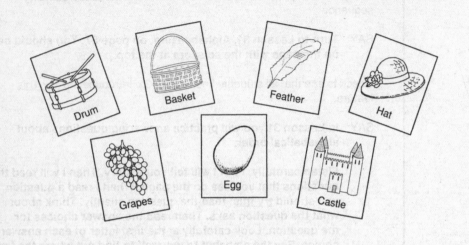

Drum

Basket

Feather

Hat

Grapes

Egg

Castle

S1 Which picture should be at the top of the page?

- ○ Hat
- ○ Feather
- ● Basket

STOP

1 Which picture should come right before the picture of the hat?

- ● Grapes
- ○ Castle
- ○ Egg

2 Which picture should come fourth on the page?

- ○ Feather
- ○ Grapes
- ● Egg

3 Which picture should come between the pictures of the feather and the hat?

- ○ Egg
- ● Grapes
- ○ Basket

STOP

Levels 6–7

57

Check to see that all students have filled in the correct answer space. Remind students that they were instructed to find the picture that should be at the top of the page.

Ask students if they have any questions about Sample 1 or about darkening the answer circle.

SAY: **Now you will practice answering more questions about alphabetical order. Read each question silently while I say it aloud. Then read the answer choices carefully. Darken the circle for the correct answer.**

Now we will begin. Put your finger on number 1.

Check to see that all students find item 1. Allow students time after each item to choose and mark their answer. Say each item only once. Do not read the answer choices to students. Say only the words that appear in boldface type.

SAY: 1 **Which picture should come right before the picture of the hat?**
2 **Put your finger on number 2. Which picture should come fourth on the page?**
3 **Put your finger on number 3. Which picture should come between the pictures of the feather and the hat?**

Look at the stop sign at the bottom of the page. You have now finished the lesson and should put your pencils down.

Review the questions and answer choices with students. Discuss with the class why one answer is correct and the others are not correct. Also check to see that students have carefully filled in their answer spaces and have completely erased any stray marks.

Lesson 32: Understanding Maps

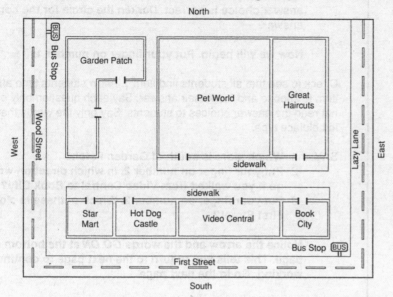

Lesson 32: Understanding Maps

North

BUS Bus Stop

Garden Patch

Pet World

Great Haircuts

West

Wood Street

sidewalk

Lazy Lane

East

sidewalk

Star Mart

Hot Dog Castle

Video Central

Book City

Bus Stop BUS

First Street

South

S1 Which of these is the smallest store?

○ Pet World

○ Hot Dog Castle

● Book City

 STOP

1 Which store is south of Garden Patch?

● Star Mart

○ Pet World

○ Great Haircuts

2 In which direction would you go if you walked from Video Central to Book City?

○ North

○ West

● East

3 Which of these is closest to First Street?

○ Garden Patch

● Hot Dog Castle

○ Great Haircuts

GO ON

Levels 6–7

58

Lesson 32: Understanding Maps

Study Skills: Using maps to locate information; determining direction and distance

SAY: **Turn to Lesson 32, Understanding Maps, on page 58.**

Check to see that all students find Lesson 32. Introduce the <u>Try This</u> feature.

SAY: **In Lesson 32 you will practice using maps to answer questions. Listen carefully. While I read a question aloud, you should <u>try this</u>: read the question silently. Then read the answer choices. Use the map to see which answer choice is correct.**

Now look carefully at the map on this page. It is a map of a shopping center. Study the map to see the different kinds of stores in the shopping center and where they are on the map.

Put your finger on <u>S1</u>. This is <u>Sample 1</u>. Now listen carefully. Which of these is the smallest store? Darken the circle for the correct answer.

Do not read the answer choices to the students. Allow students time to choose and mark their answer. Remind students to carefully fill in the answer circle and to completely erase any stray marks. Then introduce the <u>Think It Through</u> feature.

SAY: **Now we will <u>think it through</u>. We will check the answer. You should have darkened the circle for the third answer choice. *Book City* is the smallest of the stores given as answer choices.**

Check to see that all students have filled in the correct answer space. Remind students that they were instructed to find the store that is the smallest.

Ask students if they have any questions about <u>Sample 1</u> or about darkening the answer circle.

Lesson 32: Understanding Maps

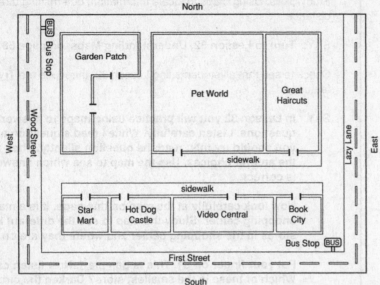

North

Bus Stop

Garden Patch

Pet World

Great Haircuts

Wood Street

West

Lazy Lane

East

sidewalk

sidewalk

Star Mart

Hot Dog Castle

Video Central

Book City

Bus Stop

First Street

South

SAY: **Now you will practice using this map to answer more questions. Read each question silently while I say it aloud. Then read the answer choices. Use the map to see which answer choice is correct. Darken the circle for the correct answer.**

Now we will begin. Put your finger on number 1.

Check to see that all students find item 1. Allow students time after each item to choose and mark their answer. Say each question only once. Do not read the answer choices to students. Say <u>only</u> the words that appear in boldface type.

SAY: 1 **Which store is south of Garden Patch?**
    2 **Put your finger on number 2. In which direction would you go if you walked from Video Central to Book City?**
    3 **Put your finger on number 3. Which of these is closest to First Street?**

Notice the arrow and the words GO ON **at the bottom of the page. This tells you to turn to the next page to continue working. Go to the next page.**

S1 Which of these is the smallest store?

  ○ Pet World

  ○ Hot Dog Castle

  ● Book City

2 In which direction would you go if you walked from Video Central to Book City?

  ○ North

  ○ West

  ● East

(STOP)

1 Which store is south of Garden Patch?

  ● Star Mart

  ○ Pet World

  ○ Great Haircuts

3 Which of these is closest to First Street?

  ○ Garden Patch

  ● Hot Dog Castle

  ○ Great Haircuts

GO ON

Levels 6–7

58

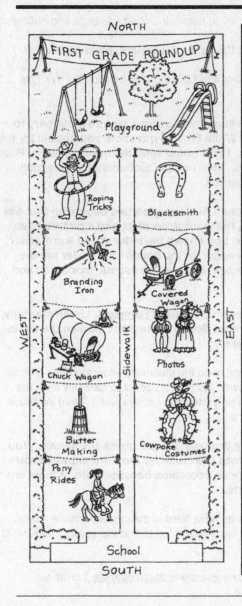

4 Where is the school building?

○   Next to the blacksmith

○   On the north end of the school grounds

●   On the south end of the school grounds

5 When the students walk from the school to the playground, which of these do they pass first?

○   Cowpoke Costumes

●   Pony Rides

○   Covered Wagon

6 Which of these is south of Chuck Wagon?

○   Branding Iron

○   Blacksmith

●   Butter Making

7 Which is farthest from the playground?

○   Chuck Wagon

●   Cowpoke Costumes

○   Covered Wagon

Levels 6–7

59

Check to see that all students find page 59.

SAY: **Now you will practice using another map to answer questions. The map on this page shows how the first-grade classes have arranged things for Western Day. Study the map to find out what it tells you about where things are.**

> **4** **Put your finger on number 4. Where is the school building?**
>
> **5** **Put your finger on number 5. When the students walk from the school to the playground, which of these do they pass first?**
>
> **6** **Put your finger on number 6. Which of these is south of Chuck Wagon?**
>
> **7** **Put your finger on number 7. Which is farthest from the playground?**

Look at the stop sign at the bottom of the page. You have now finished the lesson and should put your pencils down.

Review the questions and answer choices with students. Discuss with the class why one answer is correct and the others are not correct. Also check to see that students have carefully filled in their answer spaces and have completely erased any stray marks.

Lesson 33: Using the Dictionary

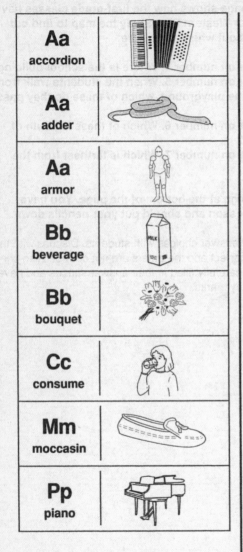

Aa accordion	
Aa adder	
Aa armor	
Bb beverage	
Bb bouquet	
Cc consume	
Mm moccasin	
Pp piano	

S1 Which of these is most like an accordion?

○ An adder

○ A beverage

● A piano

 STOP

1 How should you spell the name for a metal covering for the body?

○ armar

● armor

○ armer

2 Which would you most likely consume?

● A beverage

○ A bouquet

○ A piano

3 Which word best completes the sentence "We found the _____ coiled under a rock"?

● adder

○ armor

○ beverage

STOP

Levels 6–7

Lesson 33: Using the Dictionary

Study Skill: Using a dictionary to determine word spellings and definitions

SAY: **Turn to Lesson 33, Using the Dictionary, on page 60.**

Check to see that all students find Lesson 33. Introduce the Try This feature.

SAY: **In Lesson 33 you will practice using a picture dictionary to answer questions. While I read a question, you should try this: read along silently. Think about what the question asks. Read the answer choices. Then use the dictionary to see which answer choice is correct.**

Now look at the picture dictionary on this page. The first box shows the letter A, the word accordion, and a picture of an accordion. The next box shows the letter A, the word adder, and a picture of an adder. In the boxes after adder are the words armor, beverage, bouquet, consume, moccasin, and piano.

Now put your finger on S1. This is Sample 1. Listen carefully. Which of these is most like an accordion? Darken the circle for the correct answer.

Do not read the answer choices to the students. Allow students time to choose and mark their answer. Remind students to carefully fill in the answer circle and to completely erase any stray marks. Then introduce the Think It Through feature.

SAY: **Now we will think it through. We will check the answer. You should have darkened the circle for the third answer choice. A piano is most like an accordion because both of them are musical instruments.**

Check to see that all students have filled in the correct answer space. Remind students that they were instructed to find the object that is most like an accordion.

Ask students if they have any questions about Sample 1 or about darkening the answer circle.

Lesson 33: Using the Dictionary

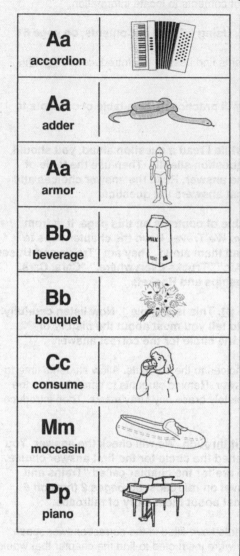

Aa accordion	
Aa adder	
Aa armor	
Bb beverage	
Bb bouquet	
Cc consume	
Mm moccasin	
Pp piano	

S1 Which of these is most like an accordion?

○ An adder

○ A beverage

● A piano

1 How should you spell the name for a metal covering for the body?

○ armar

● armor

○ armer

2 Which would you most likely consume?

● A beverage

○ A bouquet

○ A piano

3 Which word best completes the sentence "We found the _____ coiled under a rock"?

● adder

○ armor

○ beverage

STOP

Levels 6–7

60

SAY: Now you will practice using this picture dictionary to answer more questions. Read each question silently while I say it aloud. Then read the answer choices carefully. Use the dictionary to see which answer choice is correct. Darken the circle for the correct answer.

Now we will begin. Put your finger on number 1.

Check to see that all students find item 1. Allow students time after each item to choose and mark their answer. Say each question only once. Do not read the answer choices to students. Say <u>only</u> the words in boldface type.

SAY: 1 **How should you spell the name for a metal covering for the body?**

2 **Put your finger on number 2. Which would you most likely consume?**

3 **Put your finger on number 3. Which word best completes the sentence "We found the _____ (SAY: blank) coiled under a rock"?**

Look at the stop sign at the bottom of the page. You have now finished the lesson and should put your pencils down.

Review the questions and answer choices with students. Discuss with the class why one answer is correct and the others are not correct. Also check to see that students have carefully filled in their answer spaces and have completely erased any stray marks.

Lesson 34: Using a Table of Contents

Ways We Travel

Contents

	Page
Trains and Buses	2
Traveling in the Air	7
Trucks Everywhere	12
Cars, Cars, Cars	19
Spaceships and Rockets	25

S1 Which pages would tell you most about the history of railroads?

- ● 2–6
- ○ 12–18
- ○ 19–24

STOP

1 On which page should you begin to read to find out about hot-air balloons?

- ○ Page 2
- ● Page 7
- ○ Page 19

2 Which pages would tell you the most about who built the first automobile in America?

- ○ 7–11
- ○ 12–18
- ● 19–24

3 Which pages might tell about the jobs that different trucks do?

- ○ 2–6
- ○ 7–11
- ● 12–18

STOP

Levels 6–7

61

Lesson 34: Using a Table of Contents

Study Skill: Using a table of contents to locate information

SAY: **Turn to Lesson 34, Using a Table of Contents, on page 61.**

Check to see that all students find Lesson 34. Introduce the Try This feature.

SAY: **In Lesson 34 you will practice using a table of contents to answer questions.**

Listen carefully. While I read a question aloud, you should try this: read the question silently. Then use the table of contents to find the answer. Read the answer choices and look for the one that answers the question.

Now look at the table of contents on this page. It is from a book called *Ways We Travel*. Read the chapter titles to yourself while I read them aloud. They are "Trains and Buses," "Traveling in the Air," "Trucks Everywhere," "Cars, Cars, Cars," and "Spaceships and Rockets."

Put your finger on S1. This is Sample 1. Now listen carefully. Which pages would tell you most about the history of railroads? Darken the circle for the correct answer.

Do not read the answer choices to the students. Allow students time to choose and mark their answer. Remind students to carefully fill in the answer circle and to completely erase any stray marks. Then introduce the Think It Through feature.

SAY: **Now we will think it through. We will check the answer. You should have darkened the circle for the first answer choice. Pages 2 through 6 are for the chapter called "Trains and Buses." Trains travel on railroads, so *pages 2 through 6* will tell you the most about the history of railroads.**

Check to see that all students have filled in the correct answer space. Remind students that they were instructed to find the chapter that would tell the most about the history of railroads.

Ask students if they have any questions about Sample 1 or about darkening the answer circle.

Lesson 34: Using a Table of Contents

Ways We Travel

Contents

	Page
Trains and Buses	2
Traveling in the Air	7
Trucks Everywhere	12
Cars, Cars, Cars	19
Spaceships and Rockets	25

S1 Which pages would tell you most about the history of railroads?
- ● 2–6
- ○ 12–18
- ○ 19–24

STOP

1 On which page should you begin to read to find out about hot-air balloons?
- ○ Page 2
- ● Page 7
- ○ Page 19

2 Which pages would tell you the most about who built the first automobile in America?
- ○ 7–11
- ○ 12–18
- ● 19–24

3 Which pages might tell about the jobs that different trucks do?
- ○ 2–6
- ○ 7–11
- ● 12–18

STOP

Levels 6–7

61

SAY: **Now you will practice using this table of contents to answer more questions. Read each question silently while I say it aloud. Use the table of contents to find the answer. Then read the answer choices carefully. Darken the circle for the correct answer.**

Now we will begin. Put your finger on number 1.

Check to see that all students find item 1. Allow students time after each item to choose and mark their answer. Say each question only once. Do not read the answer choices to students. Say <u>only</u> the words that appear in boldface type.

SAY: 1 **On which page should you begin to read to find out about hot-air balloons?**
2 **Put your finger on number 2. Which pages would tell you the most about who built the first automobile in America?**
3 **Put your finger on number 3. Which pages might tell about the jobs that different trucks do?**

Look at the stop sign at the bottom of the page. You have now finished the lesson and should put your pencils down.

Review the questions and answer choices with students. Discuss with the class why one answer is correct and the others are not correct. Also check to see that students have carefully filled in their answer spaces and have completely erased any stray marks.

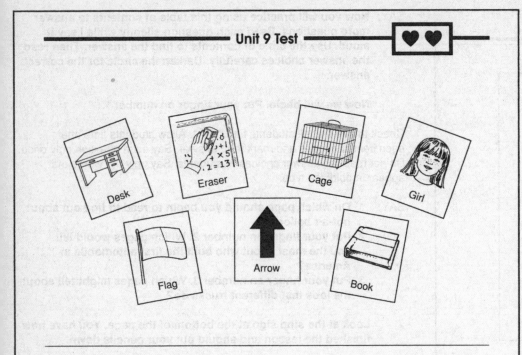

S1 Which picture should come right before the picture of the desk?

- ○ Arrow
- ● Cage
- ○ Book

STOP

1 Which picture should come last on the page?

- ○ Desk
- ○ Flag
- ● Girl

2 Which picture should come right after the picture of the flag?

- ● Girl
- ○ Eraser
- ○ Arrow

3 Which picture should come between the pictures of the book and the desk?

- ● Cage
- ○ Arrow
- ○ Eraser

STOP

Levels 6–7

Unit 9 Test

SAY: **Turn to the Unit 9 Test on page 62. You should be on the page with the hearts at the top.**

Check to see that all students find the Unit 9 Test.

SAY: **In the first part of this test, you will answer questions about alphabetical order.**

Listen carefully. Ms. Chung gave her students pictures of people and things that were in the classroom. She told the students to use the pictures to make a picture dictionary. The students were to paste the pictures in alphabetical order onto a sheet of paper, starting at the top of the page. Ms. Chung gave her students the pictures you see on this page.

Put your finger on S1. This is Sample 1. Read the question silently as I read it aloud. Which picture should come right before the picture of the desk? Darken the circle for the correct answer.

Do not read the answer choices to students. Allow students time to choose and mark their answer.

SAY: **You should have darkened the circle for the second answer choice. The picture of the *cage* should come right before the picture of the desk because *c* comes right before *d* in the alphabet.**

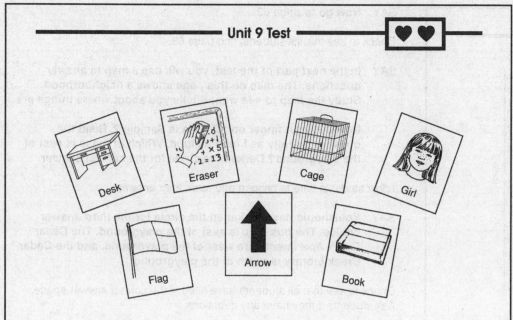

S1 Which picture should come right before the picture of the desk?

- ○ Arrow
- ● Cage
- ○ Book

STOP

1 Which picture should come last on the page?

- ○ Desk
- ○ Flag
- ● Girl

2 Which picture should come right after the picture of the flag?

- ● Girl
- ○ Eraser
- ○ Arrow

3 Which picture should come between the pictures of the book and the desk?

- ● Cage
- ○ Arrow
- ○ Eraser

STOP

Levels 6–7

Check to see that all students have filled in the correct answer space. Ask students if they have any questions.

SAY: **Now you will answer more questions about alphabetical order. Read each question silently as I read it aloud. Then read the answer choices carefully. Darken the circle for the correct answer. Put your finger on number 1.**

Check to see that all students find item 1. Allow students time after each item to choose and mark their answer. Say each question only once. Say only the words that appear in boldface type.

SAY: 1 **Which picture should come last on the page?**
2 **Put your finger on number 2. Which picture should come right after the picture of the flag?**
3 **Put your finger on number 3. Which picture should come between the pictures of the book and the desk?**

Look at the stop sign at the bottom of the page. You have finished this part of the test and should put your pencils down.

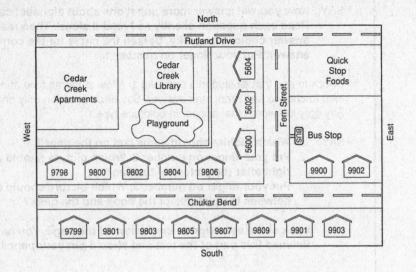

Check to see that all students find page 63.

SAY: **In the next part of the test, you will use a map to answer questions. The map on this page shows a neighborhood. Study the map to see what it tells you about where things are.**

Now put your finger on S2. This is Sample 2. Read the question silently as I read it aloud. Which of these is east of the playground? Darken the circle for the correct answer.

Allow students time to choose and mark their answer.

SAY: **You should have darkened the circle for the third answer choice. The *bus stop* is east of the playground. The Cedar Creek Apartments are west of the playground, and the Cedar Creek Library is north of the playground.**

Check to see that all students have filled in the correct answer space. Ask students if they have any questions.

SAY: **Now you will use this map to answer more questions. Read each question silently as I read it aloud. Then read the answer choices. Use the map to see which answer choice is correct. Darken the circle for the correct answer. Put your finger on number 4.**

Check to see that all students find item 4.

SAY: **4 In which direction do people who live in the Cedar Creek Apartments walk to go to Quick Stop Foods?**
    5 Put your finger on number 5. Which of these is closest to Cedar Creek Library?
    6 Put your finger on number 6. In which direction would you go if you walked from the house at 9809 Chukar Bend to the bus stop?

Look at the stop sign at the bottom of the page. You have finished this part of the test and should put your pencils down.

S2 Which of these is east of the playground?

○ Cedar Creek Apartments

○ Cedar Creek Library

● The bus stop

(STOP)

4 In which direction do people who live in the Cedar Creek Apartments walk to go to Quick Stop Foods?

○ South

● East

○ North

5 Which of these is closest to Cedar Creek Library?

○ The house at 9903 Chukar Bend

○ Quick Stop Foods

● The house at 5604 Fern Street

6 In which direction would you go if you walked from the house at 9809 Chukar Bend to the bus stop?

● North

○ South

○ West

(STOP)

Levels 6–7

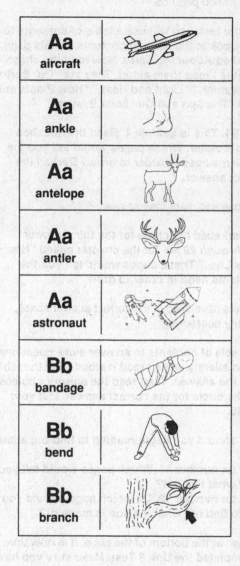

S3 Which of these is most like a branch?

○ An aircraft

○ An ankle

● An antler

🛑 **STOP**

7 How should you spell the name for a person trained to fly in a spacecraft?

○ astranaut

● astronaut

○ astronot

8 Which is most likely to have a bandage?

○ An antelope

● An ankle

○ A branch

9 Which word best completes the sentence "Can you _____ over and touch your toes"?

○ bandage

● bend

○ branch

🛑 **STOP**

Levels 6–7

SAY: **Now turn to page 64.**

Check to see that all students find page 64.

SAY: **In the next part of the test, you will use a picture dictionary to answer questions. Study the picture dictionary on this page. The first box shows the letter *A*, the word *aircraft*, and a picture of an aircraft. In the boxes after *aircraft* are the words *ankle, antelope, antler, astronaut, bandage, bend,* and *branch*.**

Put your finger on S3. This is Sample 3. Read the question silently as I read it aloud. Which of these is most like a branch? Darken the circle for the correct answer.

Allow students time to choose and mark their answer.

SAY: **You should have darkened the circle for the third answer choice. An *antler* is most like a branch because of the way it looks. An aircraft and an ankle are not in any way like a branch.**

Check to see that all students have filled in the correct answer space. Ask students if they have any questions.

SAY: **Now you will use this picture dictionary to answer more questions. Read each question silently while I read it aloud. Read the answer choices carefully. Then use the dictionary to see which answer choice is correct. Darken the circle for the correct answer. Put your finger on number 7.**

Check to see that all students find item 7.

SAY: **7 How should you spell the name for a person trained to fly in a spacecraft?**
    8 Put your finger on number 8. Which is most likely to have a bandage?
    9 Put your finger on number 9. Which word best completes the sentence "Can you _____ (SAY: *blank*) over and touch your toes"?

Look at the stop sign at the bottom of the page. You have finished this part of the test and should put your pencils down.

About the Earth

Contents

S4 Which pages would tell you the most about what plants need in order to grow?

- ○ 2–6
- ○ 7–14
- ● 21–29

(STOP)

10 On which page should you begin reading to find out about storm clouds?

- ● Page 7
- ○ Page 15
- ○ Page 21

11 Which pages would tell you the most about what fish eat?

- ○ 7–14
- ● 21–29
- ○ 15–20

12 On which page should you begin reading to find out what the sun is made of?

- ● Page 30
- ○ Page 21
- ○ Page 2

(STOP)

Levels 6–7

SAY: **Now go to page 65.**

Check to see that all students find page 65.

SAY: **In the next part of the test, you will use a table of contents to answer questions. Look at the table of contents on this page. It is from a book called *About the Earth*. Now read the chapter titles to yourself while I read them aloud. They are "Our Earth's Air and Water," "Weather," "Light and Heat," "How Plants and Animals Live," and "The Sun and Our Solar System."**

Put your finger on S4. This is Sample 4. Read the question silently while I read it aloud. Which pages would tell you the most about what plants need in order to grow? Darken the circle for the correct answer.

Allow students time to choose and mark their answer.

SAY: **You should have darkened the circle for the third answer choice. *Pages 21 through 29* are for the chapter called "How Plants and Animals Live." These pages would tell you the most about what plants need in order to grow.**

Check to see that all students have filled in the correct answer space. Ask students if they have any questions.

SAY: **Now you use this table of contents to answer more questions. Read each question silently while I read it aloud. Use the table of contents to find the answer. Then read the answer choices carefully. Darken the circle for the correct answer. Put your finger on number 10.**

10 On which page should you begin reading to find out about storm clouds?

11 Put your finger on number 11. Which pages would tell you the most about what fish eat?

12 Put your finger on number 12. On which page should you begin reading to find out what the sun is made of?

Look at the stop sign at the bottom of the page. It is now time to stop. You have completed the Unit 9 Test. Make sure you have carefully filled in your answer circles and have completely erased any stray marks. Then put your pencils down.

After the test has been scored, review the questions and answer choices with students. If students are having difficulty, provide them with additional practice.

Test Best Comprehensive Tests

Getting Ready for the Comprehensive Tests

The Comprehensive Tests are designed to simulate the Iowa Tests of Basic Skills. Each Comprehensive Test has a suggested time limit. Please remember, however, that the time limits are merely guidelines to help you schedule the tests. None of the Level 6 Iowa Tests of Basic Skills is timed; only a part of the Mathematics Computation test is timed in the Level 7 Iowa Tests of Basic Skills. It is recommended that you schedule no more than two tests in one day for Levels 6–7, providing a sufficient break between tests.

Following the suggestions presented here will enable students to experience test taking under the same structured conditions that apply when achievement tests are administered. Furthermore, students will have a final opportunity to apply the skills they have learned in *Test Best* prior to taking the Iowa Tests of Basic Skills.

The following table lists recommended test sessions and suggested time limit for each test.

Test Session	Comprehensive Test	Suggested Time Limit in Minutes
First Day	1—Vocabulary	20
	2—Word Analysis	20
Second Day	3—Reading	30
	4—Listening	10
Third Day	5—Language	25
	6—Math Concepts	25
Fourth Day	7—Math Problems	25
	8—Math Computation	25
Fifth Day	9—Sources of Information	15

Test Day

To simulate the structured atmosphere of the Iowa Tests of Basic Skills, take the following steps on each test day:

- Hang a "Do Not Disturb—Testing" sign on the classroom door to avoid interruptions.

- Seat students at an appropriate distance from one another, and make sure that their desks are clear of all materials.

- Provide students with sharpened pencils that have erasers.

- Keep supplies, such as extra pencils, readily available.

- Distribute the *Test Best* books to students and encourage them to do their best.

Before you begin, remind students to press firmly with their pencil to make a dark mark. Remind students of the importance of completely filling in the answer circles and erasing any stray marks that might be picked up as answers by the scoring machines.

While you are administering the Comprehensive Tests, make sure that students understand the directions before proceeding with each test. Circulate around the classroom, making sure that students are following the directions and that they are working on the appropriate page. Check to see that students have carefully filled in the answer spaces and have completely erased any stray marks.

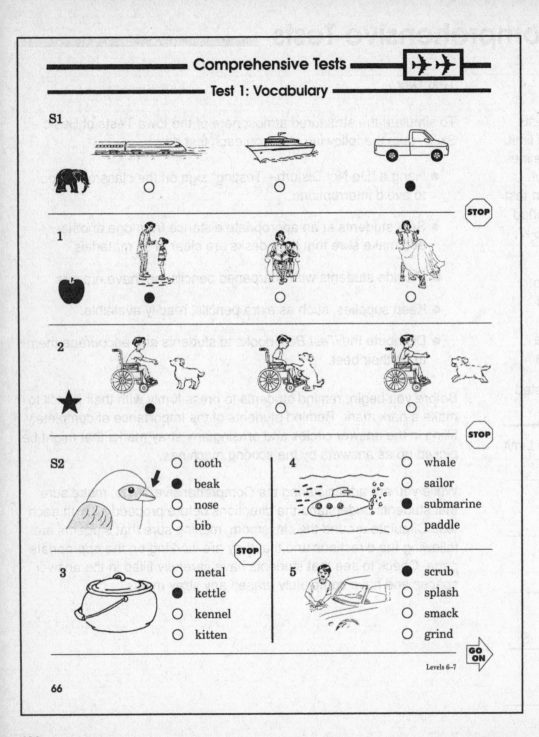

Comprehensive Tests

Test 1: Vocabulary

Allow about 20 minutes for this test. Read items at a moderate, steady pace.

SAY: **Turn to Test 1, Vocabulary, on page 66. You should be on the page with the airplanes at the top.**

Check to see that all students find Test 1.

SAY: **In the first part of this test, you will choose pictures that match words that you hear. Put your finger on <u>S1</u>. You should be on the row with the elephant. This is <u>Sample 1</u>. We will work <u>Sample 1</u> together. Look at the three pictures in <u>Sample 1</u>. Now listen carefully. Darken the circle under the picture that shows an *automobile...automobile.***

Allow students time to choose and mark their answer.

SAY: **You should have darkened the circle under the third picture. It shows an *automobile*.**

Check to see that all students have filled in the correct answer space. Ask students if they have any questions.

SAY: **Now you will choose more pictures that match words that you hear. Listen carefully to each word. Then choose your answer from the pictures given for the word. Put your finger on number 1. You should be on the row with the apple.**

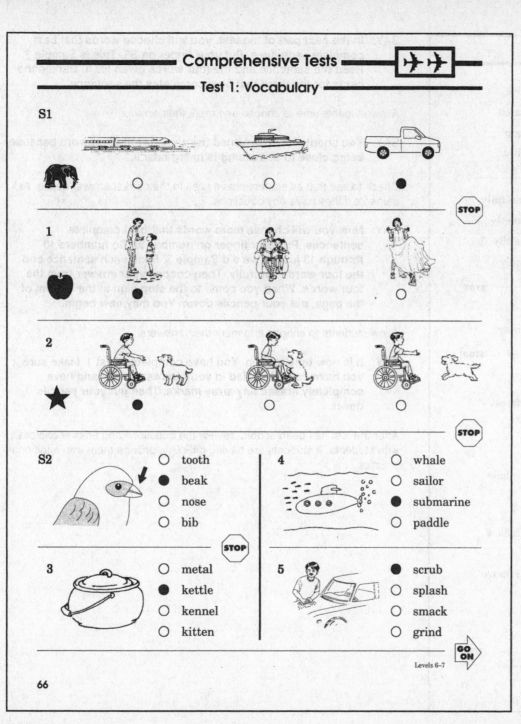

Comprehensive Tests

Test 1: Vocabulary

S1

STOP

1

2

★

STOP

S2
- ○ tooth
- ● beak
- ○ nose
- ○ bib

STOP

4
- ○ whale
- ○ sailor
- ● submarine
- ○ paddle

3
- ○ metal
- ● kettle
- ○ kennel
- ○ kitten

5
- ● scrub
- ○ splash
- ○ smack
- ○ grind

GO ON

Levels 6–7

66

Check to see that all students find item 1. Allow students time after each item to choose and mark their answer. Say each item only once. Say <u>only</u> the words that appear in boldface type.

SAY: 1 Darken the circle under the picture that shows *scold...scold* the child.

2 Put your finger on number 2. You should be on the row with the star. Darken the circle under the picture that shows the dog that is *cautious...cautious.*

Look at the stop sign at the end of the row. You have finished this part of the test and should put your pencils down.

In the next part of the test, you will choose words that match pictures. Put your finger on <u>S2</u>. This is <u>Sample 2</u>. Look at the picture. Then read the four words. Darken the circle for the word that matches the picture.

Allow students time to choose and mark their answer.

SAY: You should have darkened the circle for the second word. The picture shows a *beak. Beak* is the word that matches the picture.

Check to see that all students have filled in the correct answer space. Ask students if they have any questions.

SAY: Now you will choose more words that match pictures. Put your finger on number 3. Do numbers 3 through 9 just as we did <u>Sample 2</u>. Look at the picture and read the words carefully. Then choose your answer from the words given for the picture. Notice the arrow and the words *GO ON* at the bottom of the page. This tells you to continue working on the next page. When you come to the stop sign after number 9, put your pencils down. You may now begin.

Allow students time to choose and mark their answers.

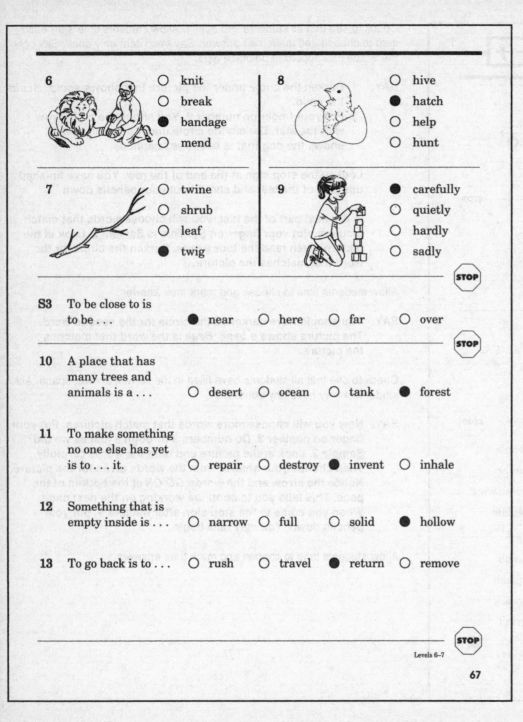

6 ○ knit
 ● break
 ● bandage
 ○ mend

8 ○ hive
 ● hatch
 ○ help
 ○ hunt

7 ○ twine
 ○ shrub
 ○ leaf
 ● twig

9 ● carefully
 ○ quietly
 ○ hardly
 ○ sadly

STOP

S3 To be close to is
to be . . .   ● near   ○ here   ○ far   ○ over

STOP

10 A place that has
many trees and
animals is a . . .   ○ desert   ○ ocean   ○ tank   ● forest

11 To make something
no one else has yet
is to . . . it.   ○ repair   ○ destroy   ● invent   ○ inhale

12 Something that is
empty inside is . . .   ○ narrow   ○ full   ○ solid   ● hollow

13 To go back is to . . .   ○ rush   ○ travel   ● return   ○ remove

STOP

Levels 6–7

67

Allow students time to choose and mark their answer.

SAY: **You should have darkened the circle for the first word because being close to something is being *near* it.**

Check to see that all students have filled in the correct answer space. Ask students if they have any questions.

SAY: **Now you will choose more words that best complete sentences. Put your finger on number 10. Do numbers 10 through 13 just as we did <u>Sample 3</u>. Read each sentence and the four words carefully. Then choose your answer from the four words. When you come to the stop sign at the bottom of the page, put your pencils down. You may now begin.**

Allow students to choose and mark their answers.

SAY: **It is now time to stop. You have completed Test 1. Make sure you have carefully filled in your answer circles and have completely erased any stray marks. Then put your pencils down.**

After the test has been scored, review the questions and answer choices with students. If students are having difficulty, provide them with additional practice.

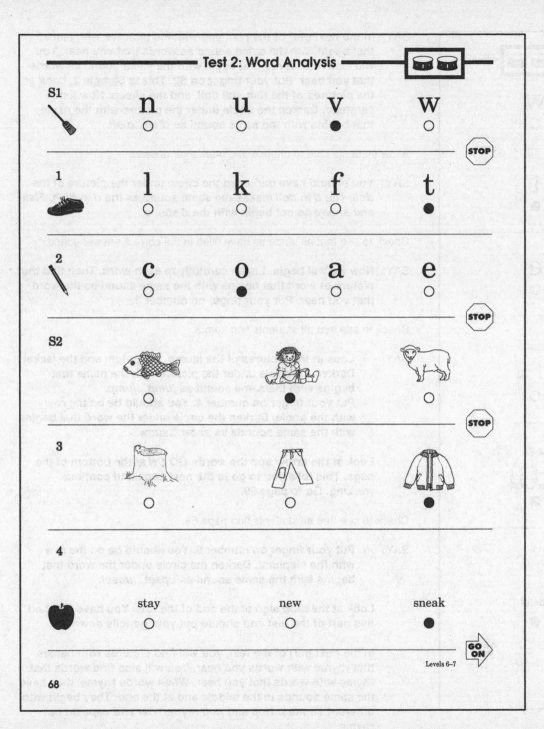

Test 2: Word Analysis

Allow about 20 minutes for this test. Read items at a moderate, steady pace.

SAY: **Turn to Test 2, Word Analysis, on page 68. You should be on the page with the drums at the top.**

Check to see that all students find Test 2.

SAY: **In the first part of this test, you will find letters that you hear. Put your finger on S1. You should be on the row with the broom. This is Sample 1. Now listen carefully. Look at the four letters in Sample 1. Darken the circle under the letter *v*.**

Do not read the letter choices to the students. Allow students time to choose and mark their answer.

SAY: **You should have darkened the circle under the *third* letter. The third letter is *v*. The first letter is *n*, the second letter is *u*, and the fourth letter is *w*.**

Check to see that all students have filled in the correct answer space. Ask students if they have any questions.

SAY: **Now you will find more letters that you hear. Listen carefully to the letter that I say. Then look at the letters listed in the row. Find the letter that you hear. Put your finger on number 1. You should be on the row with the shoe.**

Check to see that all students find item 1. Allow students time after each item to choose and mark their answer. Say each item only once. Say only the words that appear in boldface type.

SAY: 1 **Darken the circle under the letter *t*.**
      2 **Put your finger on number 2. You should be on the row with the pencil. Darken the circle under the letter *o*.**

Look at the stop sign at the end of the row. You have finished this part of the test and should put your pencils down.

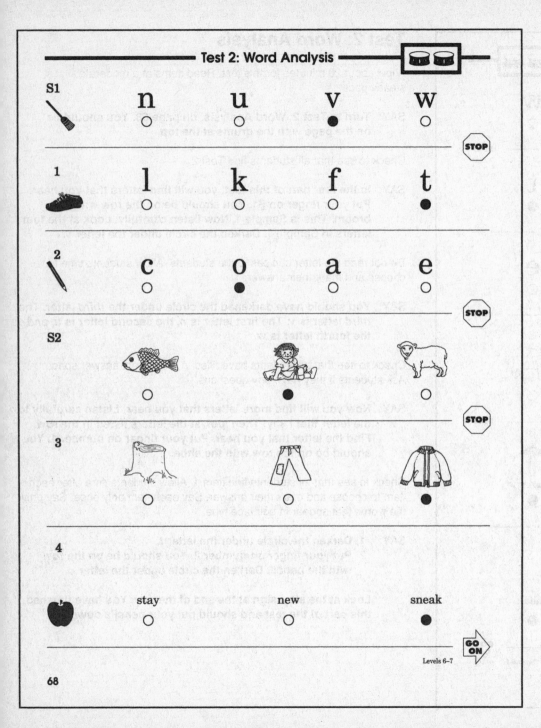

Test 2: Word Analysis

S1

n   u   **v**   w

○   ○   ●   ○

STOP

1

l   k   f   **t**

○   ○   ○   ●

2

c   **o**   a   e

○   ●   ○   ○

STOP

S2

○   ●   ○

STOP

3

○   ○   ●

4

stay   new   sneak

○   ○   ●

GO ON

Levels 6–7

68

SAY: **In the next part of the test, you will find pictures with names that begin with the same sound as words that you hear. You will also find words that begin with the same sound as words that you hear. Put your finger on S2. This is Sample 2. Look at the pictures of the fish, the doll, and the sheep. Now listen carefully. Darken the circle under the picture with the name that begins with the same sound as *dish...dish.***

Allow students time to choose and mark their answer.

SAY: **You should have darkened the circle under the picture of the *doll*. The *d* in *doll* makes the same sound as the *d* in *dish*. *Fish* and *sheep* do not begin with the *d* sound.**

Check to see that all students have filled in the correct answer space.

SAY: **Now we will begin. Listen carefully to each word. Then find the picture or word that begins with the same sound as the word that you hear. Put your finger on number 3.**

Check to see that all students find item 3.

SAY: 3   **Look at the pictures of the stump, the patch, and the jacket. Darken the circle under the picture with the name that begins with the same sound as *jump...jump.***
     4   **Put your finger on number 4. You should be on the row with the apple. Darken the circle under the word that begins with the same sounds as *snow...snow.***

Look at the arrow and the words *GO ON* at the bottom of the page. This tells you to go to the next page and continue working. Go to page 69.

Check to see that all students find page 69.

SAY: 5   **Put your finger on number 5. You should be on the row with the elephant. Darken the circle under the word that begins with the same sound as *upset...upset.***

Look at the stop sign at the end of the row. You have finished this part of the test and should put your pencils down.

In the next part of the test, you will find pictures with names that rhyme with words you hear. You will also find words that rhyme with words that you hear. When words rhyme, they have the same sounds in the middle and at the end. They begin with different sounds. *Hop* and *pop* rhyme. *Car* and *cape* do not rhyme.

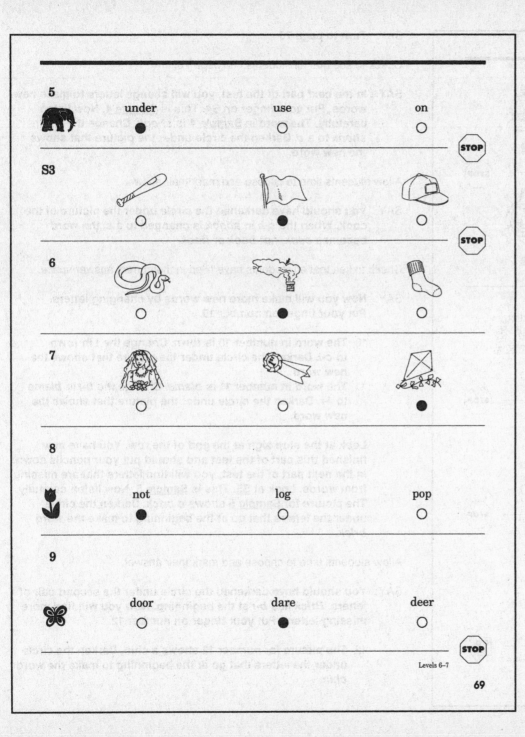

5   under   use   on

STOP

S3

STOP

6

7

8   not   log   pop

9   door   dare   deer

STOP

Levels 6–7

69

SAY: **Put your finger on S3. This is Sample 3. Look at the pictures of the bat, the flag, and the cap. Now listen carefully. Darken the circle under the picture with the name that rhymes with *drag...drag.***

Allow students time to choose and mark their answer.

SAY: **You should have darkened the circle under the picture of the *flag. Flag* rhymes with *drag.***

Check to see that all students have filled in the correct answer space.

SAY: **Now we will begin. Listen carefully to each word. Then find the picture or word that rhymes with the word that you hear. Put your finger on number 6.**

Check to see that all students find item 6.

SAY: 6   **Look at the pictures of the snake, the smoke, and the sock. Darken the circle under the picture with the name that rhymes with *joke...joke.***
      7   **Put your finger on number 7. Look at the pictures of the bride, the prize, and the kite. Darken the circle under the picture with the name that rhymes with *bite...bite.***
      8   **Put your finger on number 8. You should be on the row with the flower. Darken the circle under the word that rhymes with *dot...dot.***
      9   **Put your finger on number 9. You should be on the row with the butterfly. Darken the circle under the word that rhymes with *hair...hair.***

Look at the stop sign at the bottom of the page. You have finished this part of the test and should put your pencils down.

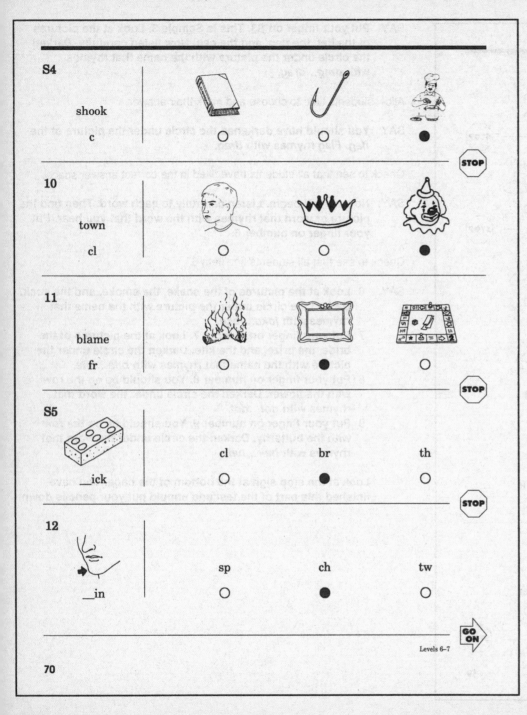

S4

shook

c

10

town

cl

11

blame

fr

S5

___ick

cl   br   th

12

___in

sp   ch   tw

Levels 6–7

SAY: **Turn to page 70.**

Check to see that all students find page 70.

SAY: **In the next part of the test, you will change letters to make new words. Put your finger on S4. This is Sample 4. Now listen carefully. The word in Sample 4 is *shook*. Change the *s-h* in *shook* to a *c*. Darken the circle under the picture that shows the new word.**

Allow students time to choose and mark their answer.

SAY: **You should have darkened the circle under the picture of the cook. When the *s-h* in *shook* is changed to a *c*, the word becomes *cook*, not *book* or *hook*.**

Check to see that all students have filled in the correct answer space.

SAY: **Now you will make more new words by changing letters. Put your finger on number 10.**

   10 **The word in number 10 is *town*. Change the *t* in *town* to *c-l*. Darken the circle under the picture that shows the new word.**

   11 **The word in number 11 is *blame*. Change the *b-l* in *blame* to *f-r*. Darken the circle under the picture that shows the new word.**

Look at the stop sign at the end of the row. You have now finished this part of the test and should put your pencils down. In the next part of the test, you will find letters that are missing from words. Look at S5. This is Sample 5. Now listen carefully. The picture for Sample 5 shows a *brick*. Darken the circle under the letters that go at the beginning to make the word *brick*.

Allow students time to choose and mark their answer.

SAY: **You should have darkened the circle under the second pair of letters. *Brick* has *b-r* at the beginning. Now you will find more missing letters. Put your finger on number 12.**

   12 **The picture for number 12 shows a chin. Darken the circle under the letters that go at the beginning to make the word *chin*.**

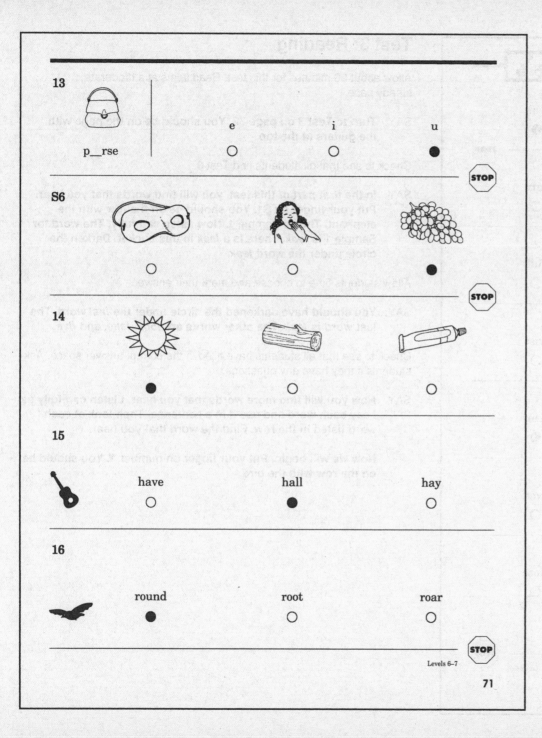

13

p__rse

e ○ i ○ u ●

STOP

S6

○ ○ ●

STOP

14

● ○ ○

15

have ○ hall ● hay ○

16

round ● root ○ roar ○

STOP

Levels 6–7

SAY: Look at the arrow and the words *GO ON* at the bottom of the page. This tells you to go to the next page and continue working on the test. Go to page 71.

13 Put your finger on number 13. The picture for number 13 shows a *purse*. Darken the circle under the letter that goes in the middle of the word to make the word *purse*.

Look at the stop sign at the end of the row. You have finished this part of the test and should put your pencils down. In the last part of the test, you will find pictures with names that have the same vowel sound as words that you hear. You will also find words that have the same vowel sound as words that you hear. Put your finger on S6. This is Sample 6. Look at the pictures in the row. Now listen carefully. Darken the circle under the picture with the name that has the same vowel sound as *place...place*.

Allow students time to choose and mark their answer.

SAY: You should have darkened the circle under the picture of the *grapes*. *Grapes* has the same vowel sound as *place*. Now we will begin. Listen carefully to the word that I say. Find the picture or word that has the same vowel sound as the word that you hear. Put your finger on number 14.

14 Darken the circle under the picture with the name that has the same vowel sound as *rug...rug*.
15 Put your finger on number 15. You should be on the row with the guitar. Darken the circle under the word that has the same vowel sound as *draw...draw*.
16 Put your finger on number 16. You should be on the row with the bird. Darken the circle under the word that has the same vowel sound as *house...house*.

Look at the stop sign at the bottom of the page. It is now time to stop. You have completed Test 2. Make sure you have carefully filled in your answer circles and have completely erased any stray marks. Then put your pencils down.

After the test has been scored, review the questions and answer choices with students. If students are having difficulty, provide them with additional practice.

Test 3: Reading

S1

look	lake	live	leak
○	○	○	●

STOP

1

more	move	most	mix
●	○	○	○

2

fill	fall	feel	full
○	○	●	○

3

wash	wish	was	wise
○	●	○	○

4

bread	branch	brown	bring
○	○	○	●

5

over	open	only	oven
○	●	○	○

6

club	clock	cloud	close
○	●	○	○

STOP

Levels 6–7

Test 3: Reading

Allow about 30 minutes for this test. Read items at a moderate, steady pace.

SAY: **Turn to Test 3 on page 72. You should be on the page with the guitars at the top.**

Check to see that all students find Test 3.

SAY: **In the first part of this test, you will find words that you hear. Put your finger on S1. You should be on the row with the elephant. This is Sample 1. Now listen carefully. The word for Sample 1 is** *leak.* **There is a** *leak* **in this bucket. Darken the circle under the word** *leak.*

Allow students time to choose and mark their answer.

SAY: **You should have darkened the circle under the** *last* **word. The last word is** *leak.* **The other words are** *look, lake,* **and** *live.*

Check to see that all students have filled in the correct answer space. Ask students if they have any questions.

SAY: **Now you will find more words that you hear. Listen carefully as I say each word and use it in a sentence. Then look at each word listed in the row. Find the word that you hear.**

Now we will begin. Put your finger on number 1. You should be on the row with the bird.

S1

look	lake	live	leak
○	○	○	●

STOP

1

more	move	most	mix
●	○	○	○

2

fill	fall	feel	full
○	○	●	○

3

wash	wish	was	wise
○	●	○	○

4

bread	branch	brown	bring
○	○	○	●

5

over	open	only	oven
○	●	○	○

6

club	clock	cloud	close
○	●	○	○

STOP

Levels 6–7

72

Check to see that all students find item 1. Allow students time after each item to choose and mark their answer. Say each item only once. Say <u>only</u> the words that appear in boldface type.

SAY: 1 **The word for number 1 is** *more*. **Wendy wants some** *more* **soup. Darken the circle under the word** *more*.

2 **Put your finger on number 2. You should be on the row with the shoe. The word for number 2 is** *feel*. **Do you** *feel* **better? Darken the circle under the word** *feel*.

3 **Put your finger on number 3. You should be on the row with the apple. The word for number 3 is** *wish*. **I** *wish* **I could go swimming. Darken the circle under the word** *wish*.

4 **Put your finger on number 4. You should be on the row with the bell. The word for number 4 is** *bring*. **Molly will** *bring* **her pet to school. Darken the circle under the word** *bring*.

5 **Put your finger on number 5. You should be on the row with the dog. The word for number 5 is** *open*. *Open* **the door for me, please. Darken the circle under the word** *open*.

6 **Put your finger on number 6. You should be on the row with the flower. The word for number 6 is** *clock*. **That** *clock* **is broken. Darken the circle under the word** *clock*.

Look at the stop sign at the bottom of the page. You have finished this part of the test and should put your pencils down.

S2	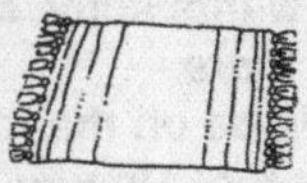	rag	rub	rug	rat
		○	○	●	○

STOP

7		coat	cup	cut	cold
		○	○	●	○

8		from	for	front	frog
		○	○	○	●

9		place	play	plane	plant
		○	●	○	○

10		window	woman	water	wagon
		●	○	○	○

11		bunk	bank	bunch	band
		○	●	○	○

STOP

Levels 6–7

73

SAY: **Go to page 73.**

Check to see that all students find page 73.

SAY: **In the next part of the test, you will find words that match pictures. Put your finger on S2. This is Sample 2. Read each word in the row. Then darken the circle under the word that matches the picture.**

Allow students time to choose and mark their answer. Remind students to carefully fill in the answer circle and to completely erase any stray marks.

SAY: **You should have darkened the circle under the *third* word. The picture shows a *rug*.**

Check to see that all students have filled in the correct answer space. Ask students if they have any questions.

SAY: **Now you will find more words that match pictures. Put your finger on number 7. Do numbers 7 through 11 just as we did Sample 2. Look at each picture and read the words listed in the row. Darken the circle under the word that matches the picture. When you come to the stop sign at the bottom of the page, put your pencils down. You may now begin.**

Allow students time to choose and mark their answers.

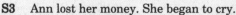

S3 Ann lost her money. She began to cry.

●   ○   ○

STOP

Check to see that all students find page 74.

SAY: **In the next part of the test, you will match pictures and words. Put your finger on <u>S3</u>. This is <u>Sample 3</u>. Read the story. Look carefully at the last word. Darken the circle under the picture that matches the last word in the story.**

Allow students time to choose and mark their answer.

SAY: **You should have darkened the circle under the *first* picture. The last word in the story is *cry*. The first picture matches the last word in the story.**

12 Please do not put your feet on the table.

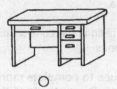   

○   ○   ●

Check to see that all students have filled in the correct answer space. Ask students if they have any questions.

SAY: **Now you will match more pictures and words. Put your finger on number 12. Do numbers 12 through 14 just as we did <u>Sample 3</u>. Read each story carefully and look at the pictures. Darken the circle under the picture that matches the last word in the story. When you come to the stop sign at the bottom of the page, put your pencils down. You may now begin.**

13 Today we saw men working on the railroad.

      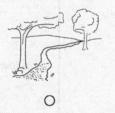

●   ○   ○

Allow students time to choose and mark their answers.

14 Ping cleaned the rabbit cage. Then he gave the rabbit a carrot.

○   ●   ○

STOP

Levels 6–7

S4 Mei likes to ____ up like her mom.

● dress   ○ look   ○ wear   ○ stay

STOP

15 Mei is wearing a ____ hat.

○ small   ○ tiny   ● large   ○ long

16 Mei thinks the necklace is ____.

○ ugly   ○ short   ○ wrong   ● pretty

17 Jay lives on a ____.

○ fan   ○ fence   ● farm   ○ frame

18 He is ____ the goats.

● feeding   ○ cleaning   ○ teasing   ○ petting

19 A baby goat has Jay's ____ in its mouth.

○ shoe   ○ cape   ○ shirt   ● cap

20 Jay looks like he feels ____.

○ angry   ○ sad   ● surprised   ○ scared

STOP

Levels 6–7

SAY: **Now look at page 75.**

Check to see that all students find page 75.

SAY: **In the next part of the test, you will use picture clues to find words that best complete sentences. Put your finger on S4. This is Sample 4. Now look carefully at the picture. Then read the sentence. Darken the circle under the word that best completes the sentence.**

Allow students time to choose and mark their answer. Remind students to carefully fill in the answer circle and to completely erase any stray marks.

SAY: **You should have darkened the circle under the word dress. The word dress best completes the sentence and matches what is shown in the picture.**

Check to see that all students have filled in the correct answer space. Ask students if they have any questions.

SAY: **Now you will use picture clues to complete more sentences. Put your finger on number 15. Do numbers 15 through 20 just as we did Sample 4. Look carefully at the picture. Then read the sentence. Darken the circle under the word that best completes the sentence. When you come to the stop sign at the bottom of the page, put your pencils down. You may now begin.**

Allow students time to choose and mark their answers.

S5   It was getting dark out. It was hard for Tina to see the book. She got up and turned on the light. Now she could see the page.

What was Tina doing?

○ Writing a letter

○ Sleeping

● Reading a book

 STOP

"What's the matter, Lucy?" asked her teacher.

"I can't find my new gloves. My grandmother made them for me. They are my favorite colors, green and white."

"Let's look for Lucy's gloves," said the teacher.

All the children searched their desks and the pockets of their coats, but no one could find Lucy's gloves. Lucy was very unhappy.

When it was time to go home, the children put on their coats and their gloves. Lucy put her hands in her pockets. She hoped her hands would stay warm on her way home. Then she started to smile. Now she knew where her gloves were.

21 Where was Lucy?

● At school

○ At a birthday party

○ At home

22 What did Lucy like about her gloves?

○ They were very warm.

○ They fit well.

● They were green and white.

23 Where were Lucy's gloves?

○ In a desk

○ In another child's coat

● In her pocket

24 What is this story mainly about?

○ Lucy's grandmother

● Lucy's gloves

○ Lucy's pocket

STOP

Levels 6–7

76

SAY: **Now turn to page 76.**

Check to see that all students find page 76.

SAY: **In the last part of the test, you will answer questions about stories that you read. Put your finger on <u>S5</u>. This is <u>Sample 5</u>. Now listen carefully. Read the story in <u>Sample 5</u>. Then read the question and the answer choices. Darken the circle for the correct answer.**

Allow students time to choose and mark their answer. Remind students to carefully fill in the answer circle and to completely erase any stray marks.

SAY: **You should have darkened the circle for the *third* answer choice. The story tells you that it was hard for Tina to see the page. You can guess that Tina was *reading a book*.**

Check to see that all students have filled in the correct answer space. Ask students if they have any questions.

SAY: **Now you will answer questions about another story. Put your finger on number 21. Do numbers 21 through 24 just as we did <u>Sample 5</u>. Read the story. Then read the question and the answer choices. Darken the circle for the correct answer. When you come to the stop sign at the bottom of the page, put your pencils down. You may now begin.**

Allow students time to choose and mark their answers.

SAY: **It is now time to stop. You have completed Test 3. Make sure you have carefully filled in your answer circles and have completely erased any stray marks. Then put your pencils down.**

After the test has been scored, review the questions and answer choices with students. If students are having difficulty, provide them with additional practice.

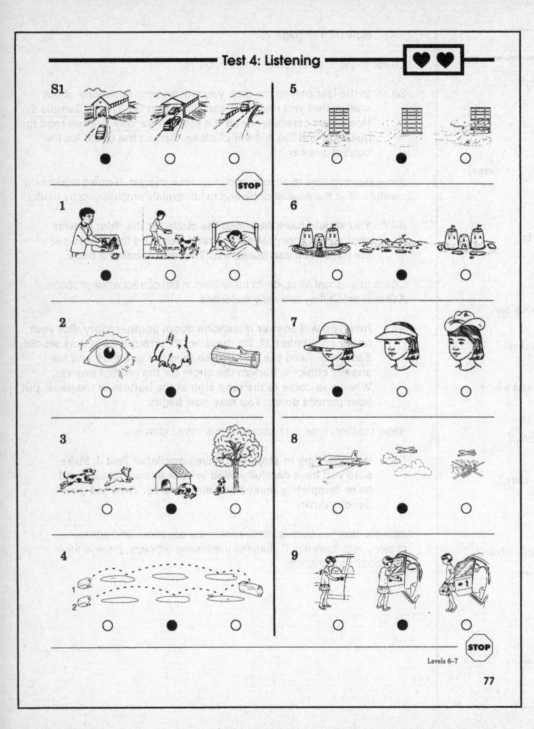

Test 4: Listening

Allow about 10 minutes for this test. Read items at a moderate, steady pace.

SAY: **Turn to Test 4, Listening, on page 77. You should be on the page with the hearts at the top.**

Check to see that all students find Test 4.

SAY: **In this test you will choose pictures that go with stories you hear. Put your finger on S1. This is Sample 1. Listen carefully. Forest Lane is an old country road. There is a covered bridge on Forest Lane that is only wide enough for one car to drive across at a time. Darken the circle under the picture that shows the bridge on Forest Lane.**

Do not identify the picture choices to the students. Allow students time to choose and mark their answer.

SAY: **You should have darkened the circle under the first picture. It shows a bridge that is only wide enough for one car to drive across at a time.**

Check to see that all students have filled in the correct answer space. Ask students if they have any questions.

SAY: **Now you will find more pictures that go with stories you hear. Listen carefully. Then look at the pictures for the story. Find the correct picture. Put your finger on number 1.**

Check to see that all students find item 1. Allow students time after each item to choose and mark their answer. Say each item only once. Say only the words that appear in boldface type.

SAY: 1 **Listen carefully. When Juan got home from school, he played with his dog, Scooter. They played until almost dark, when Juan's mother told him that it was time to come in and get ready for dinner. Darken the circle under the picture that shows something Juan did to get ready for dinner.**
  2 **Put your finger on number 2. Animals have different things that they use to protect themselves. Some, like deer and goats, have horns. Others have sharp teeth. Darken the circle that shows something else that some animals have to protect themselves.**

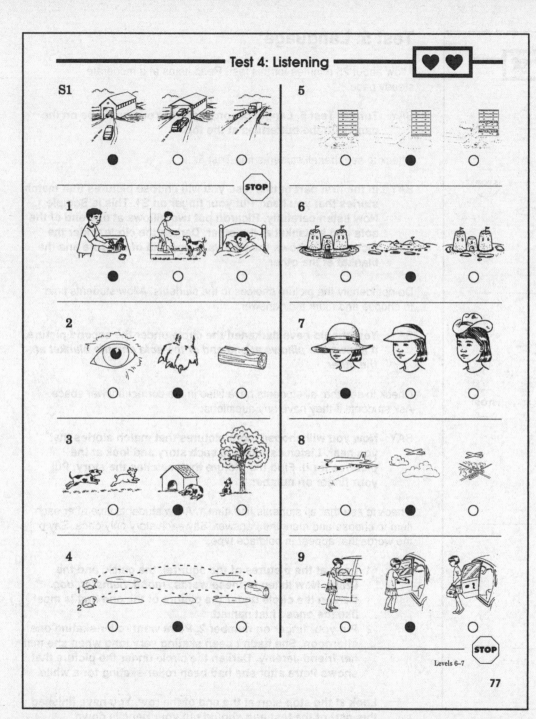

S1

1

2

3

4

5

6

7

8

9

STOP

Levels 6-7

77

SAY:

3 Put your finger on number 3. One Saturday, Holly took her dog to the park and exercised him for most of the afternoon. Darken the circle under the picture that shows what Holly's dog did when they returned home.

4 Put your finger on number 4. There are pictures of two frogs and a log. Put your pencil on frog number 2 and follow it to the log. Darken the circle under the first puddle that the frog hopped into on its way to the log.

5 Put your finger on number 5. Before Shawn goes to school every morning, he is supposed to make sure his room is neat and clean. He has to make his bed, put away all toys and clothes, and close all drawers. Darken the circle under the picture that shows how Shawn's room should look every morning when he goes to school.

6 Put your finger on number 6. Yuko's family went to the beach for the day. Yuko spent a long time making a sand castle. Just as she finished it, a big wave rolled in from the ocean. Darken the circle under the picture that shows what happened to Yuko's sand castle.

7 Put your finger on number 7. Olivia and her mother went shopping to buy some school clothes for Olivia. Olivia found a rack of hats and tried some on. Her mother laughed when Olivia tried on a hat that was so big that it covered her eyes. Darken the circle under the picture that shows what Olivia looked like when her mother laughed.

8 Put your finger on number 8. After Olivia and her mother went shopping, they went to see an airplane show. One pilot did a trick by flying his plane in circles across the sky. Darken the circle under the picture that shows how the airplane looked to Olivia when the pilot was doing tricks.

9 Put your finger on number 9. When Olivia and her mother got home, the sky was cloudy, and it looked as if it might rain. "Please get my purse, Olivia, and take it into the house," said her mother. "And please make sure that rain can't get into the car." Darken the circle under the picture that shows something Olivia did so that rain would not get into the car.

It is now time to stop. You have completed Test 4. Make sure you have carefully filled in your answer circles and have completely erased any stray marks. Then put your pencils down.

After the test has been scored, review the questions and answer choices with students. If students are having difficulty, provide them with additional practice.

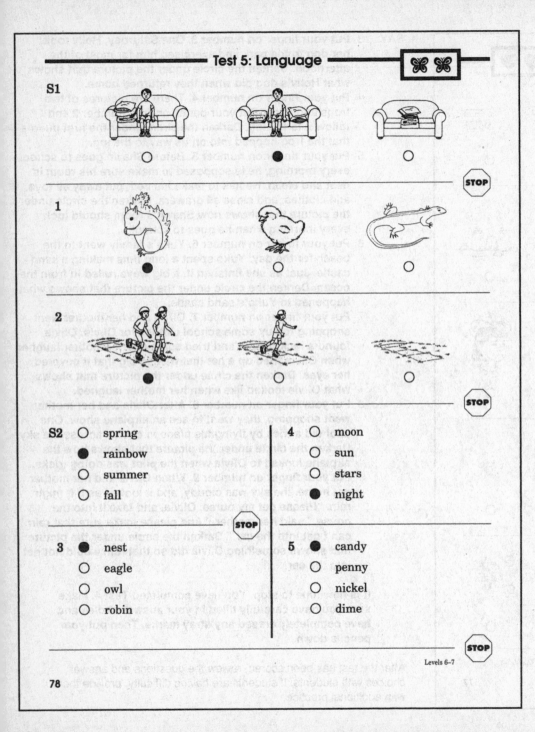

S1

STOP

1

2

STOP

S2 ○ spring
    ● rainbow
    ○ summer
    ○ fall

STOP

3 ● nest
   ○ eagle
   ○ owl
   ○ robin

4 ○ moon
   ○ sun
   ○ stars
   ● night

STOP

5 ● candy
   ○ penny
   ○ nickel
   ○ dime

STOP

Levels 6–7

78

Test 5: Language

Allow about 25 minutes for this test. Read items at a moderate, steady pace.

SAY: **Turn to Test 5, Language, on page 78. You should be on the page with the butterflies at the top.**

Check to see that all students find Test 5.

SAY: **In the first part of this test, you will choose pictures that match stories that you hear. Put your finger on S1. This is Sample 1. Now listen carefully. Ricardo put two pillows at one end of the sofa and a blanket at the other. Darken the circle under the picture that shows the pillows at one end of the sofa and the blanket at the other.**

Do not identify the picture choices to the students. Allow students time to choose and mark their answer.

SAY: **You should have darkened the circle under the second picture. It shows the *pillows at one end of the sofa and the blanket at the other.***

Check to see that all students have filled in the correct answer space. Ask students if they have any questions.

SAY: **Now you will choose more pictures that match stories that you hear. Listen carefully to each story and look at the pictures for it. Find the picture that matches the story. Put your finger on number 1.**

Check to see that all students find item 1. Allow students time after each item to choose and mark their answer. Say each story only once. Say only the words that appear in boldface type.

SAY: 1 **Look at the pictures of the squirrel, the chick, and the lizard. Now listen to these words:** *rabbit, hamster, dog.* **Darken the circle under the picture of the one that is most like the ones I just named.**

2 **Put your finger on number 2. Petra went roller-skating one afternoon. She hadn't been skating very long when she met her friend Jeremy. Darken the circle under the picture that shows Petra after she had been roller-skating for a while.**

Look at the stop sign at the end of the row. You have finished this part of the test and should put your pencils down.

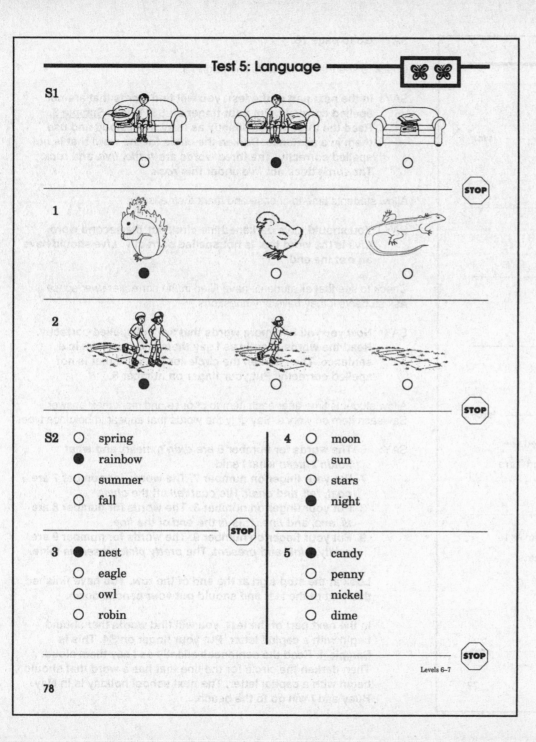

Test 5: Language

S1

STOP

1

2

STOP

S2	○ spring		**4**	○ moon
	● rainbow			○ sun
	○ summer			○ stars
	○ fall			● night

STOP

3	● nest		**5**	● candy
	○ eagle			○ penny
	○ owl			○ nickel
	○ robin			○ dime

STOP

Levels 6–7

SAY: **In the next part of the test, you choose the word that does not belong with the other words. Put your finger on S2. This is Sample 2. Read the four words silently as I say them aloud. The words are** *spring, rainbow, summer,* **and** *fall.* **Darken the circle for the word that does not belong with the other words.**

Allow students time to choose and mark their answer.

SAY: **You should have darkened the circle for the second word. The word** *rainbow* **does not belong with the other words because rainbow is not a season, like spring, summer, and fall.**

Check to see that all students have filled in the correct answer space. Ask students if they have any questions.

SAY: **Now you will choose more words that do not belong with other words. Read each word silently as I say it aloud. Then choose the word that does not belong with the other words. Put your finger on number 3.**

Allow students time after each item to choose and mark their answer. Say each word only once. Say <u>only</u> the words that appear in boldface type.

SAY: 3 **The words for number 3 are** *nest, eagle, owl,* **and** *robin.* **Darken the circle for the word that does not belong.**

4 **Put your finger on number 4. The words for number 4 are** *moon, sun, stars,* **and** *night.* **Darken the circle for the word that does not belong.**

5 **Put your finger on number 5. The words for number 5 are** *candy, penny, nickel,* **and** *dime.* **Darken the circle for the word that does not belong.**

Look at the stop sign at the bottom of the page. You have finished this part of the test and should put your pencils down.

S3
turtle	liv	rock
○	●	○

STOP

6
didnt'	mean	what
●	○	○

7
coat	fell	char
○	○	●

8
is	ende	line
○	●	○

9
prety	pink	present
○	○	○

STOP

S4
- ○ The next school holiday
- ● is in May. Huey and i
- ○ will go to the beach.

STOP

10
- ○ The snow melted too
- ● soon. we wanted it to
- ○ last forever.

11
- ● Davis and max fed the
- ○ sheep. Santos and Tara
- ○ fed the chickens.

12
- ● My horse lucky loves to
- ○ eat carrots. He eats
- ○ some every day.

STOP

Levels 6–7

SAY: **Go to page 79.**

Check to see that all students find page 79.

SAY: **In the next part of the test, you will find words that are not spelled correctly. Put your finger on S3. This is Sample 3. Read the three words silently as I say them aloud and use them in a sentence. Darken the circle for the word that is not spelled correctly. The three words are** *turtle*, *live*, **and** *rock*. **The** *turtle* **does not** *live* **under this** *rock*.

Allow students time to choose and mark their answer.

SAY: **You should have darkened the circle for the second word.** *Live* **is the word that is not spelled correctly.** *Live* **should have an** *e* **at the end.**

Check to see that all students have filled in the correct answer space. Ask students if they have any questions.

SAY: **Now you will find more words that are not spelled correctly. Read the words silently as I say them and use them in a sentence. Then darken the circle for the word that is not spelled correctly. Put your finger on number 6.**

Allow students time after each item to choose and mark their answer. Say each item only once. Say only the words that appear in boldface type.

SAY: 6 **The words for number 6 are** *didn't*, *mean*, **and** *what*. **I** *didn't mean what* **I said.**
7 **Put your finger on number 7. The words for number 7 are** *coat*, *fell*, **and** *chair*. **His** *coat fell* **off the** *chair*.
8 **Put your finger on number 8. The words for number 8 are** *is*, *end*, **and** *line*. **This** *is* **the** *end* **of the** *line*.
9 **Put your finger on number 9. The words for number 9 are** *pretty*, *pink*, **and** *present*. **The** *pretty pink present* **is mine.**

Look at the stop sign at the end of the row. You have finished this part of the test and should put your pencils down.

In the next part of the test, you will find words that should begin with a capital letter. Put your finger on S4. This is Sample 4. Read the sentences silently as I say them aloud. Then darken the circle for the line that has a word that should begin with a capital letter. The next school holiday is in May. Huey and I will go to the beach.

S3	turtle ○	liv ●	rock ○	

STOP

6	didnt' ●	mean ○	what ○

7	coat ○	fell ○	char ●

8	is ○	ende ●	line ○

9	prety ●	pink ○	present ○

STOP

S4
○ The next school holiday
● is in May. Huey and i
○ will go to the beach.

STOP

11
● Davis and max fed the
○ sheep. Santos and Tara
○ fed the chickens.

10
○ The snow melted too
● soon. we wanted it to
○ last forever.

12
● My horse lucky loves to
○ eat carrots. He eats
○ some every day.

STOP

Levels 6–7

79

Allow students time to choose and mark their answer.

SAY: **You should have darkened the circle for the second line. The word *I* should always be a capital letter.**

Check to see that all students have filled in the correct answer space. Ask students if they have any questions.

SAY: **Now you will find more words that should begin with a capital letter. Read the sentences silently as I say them aloud. Darken the circle for the line that has a word that should begin with a capital letter. Put your finger on number 10.**

Allow students time after each item to choose and mark their answer. Reread an item only if you make a mistake when saying it aloud. Say only the words that appear in boldface type.

SAY: 10 **The snow melted too soon. We wanted it to last forever.**
11 **Put your finger on number 11. Davis and Max fed the sheep. Santos and Tara fed the chickens.**
12 **Put your finger on number 12. My horse Lucky loves to eat carrots. He eats some every day.**

Look at the stop sign at the bottom of the page. You have finished this part of the test and should put your pencils down.

S5 ○ The ocean was blue
   ● and still Then the wind
   ○ began to blow.

STOP

S6 ● The cat and the dog is
   ○ sleeping together.
   ○ Don't wake them up.

STOP

13 ○ The spider has spun its
   ● web Now it waits to see
   ○ what will be trapped.

18 ○ The button on my shirt
   ● it has come off. Will
   ○ you sew it back on?

14 ● K C will raise the flag.
   ○ The other children will
   ○ take it down.

19 ● That there girl is new
   ○ in school. She sits
   ○ behind me.

15 ○ Someone is ringing
   ● the doorbell I think
   ○ I know who it is.

20 ● I have bited my small
   ○ green apple. It is very
   ○ juicy and sweet.

16 ● Oh That girl dropped
   ○ the tray of cookies that
   ○ she was carrying.

21 ○ Erin laid her glasses too
   ○ close to the edge of the
   ● table. Fell and broke.

17 ○ The giant reaches up
   ● to touch the rainbow
   ○ The elf smiles at him.

22 ○ The sandwich and the
   ○ glass of milk are for
   ● you. I is not hungry.

STOP

STOP

Levels 6–7

SAY: **Now turn to page 80.**

Check to see that all students find page 80.

SAY: **In the next part of the test, you will find missing punctuation marks in sentences. Put your finger on S5. This is Sample 5. Read the sentences silently as I say them aloud. Darken the circle for the line that is missing a punctuation mark. The ocean was blue and still. Then the wind began to blow.**

Allow students time to choose and mark their answer.

SAY: **You should have darkened the circle for the *second* line. *Still* is the last word in the first sentence. A period is needed at the end of a sentence.**

Check to see that all students have filled in the correct answer space. Ask students if they have any questions.

SAY: **Now you will find more missing punctuation marks in sentences. Read the sentences silently as I say them aloud. Darken the circle for the line that is missing a punctuation mark. Put your finger on number 13.**

Allow students time after each item to choose and mark their answer. Reread an item only if you make a mistake when saying it aloud. Say only the words that appear in boldface type.

SAY: 13 **The spider has spun its web. Now it waits to see what will be trapped.**
   14 **Put your finger on number 14. K.C. will raise the flag. The other children will take it down.**
   15 **Put your finger on number 15. Someone is ringing the doorbell. I think I know who it is.**
   16 **Put your finger on number 16. Oh! That girl dropped the tray of cookies that she was carrying.**
   17 **Put your finger on number 17. The giant reaches up to touch the rainbow. The elf smiles at him.**

Look at the stop sign at the bottom of the column. You have finished this part of the test and should put your pencils down.

S5 ○ The ocean was blue
    ● and still Then the wind
    ○ began to blow.

STOP

13 ○ The spider has spun its
    ● web Now it waits to see
    ○ what will be trapped.

14 ● K C will raise the flag.
    ○ The other children will
    ○ take it down.

15 ○ Someone is ringing
    ● the doorbell I think
    ○ I know who it is.

16 ● Oh That girl dropped
    ○ the tray of cookies that
    ○ she was carrying.

17 ○ The giant reaches up
    ● to touch the rainbow
    ○ The elf smiles at him.

STOP

S6 ● The cat and the dog is
    ○ sleeping together.
    ○ Don't wake them up.

STOP

18 ○ The button on my shirt
    ● it has come off. Will
    ○ you sew it back on?

19 ● That there girl is new
    ○ in school. She sits
    ○ behind me.

20 ● I have bited my small
    ○ green apple. It is very
    ○ juicy and sweet.

21 ○ Erin laid her glasses too
    ○ close to the edge of the
    ● table. Fell and broke.

22 ○ The sandwich and the
    ○ glass of milk are for
    ● you. I is not hungry.

STOP

Levels 6–7

SAY: **In the last part of the test, you will find mistakes in the way words are used. Put your finger on** S6. **This is** Sample 6. **Read the sentences silently as I say them aloud. Darken the circle for the line that has a mistake in the way the words are used. The cat and the dog is sleeping together. Don't wake them up.**

Allow students time to choose and mark their answer.

SAY: **You should have darkened the circle for the** first **line. The first sentence is about a more than one animal.** Are **should be used when a sentence tells about more than one thing. The cat and the dog** are **sleeping together.**

Check to see that all students have filled in the correct answer space. Ask students if they have any questions.

SAY: **Now you will find more mistakes in the way words are used. Read the sentences silently as I say them aloud. Then darken the circle for the line that has a mistake in the way the words are used. Put your finger on number 18.**

Allow students time after each item to choose and mark their answer. Reread an item only if you make a mistake when saying it aloud. Be sure you do not emphasize the words that are used incorrectly. Say only the words that appear in boldface type.

SAY: 18 **The button on my shirt it has come off. Will you sew it back on?**
      19 **Put your finger on number 19. That there girl is new in school. She sits behind me.**
      20 **Put your finger on number 20. I have bited my small green apple. It is very juicy and sweet.**
      21 **Put your finger on number 21. Erin laid her glasses too close to the edge of the table. Fell and broke.**
      22 **Put your finger on number 22. The sandwich and the glass of milk are for you. I is not hungry.**

Look at the stop sign at the bottom of the column. It is now time to stop. You have completed Test 5. Make sure you have carefully filled in your answer circles and have completely erased any stray marks. Then put your pencils down.

After the test has been scored, review the questions and answer choices with students. If students are having difficulty, provide them with additional practice.

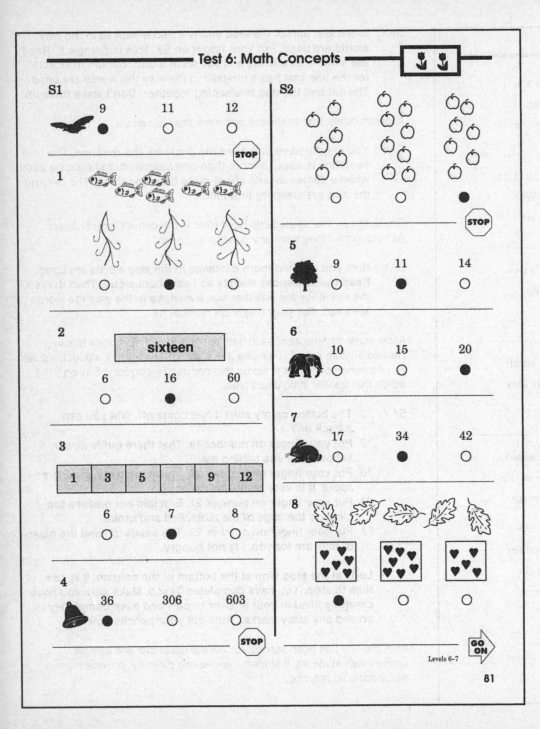

Test 6: Math Concepts

Allow about 25 minutes for this test. Read items at a moderate, steady pace.

SAY: **Turn to Test 6, Math Concepts, on page 81. You should be on the page with the flowers at the top.**

Check to see that all students find Test 6.

SAY: **In the first part of this test, you will answer math questions about numbers, patterns, and objects. Put your finger on S1. You should be on the row with the bird. This is Sample 1. Listen carefully. Look at the numbers in the row. What number comes just before 10? Darken the circle under the number that comes just before 10.**

Allow students time to choose and mark their answer.

SAY: **You should have darkened the circle under the number 9. If you count to 10, the number that comes just before 10 is 9.**

Check to see that all students have filled in the correct answer space. Ask students if they have any questions.

SAY: **Now you will answer more math questions about numbers, patterns, and objects. Put your finger on number 1.**

Check to see that all students find item 1. Allow students time after each item to choose and mark their answer. Say each item only once.

SAY: 1 **Look at the fish. Which string of hooks will hold one fish on each hook, with no hooks left over? Darken the circle under the string of hooks that will hold one fish on each hook, with no hooks left over.**
2 **Put your finger on number 2. Look at the word in the shaded box. Which number means the same as the word in the shaded box? Darken the circle under the number that means the same as the word in the shaded box.**
3 **Put your finger on number 3. Look at the numbers in the shaded box. Which number is missing? Darken the circle under the number that is missing from the box.**
4 **Put your finger on number 4. You should be on the row with the bell. Look at the numbers. Which number means the same as 3 tens and 6 ones? Darken the circle under the number that means the same as 3 tens and 6 ones.**

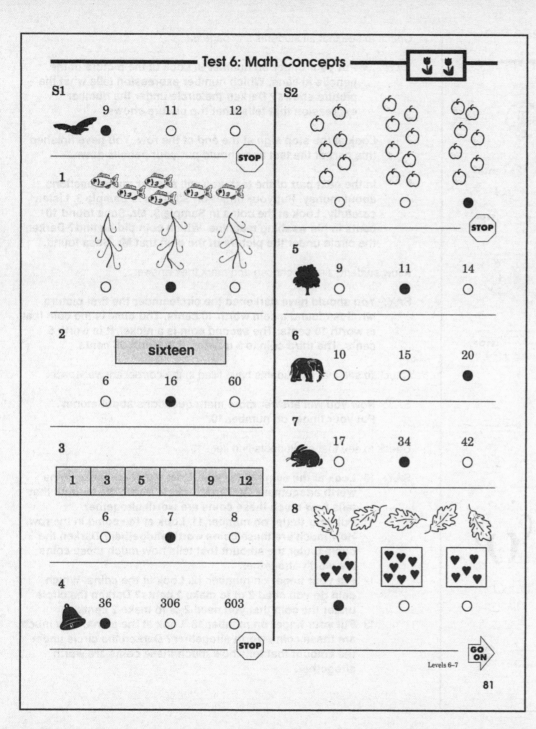

Test 6: Math Concepts

S1
9   11   12

1

2

sixteen

6   16   60

3

| 1 | 3 | 5 | | 9 | 12 |

6   7   8

4

36   306   603

STOP

Levels 6–7

81

S2

STOP

5
9   11   14

6
10   15   20

7
17   34   42

8

GO ON

SAY: Look at the stop sign at the bottom of this column. You have finished this part of the test and should put your pencils down.

In the next part of the test, you will answer math questions about numbers. Put your finger on <u>S2</u> at the top of the second column. This is <u>Sample 2</u>. Now listen carefully. Look at the groups of apples. Which group of apples needs 2 more to have 9? Darken the circle under the group of apples that needs 2 more to have 9.

Allow students time to choose and mark their answer.

SAY: **You should have darkened the circle under the *third* group of apples. It has 7 apples. If 2 more are added, the third group will have 9 apples.**

Check to see that all students have filled in the correct answer space.

SAY: **Now you will answer more math questions about numbers. Listen carefully to each question. Then find the picture or number that answers the question that you hear. Put your finger on number 5. You should be on the row with the tree.**

Check to see that all students find item 5.

SAY: 5 **Which number is between 10 and 13? Darken the circle under the number that is between 10 and 13.**
6 **Put your finger on number 6. You should be on the row with the elephant. Look at the numbers. Which number is closest in value to 22? Darken the circle under the number that is closest in value to 22.**
7 **Put your finger on number 7. You should be on the row with the rabbit. Look at the numbers in the row. Which number is between 20 and 40? Darken the circle under the number that is between 20 and 40.**
8 **Put your finger on number 8. Which box has one more heart than the number of leaves? Darken the circle under the box that has one more heart than the number of leaves.**

Notice the arrow and with the words *GO ON* at the bottom of the page. This tells you to go to the next page to continue working. Turn to page 82.

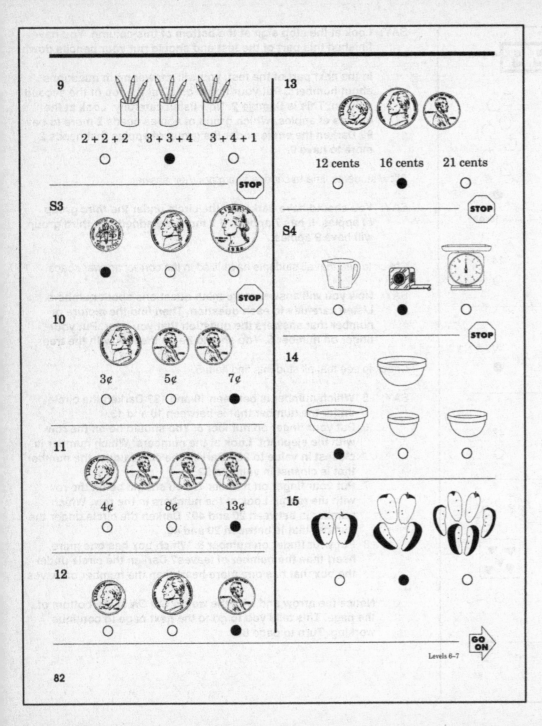

9

2 + 2 + 2　　3 + 3 + 4　　3 + 4 + 1
　○　　　　　●　　　　　○

STOP

S3

●　　　○　　　○

STOP

10

3¢　　5¢　　7¢
○　　○　　●

11

4¢　　8¢　　13¢
○　　○　　●

12

○　　○　　○

13

12 cents　16 cents　21 cents
　○　　　　●　　　　○

STOP

S4

○　　●　　○

STOP

14

○　　○　　○

15

○　　●　　○

○　　●　　○

Levels 6–7

GO ON

Check to see that all students find page 82.

SAY: **9 Put your finger on number 9. Look at the picture of the pencils in cans. Which number expression tells what the picture shows? Darken the circle under the number expression that tells what the picture shows.**

Look at the stop sign at the end of the row. You have finished this part of the test and should put your pencils down.

In the next part of the test, you will answer math questions about money. Put your finger on S3. This is Sample 3. Listen carefully. Look at the coins in Sample 3. Mr. Sosa found 10 cents in his washing machine. Which coin did he find? Darken the circle under the picture of the coin that Mr. Sosa found.

Allow students time to choose and mark their answer.

SAY: **You should have darkened the circle under the first picture. Mr. Sosa found a coin worth 10 cents. The *dime* is the coin that is worth 10 cents. The second coin is a nickel. It is worth 5 cents. The third coin is a quarter. It is worth 25 cents.**

Check to see that all students have filled in the correct answer space.

SAY: **Now you will answer more math questions about money. Put your finger on number 10.**

Check to see that all students find item 10.

SAY: **10 Look at the coins in the row. How much are these coins worth altogether? Darken the circle under the amount that tells how much these coins are worth altogether.**
11 Put your finger on number 11. Look at the coins in the row. How much are these coins worth altogether? Darken the circle under the amount that tells how much these coins are worth altogether.
12 Put your finger on number 12. Look at the coins. Which coin do you need 2 of to make 2 cents? Darken the circle under the coin that you need 2 of to make 2 cents.
13 Put your finger on number 13. Look at the coins. How much are these coins worth altogether? Darken the circle under the amount that tells how much these coins are worth altogether.

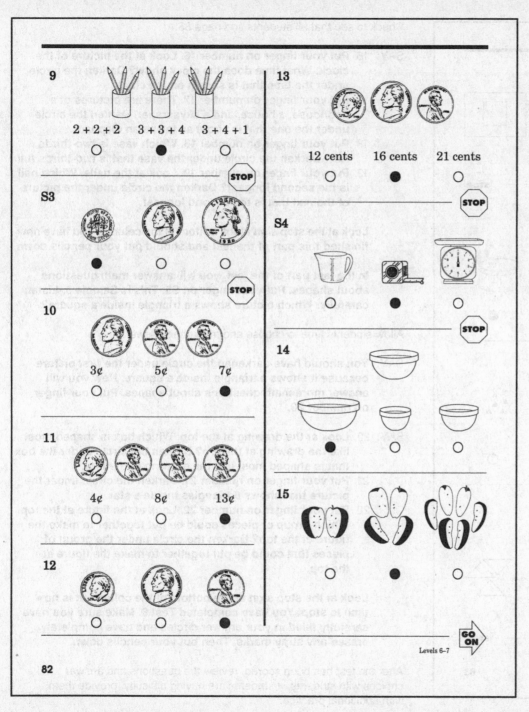

9

$2 + 2 + 2$ $3 + 3 + 4$ $3 + 4 + 1$

○   ●   ○

STOP

S3

●   ○   ○

STOP

10

3¢   5¢   7¢

○   ○   ●

11

4¢   8¢   13¢

○   ●   ○

12

○   ○   ●

13

12 cents   16 cents   21 cents

○   ●   ○

STOP

S4

○   ●   ○

STOP

14

●   ○   ○

15

○   ●   ○

GO ON

82

Levels 6–7

In the next part of the test, you will answer math questions about measurement. Put your finger on S4. This is Sample 4. Listen carefully. Mr Barnett's students had a contest to see how far they could jump. What did they use to measure how far each student could jump? Darken the circle under the picture that shows what Mr. Barnett's students used to measure how far each student could jump.

Allow students time to choose and mark their answer.

SAY: **You should have darkened the circle under the second picture. It shows a *tape measure*. A tape measure is used to measure distance.**

Check to see that all students have filled in the correct answer space.

SAY: **Now you will answer more math questions about measurement. Listen carefully to each question. Then look at each picture or number given for the question. Find the picture or number that answers the question that you hear.**

Now we will begin. Put your finger on number 14.

Check to see that all students find item 14.

SAY: 14 **Look at the bowl at the top. Which bowl holds more than the one at the top? Darken the circle under the bowl that holds more than the one at the top.**

15 **Put your finger on number 15. Look at the apples in the row. Which apple is cut into fourths? Darken the circle under the apple that is cut into fourths.**

Notice the arrow and the words *GO ON* at the bottom of the page. This tells you to go to the next page to continue working. Go to page 83.

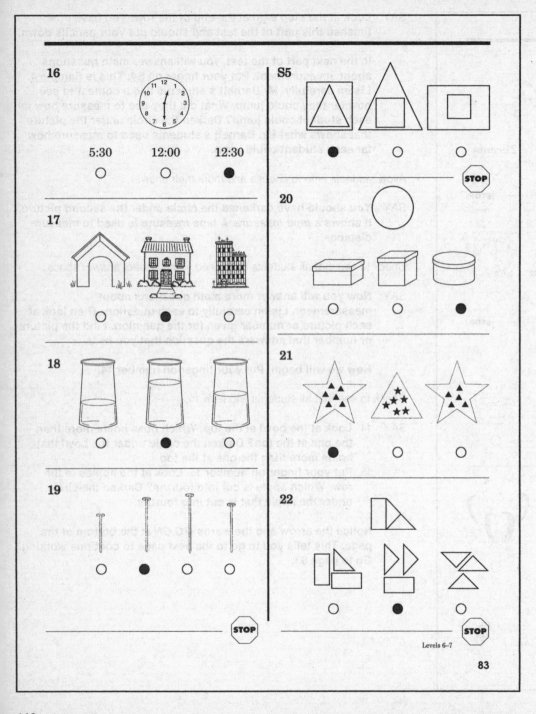

Check to see that all students find page 83.

SAY: 16 **Put your finger on number 16. Look at the picture of the clock. What time does the clock show? Darken the circle under the time that is shown on the clock.**

17 **Put your finger on number 17. There are pictures of a doghouse, a house, and a skyscraper. Darken the circle under the one that is about as tall as an elephant.**

18 **Put your finger on number 18. Which vase is two-thirds full? Darken the circle under the vase that is two-thirds full.**

19 **Put your finger on number 19. Look at the nails. Which nail is the second longest? Darken the circle under the picture of the nail that is the second longest.**

Look at the stop sign at the bottom of the column. You have now finished this part of the test and should put your pencils down.

In the last part of the test, you will answer math questions about shapes. Put your finger on S5. This is Sample 5. Listen carefully. Which picture shows a triangle inside a square?

Allow students time to choose and mark their answer.

SAY: **You should have darkened the circle under the *first* picture because it shows a triangle inside a square. Now you will answer more math questions about shapes. Put your finger on number 20.**

SAY: 20 **Look at the drawing at the top. Which box is shaped most like the drawing at the top? Darken the circle under the box that is shaped most like the drawing at the top.**

21 **Put your finger on number 21. Darken the circle under the picture that shows 6 triangles inside a star.**

22 **Put your finger on number 22. Look at the figure at the top. Which group of pieces could be put together to make the figure at the top? Darken the circle under the group of pieces that could be put together to make the figure at the top.**

Look at the stop sign at the bottom of the column. It is now time to stop. You have completed Test 6. Make sure you have carefully filled in your answer circles and have completely erased any stray marks. Then put your pencils down.

After the test has been scored, review the questions and answer choices with students. If students are having difficulty, provide them with additional practice.

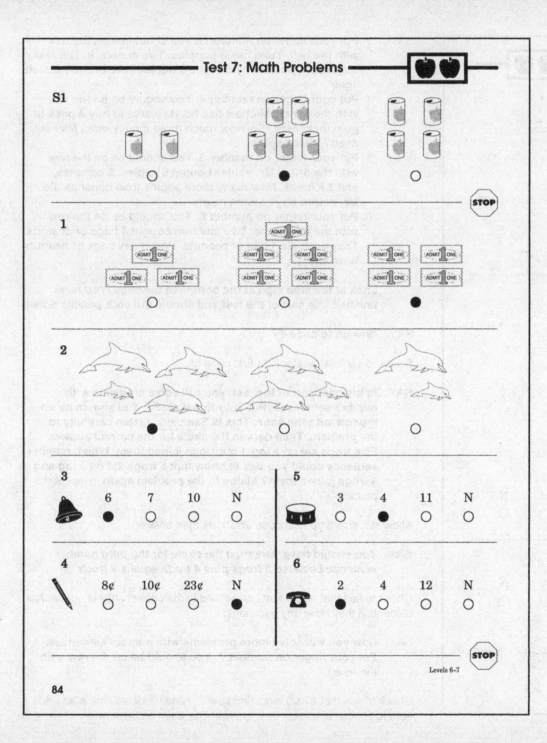

Test 7: Math Problems

Allow about 25 minutes for this test. Read items at a moderate, steady pace.

Distribute scratch paper to students. Tell them that they may use the scratch paper to work the problems.

SAY: **Turn to Test 7, Math Problems, on page 84. You should be on the page with the apples at the top.**

Check to see that all students find Test 7.

SAY: **In the first part of this test, you will solve word problems. Put your finger on S1. This is Sample 1. Listen to the problem. Then darken the circle for the correct answer. April's family took a trip to an amusement park. April packed 7 cans of juice for her family to drink on the way, but they drank only 2. How many cans of juice were left? Listen to the problem again.** (Repeat the problem.)

Allow students time to choose and mark their answer.

SAY: **You should have darkened the circle for the *second* picture. It shows *5* cans of juice. Seven cans of juice minus 2 cans of juice equals 5 cans of juice.**

Check to see that all students have filled in the correct answer space. Ask students if they have any questions.

SAY: **Now you will solve more word problems. Listen carefully to each problem. Then darken the circle for the correct answer. Darken the circle for *N* if the correct answer is not given. Put your finger on number 1.**

Check to see that all students find item 1. Allow students time after each item to choose and mark their answer. Say each problem twice.

SAY: 1 **At the amusement park, April bought 2 tickets for rides. She used 1 of them to ride the bumper cars. Then her mother gave her 3 more tickets. How many tickets did April have then? Listen again.**
2 **Put your finger on number 2. April went to see a dolphin show at the amusement park. There were 3 adult dolphins. One of them had her baby dolphin swimming with her. How many dolphins were there in all? Listen again.**

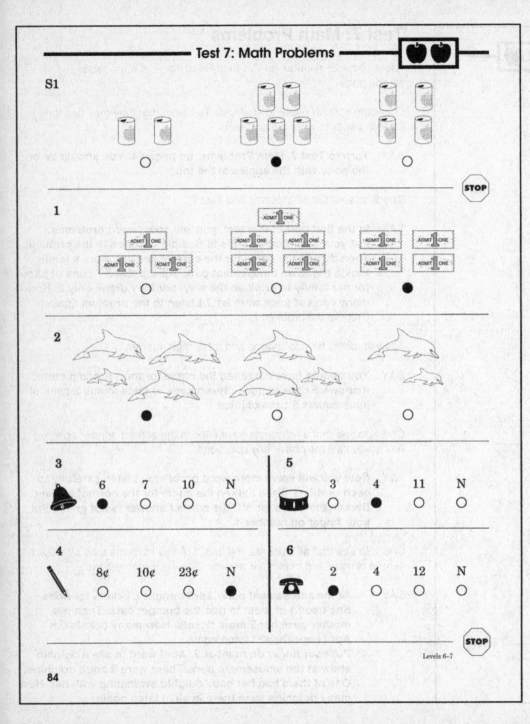

Test 7: Math Problems

S1

1

2

3 🔔 6 ● 7 ○ 10 ○ N ○

4 ✏️ 8¢ ○ 10¢ ○ 23¢ ○ N ●

5 🥁 3 ○ 4 ● 11 ○ N ○

6 ☎️ 2 ● 4 ○ 12 ○ N ○

STOP

Levels 6–7

84

SAY: 3 **Put your finger on number 3. You should be on the row with the bell. Yuko has 8 puppies. Two are black. The rest are brown. How many of Yuko's puppies are brown? Listen again.**

4 **Put your finger on number 4. You should be on the row with the pencil. Michael has 8¢. He wants to buy a pack of gum that costs 15¢. How much more money does Michael need? Listen again.**

5 **Put your finger on number 5. You should be on the row with the drum. Mr. Valdez bought 6 apples, 2 bananas, and 3 lemons. How many more apples than bananas did Mr. Valdez buy? Listen again.**

6 **Put your finger on number 6. You should be on the row with the telephone. Two children bought 4 bags of peanuts. They each ate 1 bag of peanuts. How many bags of peanuts were left?**

Look at the stop sign at the bottom of the page. You have finished this part of the test and should put your pencils down.

SAY: **Now go to page 85.**

Check to see that all students find page 85.

SAY: **In the next part of the test, you will solve problems with number sentences. Put your finger on S2. You should be on the row with the shoe. This is Sample 2. Listen carefully to the problem. Then darken the circle for the correct answer. Five frogs sat on a log. Four frogs joined them. Which number sentence could you use to show that 5 frogs sat on a log and 4 frogs joined them? Listen to the problem again.** (Repeat the problem.)

Allow students time to choose and mark their answer.

SAY: **You should have darkened the circle for the *third* number sentence because *5 frogs plus 4 frogs equals 9 frogs.***

Check to see that all students have filled in the correct answer space. Ask students if they have any questions.

SAY: **Now you will solve more problems with number sentences. Put your finger on number 7. You should be on the row with the heart.**

Check to see that all students find item 7. Allow students time after each item to choose and mark their answer. Say each problem <u>twice</u>.

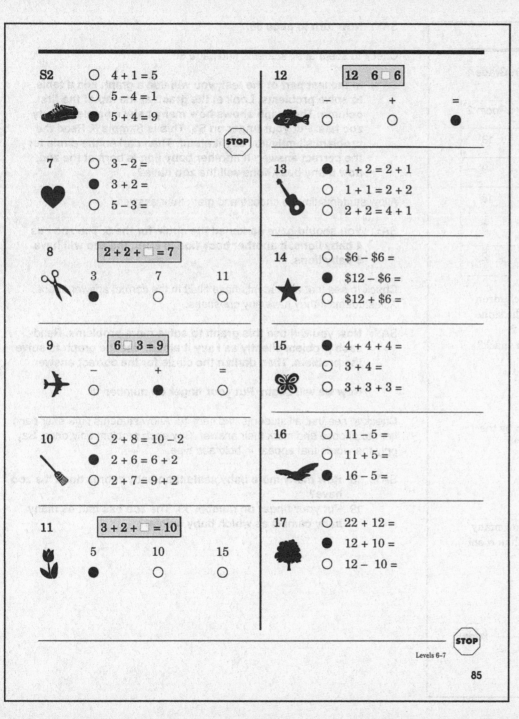

SAY: **7 Mrs. Williams bought 3 blueberry pies and 2 apple pies. Which number sentence could you use to show that Mrs. Williams bought 3 blueberry pies and 2 apple pies? Listen again.**

8 Put your finger on number 8. You should be on the row with the scissors. What number should go in the box to make the number sentence true? Listen again.

9 Put your finger on number 9. You should be on the row with the airplane. What symbol should go in the box to make the number sentence true? Listen again.

10 Put your finger on number 10. You should be on the row with the broom. Only one of the number sentences is true. Which number sentence is true? Listen again.

11 Put your finger on number 11. You should be on the row with the flower. What number should go in the box to make the number sentence true? Listen again.

12 Put your finger on number 12. You should be on the row with the fish. What symbol should go in the box to make the number sentence true? Listen again.

13 Put your finger on number 13. You should be on the row with the guitar. Only one of the number sentences is true. Which number sentence is true? Listen again.

14 Put your finger on number 14. You should be on the row with the star. Jacob had $12. He spent $6 on a Mother's Day present for his mother. Which number sentence can Jacob use to find out how much money he has left? Listen again.

15 Put your finger on number 15. You should be on the row with the butterfly. Rosa bought 3 packages of pencils. Each package had 4 pencils. Which number sentence can Rosa use to find out how many pencils she has? Listen again.

16 Put your finger on number 16. You should be on the row with the bird. Ming and his father had a string of 16 colored lights. When he plugged them in, Ming saw that 5 of the lights did not work. Which number sentence can Ming use to find out how many of the lights are working? Listen again.

17 Put your finger on number 17. You should be on the row with the tree. There are 12 boys and 10 girls in Kevin's first-grade class. Which number sentence can Kevin use to find out how many children are in his class altogether? Listen again.

Look at the stop sign at the bottom of the page. You have finished this part of the test and should put your pencils down.

Baby Animals at the City Zoo

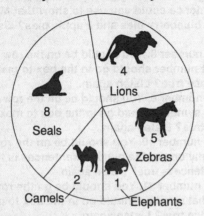

4 Lions
8 Seals
2 Camels
1 Elephants
5 Zebras

S3 If another baby lion is born at the zoo, how many baby lions will the zoo have?

   3 ○   5 ●   6 ○ **STOP**

18 How many more baby seals than baby zebras does the zoo have?

   3 ●   5 ○   13 ○

19 The zoo has half as many baby camels as which baby animal?

Elephants	Seals	Lions
○	○	●

86

Snacks Eaten by Children in Grade 1

		Room 1	Room 2
Popcorn		12	13
Cheese		6	9
Crackers		5	18
Apples		3	5
Bananas		21	2

20 The number of room 1 children who ate crackers was the same as the number of room 2 children who ate which snack?

○ Cheese
● Apples
○ Bananas

21 Which snack was eaten by the fewest room 2 children?

○ Popcorn
○ Apples
● Bananas

22 Cheese was eaten by how many more room 2 children than room 1 children?

● 3
○ 4
○ 5

STOP

Levels 6–7

SAY: **Now turn to page 86.**

Check to see that all students find page 86.

SAY: **In the last part of the test, you will use a graph and a table to solve problems. Look at the graph at the top of the first column. The graph shows how many baby animals the city zoo has. Put your finger on S3. This is Sample 3. Read the problem silently as I say it aloud. Then darken the circle for the correct answer. If another baby lion is born at the zoo, how many baby lions will the zoo have?**

Allow students time to choose and mark their answer.

SAY: **You should have darkened the circle for the 5. The zoo has 4 baby lions. If another baby lion is born, the zoo will have 5 baby lions.**

Check to see that all students have filled in the correct answer space. Ask students if they have any questions.

SAY: **Now you will use this graph to solve more problems. Read each problem silently as I say it aloud. Use the graph to solve the problem. Then darken the circle for the correct answer.**

Now we will begin. Put your finger on number 18.

Check to see that all students find item 18. Allow students time after each item to choose and mark their answer. Say each problem only once. Say only the words that appear in boldface type.

SAY: 18 **How many more baby seals than baby zebras does the zoo have?**
    19 **Put your finger on number 19. The zoo has half as many baby camels as which baby animal?**

Baby Animals at the City Zoo

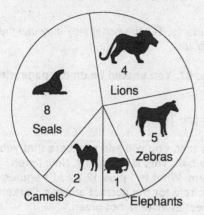

4 Lions

8 Seals

5 Zebras

2 Camels

1 Elephants

S3 If another baby lion is born at the zoo, how many baby lions will the zoo have?

3   5   6

○   ●   ○

(STOP)

18 How many more baby seals than baby zebras does the zoo have?

3   5   13

●   ○   ○

19 The zoo has half as many baby camels as which baby animal?

Elephants   Seals   Lions

○   ○   ●

Snacks Eaten by Children in Grade 1

		Room 1	Room 2
Popcorn		12	13
Cheese		6	9
Crackers		5	18
Apples		3	5
Bananas		21	2

20 The number of room 1 children who ate crackers was the same as the number of room 2 children who ate which snack?

○ Cheese

● Apples

○ Bananas

21 Which snack was eaten by the fewest room 2 children?

○ Popcorn

○ Apples

● Bananas

22 Cheese was eaten by how many more room 2 children than room 1 children?

● 3

○ 4

○ 5

(STOP)

Levels 6–7

SAY: Now look at the table at the top of the second column. One day two rooms of children in grade 1 made a table showing the kinds of snacks they ate. This table shows the number of children in each room who ate each kind of snack.

20 Put your finger on number 20. The number of room 1 children who ate crackers was the same as the number of room 2 children who ate which snack?

21 Put your finger on number 21. Which snack was eaten by the fewest room 2 children?

22 Put your finger on number 22. Cheese was eaten by how many more room 2 children than room 1 children?

It is now time to stop. You have completed Test 7. Make sure you have carefully filled in your answer circles and have completely erased any stray marks. Then put your pencils down.

After the test has been scored, review the questions and answer choices with students. If students are having difficulty, provide them with additional practice.

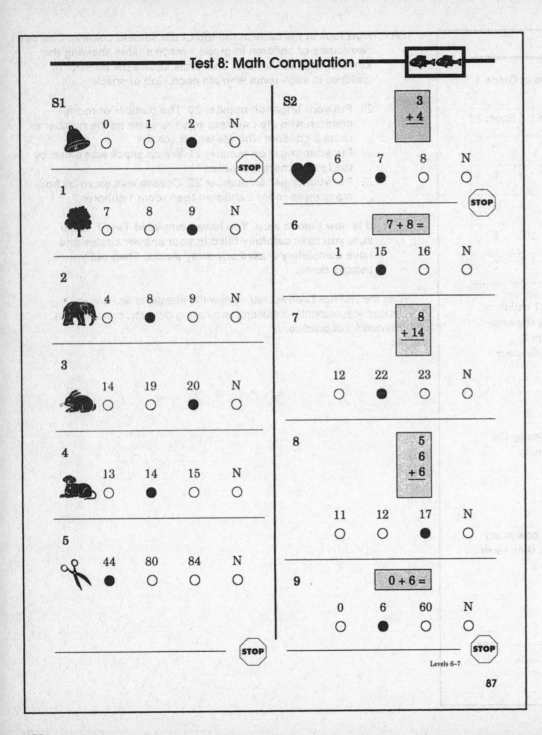

Test 8: Math Computation

Allow about 25 minutes for this test. Read items at a moderate, steady pace.

Distribute scratch paper to students. Tell them that they may use the scratch paper to work the problems.

SAY: **Turn to Test 8 on page 87. You should be on the page with the fish at the top.**

Check to see that all students find Test 8.

SAY: **In the first part of this test, you will add numbers that you hear. Put your finger on the bell. This is** Sample 1. **Now listen carefully to the problem. What is 1 plus 1? 1 add 1 equals what number? Darken the circle for the correct answer. Darken the circle for** N **if the correct answer is not given.**

Allow students time to choose and mark their answer.

SAY: **You should have darkened the circle for the** 2. **1 plus 1 is** 2.

Check to see that all students have filled in the correct answer space. Ask students if they have any questions.

SAY: **Now you will add more numbers in problems that you hear. Listen carefully to each problem. Add the numbers. Then darken the circle for the correct answer. Put your finger on the tree.**

Check to see that all students find item 1. Allow students time after each item to choose and mark their answer. Say each problem only once. Say only the words that appear in boldface type.

SAY: 1 **What is 1 plus 8? 1 add 8 equals what number?**
2 **Put your finger on the elephant. What is 6 plus 2? 6 add 2 equals what number?**
3 **Put your finger on the rabbit. What is 17 plus 3? 17 add 3 equals what number?**
4 **Put your finger on the dog. What is 2 plus 12? 2 add 12 equals what number?**
5 **Put your finger on the scissors. What is 40 plus 4? 40 add 4 equals what number?**

Look at the stop sign at the bottom of this column. You have finished this part of the test and should put your pencils down.

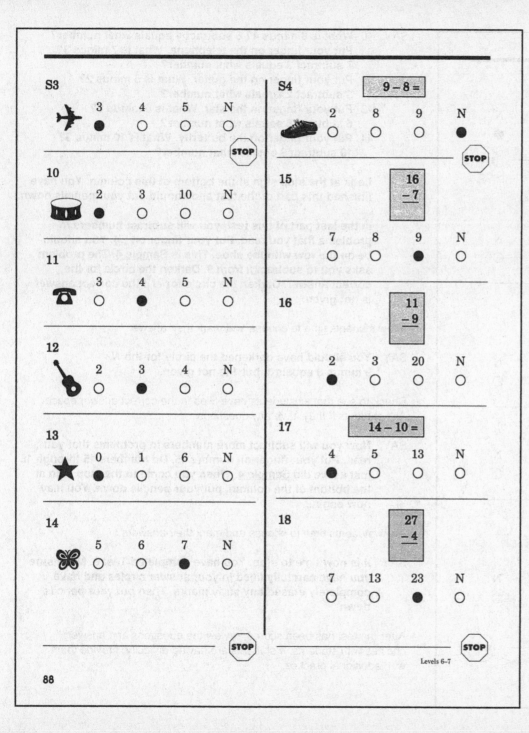

S3

3   4   5   N
●   ○   ○   ○

STOP

10

2   3   10   N
●   ○   ○   ○

11

3   4   5   N
○   ●   ○   ○

12

2   3   4   N
○   ●   ○   ○

13

0   1   6   N
●   ○   ○   ○

14

5   6   7   N
○   ○   ●   ○

STOP

S4 $9 - 8 =$

2   8   9   N
○   ○   ○   ●

STOP

15 $\begin{array}{r} 16 \\ -\ 7 \\ \hline \end{array}$

7   8   9   N
○   ○   ●   ○

16 $\begin{array}{r} 11 \\ -\ 9 \\ \hline \end{array}$

2   3   20   N
●   ○   ○   ○

17 $14 - 10 =$

4   5   13   N
●   ○   ○   ○

18 $\begin{array}{r} 27 \\ -\ 4 \\ \hline \end{array}$

7   13   23   N
○   ○   ●   ○

STOP

Levels 6–7

88

SAY: **In the second part of this test, you will add numbers in problems that you read. Put your finger on S2. You should be on the row with the heart. This is Sample 2. The problem asks you to add 3 and 4. Darken the circle for the correct answer. Darken the circle for N if the correct answer is not given.**

Allow students time to choose and mark their answer.

SAY: **You should have darkened the circle for the 7. 3 plus 4 equals 7.**

Check to see that all students have filled in the correct answer space.

SAY: **Now you will add more numbers in problems that you read. Put your finger on number 6. Do numbers 6 through 9 just as you did Sample 2. Read the problems carefully. When you come to the stop sign at the bottom of the column, put your pencils down. You may now begin.**

Allow students time to choose and mark their answers.

SAY: **You have finished this part of the test and should put your pencils down. Turn to page 88.**

Check to see that all students find page 88.

SAY: **In the next part of the test, you will subtract numbers in problems that you hear. Put your finger on the airplane. This is Sample 3. Now listen carefully. What is 4 minus 1? 4 subtract 1 equals what number? Darken the circle for the correct answer. Darken the circle for N if the correct answer is not given.**

Allow students time to choose and mark their answer.

SAY: **You should have darkened the circle for the 3. 4 minus 1 equals 3.**

Check to see that all students have filled in the correct answer space. Ask students if they have any questions.

SAY: **Now you will subtract more numbers in problems that you hear. Listen carefully to each problem. Subtract the numbers. Then darken the circle for the correct answer. Put your finger on the drum.**

Check to see that all students find item 10. Allow students time after each item to choose and mark their answer. Say each problem only once. Say <u>only</u> the words that appear in boldface type.

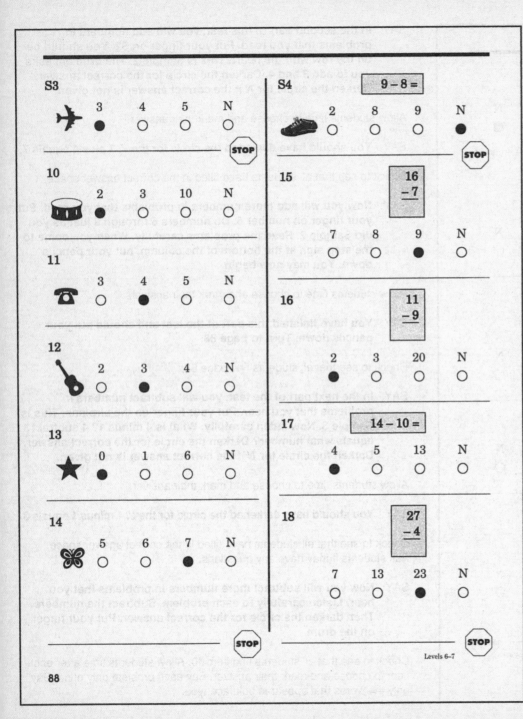

S3 ✈ 3 ● | 4 ○ | 5 ○ | N ○ **STOP**

10 🥁 2 ● | 3 ○ | 10 ○ | N ○

11 ☎ 3 ○ | 4 ● | 5 ○ | N ○

12 🎸 2 ○ | 3 ● | 4 ○ | N ○

13 ★ 0 ● | 1 ○ | 6 ○ | N ○

14 🦋 5 ○ | 6 ○ | 7 ● | N ○ **STOP**

S4 | 9 − 8 =
👟 2 ○ | 8 ○ | 9 ○ | N ● **STOP**

15 | 16 − 7
7 ○ | 8 ○ | 9 ● | N ○

16 | 11 − 9
2 ● | 3 ○ | 20 ○ | N ○

17 | 14 − 10 =
4 ● | 5 ○ | 13 ○ | N ○

18 | 27 − 4
7 ○ | 13 ○ | 23 ● | N ○ **STOP**

Levels 6–7

88

SAY: 10 What is 6 minus 4? 6 subtract 4 equals what number?
11 Put your finger on the telephone. What is 7 minus 3? 7 subtract 3 equals what number?
12 Put your finger on the guitar. What is 5 minus 2? 5 subtract 2 equals what number?
13 Put your finger on the star. What is 6 minus 6? 6 subtract 6 equals what number?
14 Put your finger on the butterfly. What is 10 minus 3? 10 subtract 3 equals what number?

Look at the stop sign at the bottom of this column. You have finished this part of the test and should put your pencils down.

In the last part of this test, you will subtract numbers in problems that you read. Put your finger on S4. You should be on the row with the shoe. This is Sample 4. The problem asks you to subtract 8 from 9. Darken the circle for the correct answer. Darken the circle for N if the correct answer is not given.

Allow students time to choose and mark their answer.

SAY: You should have darkened the circle for the N. 9 minus 8 equals 1, but 1 is not given.

Check to see that all students have filled in the correct answer space. Ask students if they have any questions.

SAY: Now you will subtract more numbers in problems that you read. Put your finger on number 15. Do numbers 15 through 18 just as we did Sample 4. When you come to the stop sign at the bottom of the column, put your pencils down. You may now begin.

Allow students time to choose and mark their answers.

SAY: It is now time to stop. You have completed Test 8. Make sure you have carefully filled in your answer circles and have completely erased any stray marks. Then put your pencils down.

After the test has been scored, review the questions and answer choices with students. If students are having difficulty, provide them with additional practice.

S1 Which picture should be at the top of the page?

○ Tiger
○ Owl
● Newt

STOP

1 Which picture should come fifth on the page?

○ Panda
● Raccoon
○ Tiger

2 Which picture should come right before the picture of the tiger?

○ Raccoon
● Swan
○ Newt

3 Which picture should come between the pictures of the panda and the raccoon?

○ Swan
● Quail
○ Panda

STOP

Levels 6–7

Test 9: Sources of Information

Allow about 15 minutes for this test. Read items at a moderate, steady pace.

SAY: Turn to Test 9, Sources of Information, on page 89. You should be on the page with the bells at the top.

Check to see that all students find Test 9.

SAY: In the first part of this test, you will answer questions about alphabetical order. Now listen carefully. Mr. Compton gave his students pictures of the animals they saw at the zoo. He asked his students to paste the pictures in alphabetical order on a sheet of paper, starting at the top of the page. Mr. Compton gave his students the pictures you see on this page. Put your finger on S1. This is Sample 1. Read the question silently as I say it aloud. Which picture should be at the top of the page? Darken the circle for the correct answer.

Do not read the answer choices to students. Allow students time to choose and mark their answer.

SAY: You should have darkened the circle for the third answer choice. The picture of the *newt* should be at the top of the page because *n* comes before *o* and *t* in the alphabet.

Check to see that all students have filled in the correct answer space.

SAY: Now you will answer more questions about alphabetical order. Put your finger on number 1.

Check to see that all students find item 1. Allow students time after each item to choose and mark their answer. Say each question only once. Say only the words that appear in boldface type.

SAY: 1 Which picture should come fifth on the page?
2 Put your finger on number 2. Which picture should come right before the picture of the tiger?
3 Put your finger on number 3. Which picture should come between the pictures of the panda and the raccoon?

Look at the stop sign at the bottom of the page. You have finished this part of the test and should put your pencils down.

NORTH

SEA LAND PARK

Whale Pool

Penguins

Seals

SEA LAND Gift Shop

Dolphins

Underwater Theater

Sharks

Snack Stand

Picnic Tables

Ticket Booth

WEST

EAST

SOUTH

S2 Where is the ticket booth?

○ On the north side of the park

○ On the east side of the park

● On the south side of the park

STOP

4 If you walked south from the penguins, where would you be?

● The gift shop

○ The whale pool

○ The dolphins

5 Which of these is east of the underwater theater?

● The sharks

○ The penguins

○ The whale pool

6 In which direction would you go if you walked from the picnic tables to the sharks?

● North

○ South

○ East

STOP

Levels 6–7

SAY: **Now turn to page 90.**

Check to see that all students find page 90.

SAY: **In the next part of the test, you will use a map to answer questions. The map on this page shows Sea Land Park. Study the map to see what it tells you about where things are.**

Now put your finger on S2. This is Sample 2. Read the question silently as I say it aloud. Where is the ticket booth? Darken the circle for the correct answer.

Do not read the answer choices to students. Allow students time to choose and mark their answer.

SAY: **You should have darkened the circle for the third answer choice. The ticket booth is** *on the south side of the park.*

Check to see that all students have filled in the correct answer space. Ask students if they have any questions.

SAY: **Now you will use this map to answer more questions. Read each question silently as I say it aloud. Then read the answer choices. Use the map to see which answer choice is correct. Darken the circle for the correct answer. Put your finger on number 4.**

Check to see that all students find item 4. Allow students time after each item to choose and mark their answer. Say each question only once. Say only the words in boldface type.

SAY: 4 **If you walked south from the penguins, where would you be?**

5 **Put your finger on number 5. Which of these is east of the underwater theater?**

6 **Put your finger on number 6. In which direction would you go if you walked from the picnic tables to the sharks?**

Look at the stop sign at the bottom of the page. You have finished this part of the test and should put your pencils down.

Aa advertisement	SHOE SALE!
Bb badge	POLICE
Bb border	
Ee edge	
Gg geyser	
Mm mend	
Pp peak	
Vv vest	

S3 Which would you most likely find in a newspaper?

- ● An advertisement
- ○ A badge
- ○ A geyser

STOP

7 Which of these would you mend?

- ○ An advertisement
- ○ A geyser
- ● A vest

8 Which word best completes the sentence "The pen rolled off the _____ of the table"?

- ○ badge
- ● edge
- ○ peak

9 How should you spell the name for a line that separates one country from another?

- ○ bordar
- ○ barder
- ● border

STOP

Levels 6–7

91

SAY: **Now go to page 91.**

Check to see that all students find page 91.

SAY: **In the next part of the test, you will use a picture dictionary to answer questions. Study the picture dictionary on this page. The first box shows the letter *A*, the word *advertisement*, and a picture of an advertisement. In the boxes after *advertisement* are the words *badge*, *border*, *edge*, *geyser*, *mend*, *peak*, and *vest*.**

Put your finger on S3. This is Sample 3. Read the question silently as I say it aloud. Which would you most likely find in a newspaper? Darken the circle for the correct answer.

Do not read the answer choices to students. Allow students time to choose and mark their answer.

SAY: **You should have darkened the circle for the first answer choice. An *advertisement* is the thing you would most likely find in a newspaper. You would not find a badge or a geyser in a newspaper.**

Check to see that all students have filled in the correct answer space. Ask students if they have any questions.

SAY: **Now you will use this picture dictionary to answer more questions. Read each question silently while I say it aloud. Read the answer choices carefully. Then use the dictionary to see which answer choice is correct. Put your finger on number 7.**

Check to see that all students find item 7. Allow students time after each item to choose and mark their answer. Say each item only once. Say <u>only</u> the words that appear in boldface type.

SAY: 7 **Which of these would you mend?**
8 **Put your finger on number 8. Which word best completes the sentence "The pen rolled off the _____ (SAY: *blank*) of the table"?**
9 **Put your finger on number 9. How should you spell the name for a line that separates one country from another?**

Look at the stop sign at the bottom of the page. You have finished this part of the test and should put your pencils down.

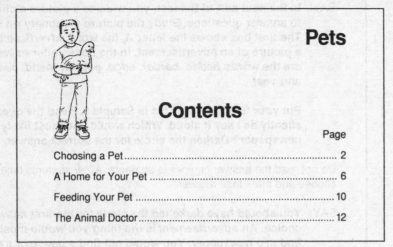

Pets

Contents

S4 On which page should you probably begin reading to find out the best kind of cage for a hamster?

○ Page 2
● Page 6
○ Page 10

STOP

10 Which pages might tell about the kind of food to give your cat?

○ 2–5
○ 6–9
● 10–11

11 On which page should you begin reading to find out why your pet rabbit is sick?

○ Page 2
○ Page 10
● Page 12

12 Which pages would tell you the best pet to select if you live in an apartment?

● 2–5
○ 6–9
○ 10–11

STOP

Levels 6–7

92

SAY: **Now turn to page 92.**

Check to see that all students find page 92.

SAY: **In the next part of the test, you will use a table of contents to answer questions. Look at the table of contents on this page. It is from a book called *Pets*. Read the chapter titles to yourself while I read them aloud. They are "Choosing a Pet," "A Home for Your Pet," "Feeding Your Pet," and "The Animal Doctor." Now put your finger on S4. This is Sample 4. Read the question silently while I say it aloud. On which page should you probably begin reading to find out the best kind of cage for a hamster? Darken the circle for the correct answer.**

Do not read the answer choices to students. Allow students time to choose and mark their answer.

SAY: **You should have darkened the circle for the second answer choice. *Page 6* begins the chapter called "A Home for Your Pet." You should probably begin reading on that page to find out what the best kind of cage is for a hamster.**

Check to see that all students have filled in the correct answer space.

SAY: **Now you will use this table of contents to answer more questions. Put your finger on number 10.**

Check to see that all students find item 10. Allow students time after each item to choose and mark their answer. Say each question only once. Say only the words that appear in boldface type.

SAY: 10 **Which pages might tell about the kind of food to give your cat?**
11 **Put your finger on number 11. On which page should you begin reading to find out why your pet rabbit is sick?**
12 **Put your finger on number 12. Which pages would tell you the best pet to select if you live in an apartment?**

Now it is time to stop. You have finished Test 9. Check to see that you have completely filled in your answer circles and have erased any stray marks. Then put your pencils down and close your books.

After the test has been scored, review the questions and answer choices with students. If students are having difficulty, provide them with additional practice.